Negotiating Relief

The Development of Social Welfare Programs in
Depression-Era Michigan, 1930–1940

SUSAN STEIN-ROGGENBUCK

The Ohio State University Press
Columbus

Library of Congress Cataloging-in-Publication Data
Stein-Roggenbuck, Susan.
Negotiating relief : the development of social welfare programs in Depression-era Michigan,
1930–1940 / Susan Stein-Roggenbuck.
   p. cm.
Includes bibliographical references and index.
ISBN 978-0-8142-1089-5 (cloth : alk. paper)
1. Public welfare—Michigan—History. 2. Welfare recipients—Michigan—History. 3. Social
service—Michigan—History. 4. Depressions—1929—Michigan. I. Title.
HV98.M5S74 2008
361.609774'09033—dc22
                  2008016900

This book is available in the following editions:
Cloth (ISBN 978-0-8142-1089-5)
CD-ROM (ISBN 978-0-8142-9169-6)

Cover design by Laurence J. Nozik
Type set in Adobe Minion Pro by Juliet Williams
Printed by Thomson-Shore, Inc.

CONTENTS

CHAPTER SIX

CHAPTER SEVEN

CONCLUSION

ILLUSTRATIONS

FIGURES

MAPS

TABLES

ACKNOWLEDGMENTS

MANY PEOPLE ASSISTED in the long process of completing this project. The book started as a dissertation in Michigan State University's history department under the direction of Lisa Fine. She was a wonderful adviser and model of a teacher and scholar. She helped my early thinking on the book and continued to encourage me throughout this process. I also thank committee members Julia Grant, Mark Kornbluh, and Peter Levine. Travel grants from the Department of History helped fund research in the early stages. I am particularly indebted to the American Association of University Women, whose American Fellowship enabled me to finish the dissertation in a much more timely manner. The year devoted to research and writing was invaluable. I appreciate the organization's commitment to women's education.

Conference presentations were extraordinarily useful in my work on this project. Parts of the manuscript were presented at the North American Labor History conference, the Great Lakes History conferences, and the Social Science History Association conferences. Audiences and those who commented provided valuable feedback that sharpened my thinking and analysis. Travel funds from James Madison College at Michigan State University fostered my attendance at these conferences, for which I am grateful.

No history project is possible without archivists, and I have been fortunate to work with many dedicated and skilled professionals. Archivists at the National Archives, Bentley Historical Library, and Burton Historical Collections helped to locate useful sources. David Klassen at the Social Welfare History Archives at the University of Minnesota was extraordinarily helpful on all my visits. He and his staff always were interested and friendly, and my time researching there was among the most pleasant of this project. I would especially like to thank the staff at the Archives of Michigan in Lansing, where I spent a considerable amount of time. LeRoy Barnett and Mark Harvey, his successor, were always helpful and courteous. Staff members, especially Charlie Cusack, Mary Zimmeth, and Julie Meyerle, were also great. The friendliness and professionalism of everyone in the Archives of Michigan have always impressed me and have made it a very pleasant place to work. I also thank Kathleen Baker, who was a graduate student working in MSU's Digital Services Center, for her work on the maps for this study.

Many people read parts of this manuscript at different stages. Kyle Ciani and Patricia Rogers were among those in my graduate-school writing group, which provided both social and intellectual support. Maria Quinlan Leiby and Tammy Stone-Gordon, also group members, were particularly helpful throughout the manuscript process. Maria's knowledge of Michigan history and her keen ability to critique were especially valuable. All made this manuscript much stronger. Carolyn Shapiro-Shapin provided very helpful comments and is a continued source of collaboration on Michigan history in the 1930s. Mary Thompson and Mary Ann Sherby are intellectual sounding boards and sources of great humor and friendship.

The interdisciplinary nature of James Madison College has made this a better and stronger work. Colleagues were helpful in their support. Faculty in the fields of both writing and social policy shared interest in my work and its outcome. Madison students are a joy to teach, and their willingness to engage with issues of interest to me and my research proved very beneficial. Teaching helps me to place my focused study in the bigger picture. This was particularly true of students in my social-policy class in the spring of 2007. I was in the final revision stages of this book, and my students' comments and questions during our debates about policy helped me think through the significance of this project. I thank them.

The Ohio State University Press showed early interest in this project, and Sandy Crooms has been a wonderful editor. She inherited the project from her predecessor, and I have appreciated her interest and professional guidance. I thank Ben George, freelance copyeditor for the press, whose skillful copyediting improved the manuscript. I also thank the two reviewers of the manuscript, particularly Eileen Boris. Her comments improved the final product immeasurably, but I am responsible for any remaining errors. Parts of this manuscript, in different form, have appeared in publications, and I thank them for their permission to reprint parts. They include "A Contest for Local Control: Emergency Relief in Depression-Era Michigan" in the *Michigan Historical Review* and "'Wholly within the Discretion of the Probate Court': Judicial Authority and Mothers' Pensions in Michigan, 1913–1940" in *Social Service Review*.

The people I wish most to thank are my family and friends who helped me see the end of this project. Navigating the world of fixed-term faculty can be an isolating experience, and these people kept me grounded in what was important. My parents, Gerald and Lois Stein, fostered my love of reading and learning at an early age and encouraged me at all stages of my education. My sister, Cheryl Crowley, and her husband, Dave, are good friends as well as computer consultants. Mary VanderWilt shared my interest in this project from the start and has been a valued friend since our undergraduate days at the University of Michigan. The St. Vincent de Paul Society at St. John Student Parish in East Lansing shares my concerns about the persistence of poverty and how to address it, and I appreciate our collective effort to relieve some of its effects. I especially thank Kathleen Caruso, Amy O'Brien, and Marge Pestka. Terri Biron, Jacob's caregiver, offers me great peace of mind when he is not with us. I appreciate Frank's family's pride in my PhD and the work on this project. Most thanks, however, go to Frank and Jacob. They are the center of my life. Without them, none of this would have meaning. Words cannot describe their importance in my life. I thank them both with much love.

ABBREVIATIONS

ADC	Aid to Dependent Children
AFL	American Federation of Labor
AASW	American Association of Social Workers
CCC	Civilian Conservation Corps
CIO	Congress of Industrial Organizations
CWA	Civil Works Administration
DPW	Department of Public Welfare
DSW	Department of Social Welfare
ERA	Emergency Relief Administration
FERA	Federal Emergency Relief Administration
FWA	Family Welfare Association
NASW	National Association of Social Work
NYA	National Youth Administration
OAA	Old Age Assistance
SERA	State Emergency Relief Administration
SEWRC	State Emergency Welfare Relief Commission
SSA	Social Security Act
WCSWA	Wayne County Social Workers Association
WPA	Works Progress Administration
WRC	Welfare Relief Commission
WRSC	Welfare and Relief Study Commission

INTRODUCTION

MICHIGAN GOVERNOR JOHN ENGLER eliminated the state's General Assistance program, which provided relief to unemployed individuals, in October 1991. Other states followed his course, and the number of states providing General Assistance benefits dropped from twenty-three to thirteen.[1] Engler's efforts to reduce welfare costs were mirrored at the national level, culminating in the 1996 Personal Responsibility and Work Opportunity Act. The presumption behind many of these reforms was that welfare recipients could work but refused to do so. Michael Katz argues that the 1996 law "signaled the victory of three great forces—the war on dependence, the devolution of public authority, and the application of market models to public policy."[2] The 1996 reforms emphasized the link between work and citizenship, and the 1996 law redefined work to exclude any training program that took more than one year; recipients could no longer pursue post-secondary education and have it

---

1. Ruth Connif, "Welfare, Ground Zero: Michigan Tries to End It All," *The Nation* (May 27, 1996): 16; Michael B. Katz, *The Price of Citizenship: Redefining the American Welfare State* (New York: Henry Holt, 2001), 86–88; John A. Begala and Carol Bethel, "A Transformation within the Welfare State," in *The Council of State Governments* 65.1 (1992): 26; Lyke Thompson, "The Death of General Assistance in Michigan," in *The Politics of Welfare Reform*, eds. Donald F. Norris and Lyke Thompson (Thousand Oaks, CA: Sage Publications, 1995), 79–80.

2. Katz, *The Price of Citizenship*, 1. Katz argues that welfare "reform" has redefined citizenship and strengthened the link between employment and benefits.

considered a "work-related activity."[3] Work was only work if it paid wages. The goal of early-twentieth-century maternalists—to provide mothers' pensions to enable mothers to care for their children at home—fully disappeared. Child care qualified as "work" only if one was watching someone else's children.[4] The emphasis of these reforms was on one's responsibility to provide for oneself and one's family.

A key goal of the reforms of the 1990s was to return control over welfare to the states. Proponents of such reforms, like Engler, questioned the role of the federal government in welfare provision. The shift to federalism dates to the 1930s, when the federal government first entered the arena of public welfare. According to Katz, "Instead of the constitutional allocation of government functions by level, federalism became a system in which major functions were shared among local, state, and national governments." Welfare became a partnership between the different levels of government, and financial responsibility and administrative control shifted, in part, from the county and township levels to the state and federal governments. Engler and other governors sought to reverse that in the early 1990s, arguing that it was not the federal government's role to end poverty. Engler was extremely critical of the programs of the Great Society in the 1960s, and believed they should be dismantled and authority returned to the states: "These programs," he claimed, "have worked untold mischief on the American republic."[5] Engler led the charge to return the power to develop programs to the states; he welcomed federal funds, but argued that states could more effectively administer those funds, resulting in more cost-effective programs that would encourage independence.

My goal is to provide a historical foundation to this narrative by studying the debates of the 1930s, which led to the federal and state partnership that Engler and other welfare-reform advocates sought to dismantle. I do this by analyzing the experiences in Michigan from 1930 to 1940, the period in which the administration of relief policies shifted, at least in part, from local communities to the state and federal governments. The New Deal was, in fact, a compilation of many "little New Deals" at the state and local levels; implementation of the Federal Emergency Relief Act of 1933 and the Social Security Act of 1935 varied tremendously across the nation.[6] Edwin Amenta

3. Jyl J. Josephson, "Gender and Social Policy," in *Gender and American Politics: Women, Men, and the Political Process*, eds. Sue Tolleson-Rinehart and Jyl J. Josephson (Armonk, NY: M. E. Sharpe, 2000), 149–50.

4. Gwendolyn Mink, "The Lady and the Tramp (II): Feminist Welfare Politics, Poor Single Mothers, and the Challenge of Welfare Justice," *Feminist Studies* 24 (Spring 1998): 59–61; see also Mink, *Welfare's End* (Ithaca: Cornell University Press, 1998), 22, 108–9.

5. Katz, *The Price of Citizenship*, 79, 84.

6. Edwin Amenta, *Bold Relief: Institutional Politics and the Origins of Modern American*

argues that the limited and uneven change brought by the New Deal resulted from this variance in the states' implementation of those programs. States with limited public welfare before the Great Depression saw the greatest change, as the New Deal programs fostered the creation of a public welfare system. States with a strong network of private welfare agencies saw at least a partial shift to public welfare programs under the Social Security Act. Other states, such as Michigan, whose needy residents relied on public welfare, saw a mix of change and continuity. Despite the new laws, Michigan's welfare system reestablished local control, within the legal limits of the Social Security Act, in 1939. The question of which level of government—local, state, or federal—would create and implement public welfare policy was a major issue in Michigan's debates.

Defense of local control, and thus of democracy, is central to understanding the development of welfare programs in Michigan. Early efforts to respond to the economic crisis of the Great Depression were framed by what I term fiscal localism: the attempt to minimize local expenditures and provide tax relief, even at the expense of welfare services. A fear of creating dependence and a reliance on the private sector for solutions to the economic downturn were central to this idea. A significant antitax sentiment fueled fiscal localism, which overlapped and at times merged with a belief in home rule. Local officials did not seek an end to public relief programs and believed such programs were necessary for the truly needy and deserving; they also welcomed state and federal funds. They did argue, however, that they could best administer the programs, with minimal state or federal oversight. Home rule advocates shared a hostility to professional social work, arguing that business professionals were the most competent welfare administrators. Home rule advocates believed local control was the best means to limit taxation and to achieve fiscal efficiency. Both home rule and fiscal localism appear throughout the decade.

The emergency-relief period did not end in Michigan until 1940, when the 1939 Welfare Reorganization Act was applied. Although Michigan qualified for funds under the Social Security Act's Aid to Dependent Children, Aid to Blind, and Old Age Assistance programs beginning in 1936, administration of those programs continued under the emergency-relief administrative structure (local welfare-relief commissions and the State Emergency Relief Administration) until 1940.[7] The emergency-relief structure remained in

---

Social Policy (Princeton: Princeton University Press, 1998). See particularly chapter 5, "Some Little New Deals Are Littler than Others." For a similar argument regarding court reform in the Progressive Era, see Michael Willrich, City of Courts: Socializing Justice in Progressive Era Chicago (New York and Cambridge: Cambridge University Press, 2003).

7. SERA administered relief efforts at the state level, using local welfare-relief commissions (also referred to as county emergency-relief administrations). Both terms were used in the

place in Michigan, and in other states, well beyond the demise of the Federal Emergency Relief Administration in December of 1935. Those years saw the overlap and intertwining of numerous welfare programs, including traditional poor relief, county infirmary care, mothers' and old-age pensions, direct relief, work relief, and the categorical aid programs. The 1939 Welfare Reorganization Act attempted to consolidate the state's welfare system while conforming to the requirements of the Social Security Act to permit the state to continue to receive federal funding.

The decade witnessed significant debate and conflict over the state's social welfare policy. Debates operated at numerous levels in Michigan's diverse demographics: rural and urban, industrial and agricultural, native-born white and immigrant or nonwhite. Through these counties we see the negotiations of relief at all levels. In my research, I analyze four counties: Marquette, Saginaw, Van Buren, and Wayne. Collectively they illuminate Michigan's combined rural and urban and agricultural and industrial economy, as well as its population demographics. It is at this level that we see the actual *implementation* of the New Deal programs, rather than just what the federal government envisioned when the laws were written.

Numerous state and local studies of the New Deal have appeared in recent years, adding to our understanding of the operation of these programs at the local and state levels. The New Deal encompassed a range of programs and issues, and scholars vary in their emphasis by necessity; an all-inclusive study of the New Deal is impossible in a single monograph. Many state studies assess the New Deal programs, and the relationships between federal and state governments, as well as the effects of the programs on different groups: farmers, workers, minorities, etc. The studies are often organized around the specific programs, including the Federal Emergency Relief Administration, the Works Progress Administration, the Agricultural Adjustment Act, and the Social Security Act. Some emphasize labor or farm issues.[8]

Studies such as those by Jo Ann Argersinger and Douglass Smith examine the impact of the programs on urban politics: Argersinger in Baltimore, and Smith in four southern cities. Cecelia Bucki examines the role of the Socialist Party, and third-party politics in general, in Bridgeport, Connecticut, in the fifteen years leading to the Depression and the New Deal years. Other studies,

---

1930s, but I tend to rely on the former (WRC).

8. For example, see George T. Blakey, *Hard Times and New Deal in Kentucky, 1929–1939* (Lexington: University of Kentucky Press, 1986); Jack Irby Hayes Jr., *South Carolina and the New Deal* (Columbia: University of South Carolina Press, 2001); and Ronald L. Heinemann, *Depression and New Deal in Virginia: The Enduring Dominion* (Charlottesville: University Press of Virginia, 1983).

such as Karen Ferguson's *Black Politics in New Deal Atlanta,* look at the issue of race and black activism during the New Deal.[9]

A key goal in this study is to examine these years through the lens of relief and welfare, and thus other issues, including farm and labor programs, are given minimal attention.[10] I consider programs, particularly work relief, as they intersected with welfare programs and were conceived as an alternative to "the dole." The title, *Negotiating Relief,* refers to the multiple negotiations that took place between various groups during the debates about how best to provide for the state's needy residents. Local officials, state officials, local welfare-relief commissions, relief workers, professional social workers, and the recipients of relief—all took part in these negotiations and helped to shape the outcome of relief administration. These multiple perspectives reveal the often-competing narratives of relief that emerged during the 1930s in Michigan. Frequently local government representatives, particularly those from rural areas of the state, were at odds with those who sought progressive change in welfare administration. Time and again recipients had different ideas about relief and, although in positions of minimal power, used the system to gain support for their families.

Competing professional visions in welfare administration took center stage in the 1930s in Michigan. The debate centered on what expertise and training were required to administer relief. In its most basic form, the debate pitted home rule advocates who favored a return to pre–New Deal local control of relief (although they welcomed the state and federal monies of the New Deal) against those who advocated a centralized welfare system staffed by professional social workers. The first group saw welfare as a business; therefore, business expertise, and not social work experience, was central to the administration of welfare. Two groups of professionals were behind these debates: local officials and their professional organizations, including the Michigan State Association of Supervisors and the State Association of the Superintendents of the Poor, and professional social workers educated in college social

9. See Jo Ann R. Argersinger, *Toward a New Deal in Baltimore* (Chapel Hill: University of North Carolina Press, 1988); Douglas L. Smith, *The New Deal in the Urban South.* (Baton Rouge: Louisiana State University Press, 1988); Cecilia Bucki, *Bridgeport's Socialist New Deal, 1915–1936* (Urbana and Chicago: University of Illinois Press, 2001); and Karen Ferguson, *Black Politics in New Deal Atlanta* (Chapel Hill: University of North Carolina Press, 2002).

10. Jerry Bruce Thomas analyzes the evolution of welfare programs as a part of his study of West Virginia, but most scholars spend minimal time on that issue. See *An Appalachian New Deal: West Virginia and the Great Depression* (Lexington: University Press of Kentucky, 1998), particularly chapters 6 and 7. Susan Traverso analyzes the roles of religion, ethnicity, and gender in welfare developments in Boston from 1910 and 1940. See *Welfare Politics in Boston, 1910–1940* (Amherst and Boston: University of Massachusetts Press, 2003).

work programs. Social workers believed that social work training, including casework methods and family counseling, was critical. The reaction against the passage of the 1937 law reorganizing welfare, which implemented in large measure the recommendations of the 1936 Welfare and Relief Study Commission, illustrates these polar views. The subsequent 1939 Welfare Reorganization Act was a blend of more-traditional practices and more-modern ideas about social welfare.

The story of welfare reorganization is intertwined with the development of the profession of social work. Social workers entered public welfare in an unprecedented way with the onset of the emergency-relief programs of 1933, and were critical negotiators of relief, both with local officials and individual recipients. The profession faced its own internal conflicts during the 1930s, including debates about the role of the "new" relief worker, who did not fit the professional model constructed so carefully by professional organizations in the previous decades. The professional social work system was hard-pressed to meet the training and educational demands of its untrained emergency workers. The status of social work as a profession was contested, and like others employed in the "semiprofessions" or female-dominated fields, social workers were underpaid, but the administrative costs of the emergency-relief system, in particular the salaries paid to caseworkers, were at the heart of criticisms by opponents of professional social work. Competing visions of professionalization, or how to define or use it, existed within the ranks of relief workers. Some wanted no part of the "profession," opting instead to use unionization to address issues such as working conditions, low pay, and high caseloads, and some allied with relief recipients to secure more adequate benefits.

Michigan's debates about welfare and relief speak to larger issues operating throughout the nation during this difficult and turbulent period. Fears about the centralization of government and the decline of the local community, and the values associated with notions of community, were at the center of several New Deal–era movements, and also have a larger history in the American past. The reaction against social work, and centralized, state-supervised relief administration, was rooted in these larger national issues, although it manifested itself in the relief debates in this state. Criticisms of local government actually predate the Depression, and political scientists and policy makers questioned the quality and efficiency of county and township governments. The Depression's severity, and the inability of local governments to respond fully to that crisis, further called into question local government structure. But belief in the sanctity of local control ran deep, as William Brock argues:

> Whatever professional critics might say, local government was, in popular estimation, the seed bed of American democracy. If the depression brought

it to the verge of ruin, more would be at stake than the functions of county commissioners, boards of supervisors, township trustees, and overseers of the poor; however pressing the case for centralization, many Americans would consider that the erosion of local responsibility had inflicted fatal injury upon self-government.[11]

Alan Brinkley's study of Huey Long and Father Charles Coughlin, the popular "radio priest" based in a parish in Royal Oak, Michigan, presents an example of this belief in local control and autonomy. Brinkley argues that the importance of these two men and their movements extended far beyond their limited constituencies: "They were manifestations of one of the most powerful impulses of the Great Depression, and of many decades of American life before it: the urge to defend the autonomy of the individual and the independence of the community against encroachments from the modern industrial state."[12] This study of Michigan's relief debates further validates the resonance of those feelings. The hopes and fears tapped by Long and Coughlin, and described by Brock, were remarkably similar to those evidenced in these debates, and in part explain why opponents of professional welfare administration were ultimately successful. Fueled by anti-intellectualism, antiradicalism, antitax sentiment, partisan politics, and growing opposition to the New Deal programs by 1935, opponents of welfare reform advocated a return to local administration of relief, to ensure that relief administration did not become too far removed from the electoral reach of Michigan voters. The rhetoric they employed struck a familiar chord among Michigan voters in the 1938 referendum on welfare reform.

One of my central arguments is analyzing the continuities in social welfare history, as well as the key changes resulting from the New Deal. The hardship of the Great Depression in the 1930s prompted some of the boldest initiatives in social welfare in American history. Two centuries of American poor law, with responsibility for social welfare firmly rooted in local communities, changed as a result, but at times in limited ways. Although a major period that witnessed significant changes and sparked heated debates, the New Deal continued many practices found in pre-Depression relief. The New Deal did introduce the professional social worker to public welfare on a much greater scale than earlier, shifted the source of funding from primarily local to a financial partnership between local, state, and federal governments, and of course changed the magnitude and scope of welfare. In fact numerous continuities

---

11. William R. Brock, *Welfare, Democracy, and the New Deal* (New York and Cambridge: Cambridge University Press, 1988), 45, 50–52.

12. Alan Brinkley, *Voices of Protest: Huey Long, Father Coughlin, and the Great Depression* (New York: Vintage Books, 1983), xi.

existed between pre–New Deal relief and the establishment of the Social Security Act's Aid to Dependent Children and Old Age Assistance programs, as well as general-relief programs under the 1939 state law.

One area of continuity was the distinction between earned benefits and public assistance. As Barbara Nelson and other scholars have argued, the New Deal entrenched the "two track" welfare system, separating those who were entitled to help from those who needed benefits. Connected to this was the notion that some recipients deserved assistance, such as widowed mothers of a certain ethnicity or culture, while others did not. The issues of gender and race played important roles. Women and nonwhites often were among those who did not work in paid employment areas included in the early workers' compensation or the Social Security Act's insurance program; instead, they often fell under the area of dependent mothers.[13] A key change from mothers' pensions was the administrative placement of the program; no longer a part of the Probate Court, ADC was situated squarely in public assistance. This was a significant shift, and a contested one, in some counties, while in others it simply codified the administrative practices of mothers' pensions.

Welfare reorganization created what I term a "third track" of welfare, or the general-relief programs which were outside the federal arena, the same aid (General Assistance) eliminated in 1991. Home rule advocates had successfully regained control of these services in the 1939 law. These programs, often forgotten in the analysis of federal welfare under the Social Security Act, served those people not eligible for aid under Aid to Dependent Children, Old Age Assistance, or Aid to the Blind: often the disabled or those unable to work but too young for OAA. The state government began to contribute funds to general relief after the 1939 reorganization, a key change from pre–New Deal years. Control over this third track of welfare was a contentious part of the debates over welfare reorganization in the 1930s, as local officials fought to prevent the centralization of all relief. For many counties, that translated into a wholesale return to poor-relief practices and traditions. Local officials, particularly township supervisors, continued to wield extraordinary influence in the administration of relief. General relief became the "third track" of welfare provision, and perhaps the most stigmatized of all the welfare programs. The

---

13. Alice Kessler-Harris, *In Pursuit of Equity: Women, Men, and the Quest for Economic Citizenship in 20th-Century America* (New York and Oxford: Oxford University Press, 2001), 95–96, 105–6. Kessler-Harris argues that the social insurance program under the Social Security Act excluded 55 percent of all black workers, 80 percent of all women workers, and 87 percent of all black women workers. See also Barbara Nelson, "The Origins of the Two-Channel Welfare State: Workmen's Compensation and Mothers' Aid," in *Women, the State, and Welfare*, ed. Linda Gordon (Madison: University of Wisconsin Press, 1990).

state replaced these county programs in 1976 with General Assistance, with the state fully funding the program, completing the centralization of relief started in the 1930s.[14] The arguments for the welfare reforms of the 1990s hearken to those put forth in the 1930s by groups and individuals opposed to the federalism created by the New Deal. Michigan's General Assistance program, which provided both cash aid and health care for unemployed residents, evolved from the changes of the 1930s.[15]

Another area of continuity, intertwined with the issue of gender, was the role of the family in welfare administration. Central to that administration is the ideology of family responsibility, closely linked to the family wage. Social welfare law in Michigan, and in most other states as well, contained stipulations that family members had a legal responsibility to support other family members, if able to do so. For young children, fathers were the logical first step as the expected family breadwinner. If the father could not provide, that duty extended to other family members. The responsible-relative clause dates to Michigan's earliest poor laws in the nineteenth century, and it remained in force in Public Act 146 of 1925, which consolidated Michigan's relief system. Township supervisors or county superintendents of the poor enforced support of relatives in the county's probate court. Children who had been deserted or abandoned by parents before they reached the age of sixteen were exempt from the responsibility, but they had to prove that they were in fact deserted.[16] The 1935 Social Security Act did not require that states enforce any family responsibility in administration of the categorical aid programs, but a large number of states, including Michigan, nevertheless retained those provisions in their laws.[17] The responsible-relative clause persisted in emergency-relief

14. Josephson, "Gender and Social Policy," 141; *Report of the Michigan Department of Social Services for 1976* (Lansing: 1976), 12; Public Act 237 of 1975, *Public and Local Acts of the Legislature of the State of Michigan*, 607–11.

15. Opponents of the program argued that recipients were employable, able-bodied adults who refused to work. Katz points out that more than 40 percent of GA recipients in Michigan were over the age of forty and 61 percent were never employed; the majority of the latter category were "many newly widowed or divorced women." Only 38 percent found work within two years, and only 26 percent earned an income comparable to their benefits under GA. Katz, *The Price of Citizenship*, 87–88. The program served many of the state's seasonal workers, employed in construction, tourism, and agriculture, as well as some auto workers. Thompson, "The Death of General Assistance," 81–82.

16. Edith Abbott, *Public Assistance: American Principles and Policies, Vol. I* (New York: Russell & Russell, 1966), 277–80; Isabel Campbell Bruce and Edith Eickhoff, *The Michigan Poor Law: Its Development and Administration* (Chicago: University of Chicago Press, 1936), 31.

17. A Works Progress Administration study found that just nine states, and the District of Columbia, had no provisions for relatives' support. Another nine states included grandparents, grandchildren, and siblings among the responsible relatives, and nine others excluded only siblings. The *Social Security Bulletin* reported in 1939 that twenty-seven of the fifty-one Old

administration practices, and also in the 1937 and 1939 welfare-reorganization laws in Michigan.[18]

All relief programs, whether direct relief or work programs, framed aid through the lens of the family. Whether it was the earnings of a father or brother with a Works Progress Administration assignment, or of a young man sent to a Civilian Conservation Corps camp, such aid was for the family's needs, and was budgeted accordingly. Program administration often ignored individual needs and dissension within the family in their focus on the family as a unit. The WPA, CCC, and other work-relief assignments operated with the expectation that wages would support the family and household. The enforcement of the responsible-relative clause was a key source of conflict among social workers, relief recipients, and their families before, during, and after the New Deal. Often when families balked at helping other members, particularly elderly parents on OAA or mothers receiving ADC, the recipient paid the price in terms of delayed or lost benefits. Although the intention of the law was to use the state as a means of support as a last resort, the outcome at times was to punish those who needed the aid the most, and who often had the least power to persuade family members to contribute. Gender played a critical role in this debate, both in what social workers expected of recipients and in the positions individuals held in the negotiation of relief in households and families.

Recipients were very much a part of the relief story, and provided their own narrative of the experience of receiving relief during the 1930s. Case records from the emergency-relief programs and the early years of the categorical-aid programs permit the inclusion of their voices, although filtered through the lens of the caseworker. Four counties serve as case studies based in part on the availability of case-file materials from those localities; all four counties' case records from the New Deal programs have survived to some extent.[19]

Age Assistance programs required relatives' support, and another fourteen states had such requirements in their general poor laws. Robert C. Lowe, *State Public Welfare Legislation* (Washington, D.C.: U.S. Government Printing Office, 1939), 63–67; "Public Assistance," *Social Security Yearbook: Annual Supplement to the Social Security Bulletin* 3 (1939): 161.

18. See Public Act 146 of 1925, Chapter 1, Sections 1–21; Public Act 258 of 1937, Sections 30–31; Public Act 280 of 1939, Sections 76–77, *Public and Local Acts of the Legislature of the State of Michigan*; "Local Public Welfare," n.d., WRSC Records, RG 35 Box 5, Folder 10, 96; Bruce and Eickhoff, 3, 10, 26, and 31. Under a 1953 law, grandparents were relieved of the burden of caring for grandchildren when the grandchildren reached the age of sixteen, but the responsibility of other relatives to support family members did not undergo significant change until 1970. See Public Act 148 of 1953 and Public Act 88 of 1970, chapter 1.

19. All case files of the Department of Human Services have restricted access in the archives. Researchers must obtain permission from the department to see the files, and they cannot record any proper names of recipients. Thus my records include only case numbers and

(See maps I.1 and I.2.) Van Buren County's Emergency Relief Administration case-file collection includes 102 case files dating from 1930 to 1940, and is the most complete source base I have located.[20] I also analyzed the OAA and ADC case files from Saginaw County, in the thumb area of Michigan, on the east side of the state; Marquette County, on the shores of Lake Superior, in the Upper Peninsula; and Wayne County, which includes Detroit, the state's largest city. I focused on cases initiated before the close of 1940, when the emergency-relief period ends. These case files include original application forms, verification investigations conducted by social workers, detailed case histories chronicling case visits, and correspondence.[21] Particularly valuable are letters or other correspondence written by recipients voicing their views on the relief programs serving them. These records make it possible not only to study the basic questions of who sought relief and why, but also to reconstruct the interactive relationships between the various individuals and agencies involved in the administration and receipt of welfare aid. In addition, the records enabled me to assess how both groups viewed welfare policy and their individual case, and how relief recipients influenced the program's administration.[22]

---

the personal characteristics of the recipient. All recipients' names are fictitious, although I have endeavored to retain ethnic characteristics in the selection of a name. All case numbers, and footnote references to archival locations and microfilm reel numbers, are accurate; anyone who obtains permission from the department can identify specific cases using the case number.

20. The full collection includes 133 records through 1945, but as with the ADC and OAA files, I examined only those initiated before or during 1940. Samples of other counties' ERA records survive for Kent and Bay counties but contain only a handful of case files. While useful for anecdotal purposes, they are too limited for any statistical analysis or for the county's administrative practices. Most counties' emergency-relief records were apparently lost, although many of the categorical-aid records include ERA information. A large number of OAA and ADC recipients in the late 1930s also received direct relief under FERA.

21. Saginaw's collection is the most complete, including 409 ADC cases and 218 OAA cases. I analyzed the complete run of surviving ADC files and a sampling (every tenth case) of OAA records. A sampling of Wayne County's collection (every fiftieth case) yielded a base of 319 ADC and 285 OAA cases. Marquette's collection is much smaller, with just 16 ADC cases and 39 OAA cases. Only about a quarter of Michigan counties are represented in the collections with a significant number of case files; most collections contain only a 2 percent sample, thus limiting the counties available for study.

22. The ERA case files and the categorical-aid records represent different relief populations. ERA records reflect a variety of case types, from unemployment to ill health to dependent mothers. They include anyone who applied for relief during the emergency-relief period. In contrast, the ADC and OAA programs served unemployable individuals, or those people who either could not work, physically, or should not work, according to policy makers, because of parental responsibilities. Many of the categorical-aid recipients also received emergency relief and were simply transferred to the ADC and OAA programs in 1936. Although they were categorized as ADC or OAA, the local welfare-relief commission continued to administer those programs until the 1939 law was implemented. Thus they continued under the New Deal emergency-relief umbrella until the end of the decade.

Map I.1 Michigan counties

Although New Deal programs were opposed and criticized from the start, they were important to Michigan residents, providing relief and employment when there were few other outlets. The state of Michigan suffered high unemployment and relief rates during the Depression years, and its economic problems dated to the 1920s. Much of the state was already in a recession by the crash of 1929, and the problems only worsened in the 1930s. By 1933 between 13 and 16 percent of all Michigan residents depended on some kind of relief, and those numbers approached 20 to 30 percent in the northern parts of the state, especially the Upper Peninsula.[23]

Michigan was a diverse state in terms of demographics and economics in the 1930s, and thus its residents experienced the Depression in different

23. William Haber and Paul L. Stanchfield, *Unemployment, Relief, and Economic Security: A Survey of Michigan's Relief and Unemployment Problem* (Lansing: State Emergency Welfare Relief Commission, 1936), 19, 39.

Map I.2 Key locations in the development of social welfare, 1930–40

ways, depending upon one's region, race, nativity, citizenship, sex, age, and occupation. Although Michigan contained a relatively small minority population (just 4 percent in 1930, the vast majority of which was African-American), its foreign-born population was 19.8 percent in 1920 and 17.4 percent in 1930. Its economy varied from the industrial centers of Detroit and Flint to the agricultural centers in southwestern Michigan, mid-Michigan, and the thumb area on the east side of the state between Saginaw Bay and Lake Huron. The Upper Peninsula and the northern Lower Peninsula centered on lumbering and lake commerce, and mining also was a critical industry in the Upper Peninsula. The counties selected for this case study reflect this diversity in population demographics and economics, both of which are intertwined with the need for and delivery of relief and social welfare services in the 1930s. Representing that diversity, in conjunction with securing the case-file source base, were critical factors in selecting the counties for study. Historians know much more about social welfare, relief, and the New Deal programs in large urban centers than they do about smaller towns and rural areas. My study seeks to illuminate both the rural and urban nature of relief.

Van Buren County, largely white and native born, represents the rural, agricultural experience in Michigan, while Marquette County illustrates the mining and lumbering (and some agriculture) economy of the Upper Peninsula. Saginaw County, with its racial and ethnic diversity, represents the "simultaneous growth of industry and agriculture" characteristic of Michigan and other Midwestern states.[24] Its economy centered on sugar beets and other agriculture, but industry also played an increasing role, particularly with the rise of the automotive and steel industries, and later the defense plants of the 1940s.[25] These job opportunities attracted African-Americans and Mexicans, offering an opportunity to assess the role of race and citizenship in the welfare process. Race was and is a critical issue in welfare policy, but citizenship also played an important role. Noncitizens of all nationalities experienced discrimination in welfare programs as well as in employment opportunities, and both Saginaw and Wayne counties offer the basis for this analysis. Mexican populations in Saginaw and Wayne counties also faced repatriation efforts in the 1930s, a strategy used at the state and local level to remove noncitizens who might take jobs, or relief benefits, from citizens and residents.

Wayne County was the center of Michigan's automotive industry (and later the defense industry). It had the highest population of any county, and its racial demographics were very similar to Saginaw County (see table I.1). Those two counties contained the majority of the state's African-American and Mexican populations. Wayne County had more than half of all Mexicans who lived in the state, but the Mexican population in Saginaw made up a greater percentage of the county's overall population.[26] Wayne County (and Detroit) experienced a unique relief situation. Detroit professionalized its social welfare department in the 1920s, and thus does not represent the larger experiences in the state. Detroit's size also permitted it to create a Department of Social Welfare separate from Wayne County under the 1939 Welfare Reorganization Act.

Van Buren County, largely rural, with only one city (South Haven) in the 1930s, had a population of 32,637 in 1930. At that time, the county's popula-

24. Daniel Nelson, *Farm and Factory: Workers in the Midwest, 1880–1990* (Bloomington: Indiana University Press, 1995), vii.

25. Alan Clive, *State of War: Michigan in World War II* (Ann Arbor: University of Michigan Press, 1979), 20–22.

26. Wayne County's 1930 census listed 7,104 Mexicans—more than half of the state's 13,336 Mexicans. Saginaw had the next greatest number (2,270), which represented nearly 2 percent of the county's population. See *Fifteenth Census of the United States: 1930, Vol. I, Population* (Washington, D.C.: U.S. Government Printing Office, 1931), 1152.

TABLE I.1
FOREIGN-BORN AND MINORITY POPULATIONS IN 1930

County	1930 Census Population	% Foreign-Born	% African-American	% Mexican
Marquette	44,076	22.8	0.4	0.0
Saginaw	120,717	9.1	3.9	1.9
Van Buren	32,637	10.3	1.4	0.0
Wayne	1,888,946	25.3	7.0	0.37
State of Michigan	4,842,325	7.4	3.5	0.3

Source: *Fifteenth Census of the United States: 1930, Vol. I, Population*, 1115, 1152.

tion was 88 percent native-born white, 10.5 percent foreign-born white and 1.4 percent African-American (see table I.1).[27] More than half of its employed residents labored in the farming industry, either on their own farms or as laborers. Other key areas of employment included retail, construction, and domestic work (for women).[28]

Van Buren County residents made their living through the century from fruit production, including berries (blueberries, strawberries, and cherries), apples, pears, and peaches. Grape vineyards not only yielded fruit but also fed the wine and juice industries. Juice companies had organized in the early years of the twentieth century, with companies in Lawton and Paw Paw. Welch Grape Juice Company, for instance, started business in Van Buren during World War I, manufacturing grape jelly for the armed forces. With the demise of Prohibition, in 1933, came the growth of the wine-making industry, and by 1937 the county boasted five wineries.[29] Some residents also labored in the paper mills of Watervliet, in nearby Berrien County, as well as in Kalamazoo and Grand Rapids.

Marquette County, like much of the Upper Peninsula, had a significant foreign-born population. It was slightly larger than Van Buren, with a population in 1930 of 44,076. Nearly one-quarter of its residents were non-native-born whites; the foreign-born population was 22.8 percent. However, as was true for much of Michigan, Marquette had few nonwhite residents, with just 0.4 percent of its population listed as African-American.[30] Immigrants from Scandinavian countries—especially Finland, Norway, and Sweden—and also from

27. *Fifteenth Census,* 1140.
28. *Fifteenth Census,* 1164.
29. Douglas L. Semark, ed., *A History of Van Buren County, Michigan* (Hartford, MI: Van Buren County Historical Society, 1983), 1, 3–5.
30. *Fifteenth Census,* table 13, 1138, 1140.

Ireland, Scotland, England, and Canada, helped to settle Marquette. Some came under contract with mining companies, while others migrated for land in addition to the promise of employment.[31]

Like much of the Lake Superior shore of the Upper Peninsula, Marquette centered its economic base on extractive industries such as mining and lumbering, dating to the mid-nineteenth century. For the Marquette area, iron ore was the major material, as compared to copper in the Keewenaw Peninsula. Iron ore was first found in the region in 1844, and by 1845 the first mine—Jackson Mine—opened, and became the site of the city of Negaunee in Marquette County.[32] Other mining ventures soon followed, including the Cleveland-Cliffs Iron Company. The county's location on the shores of Lake Superior made it a natural choice as an urban center for the Upper Peninsula and the mining industry, and completion of the shipping locks in 1855 at Sault Ste. Marie—connecting Lake Superior with the lower Great Lakes—only facilitated the industry's growth. Until the late nineteenth century, all of Michigan's iron-ore industry was concentrated in the Marquette range.[33]

Of the companies founded during the peak of Marquette's mining industry, the Cleveland-Cliffs Iron Company, the largest, continued to operate into the mid-twentieth century, and gained ownership of several smaller mines throughout the late nineteenth and early twentieth centuries. Mining continued to be a key employer in the area by 1930.[34] In addition to its role as a shipping center, Marquette also developed other industries, including chemical production (nitroglycerin), sawmills, brownstone quarries, flour mills, and a brickyard, in addition to agriculture. Its key industries—mining, forestry, and railroads—were all on the decline by the Depression, however, and the short growing season made agriculture less than ideal in the Upper Peninsula.[35] But its more diverse industrial base saved it from disappearing, as some mining towns did.

Saginaw County represents the state's mix of industry and agriculture. Originally founded as a major lumber town, Saginaw, both the city and the

31. Warren Vander Hill, "So Many Different People," in *A Most Superior Land*, ed. Susan Newhof Pyle (Lansing: TwoPeninsula Press, 1983), 19–23.

32. John S. Burt, "'Boys, look around and see what you can find,'" *Michigan History* 78.6 (November/December 1994): 11, 14.

33. "A Bond of Interest," in *Harlow's Wooden Man: Quarterly Journal of the Marquette County Historical Society* XIII, no. 5 (Fall 1978): 6–10; Kathleen Marie Blee, "The Impact of Family Settlement Patterns on the Politics of Lake Superior Communities, 1890–1920" (PhD dissertation, University of Wisconsin, 1982), 87–88.

34. "A Bond of Interest," 16; Blee, "The Impact of Family Settlement Patterns," 87–88.

35. *Fifteenth Census*, 1162; *Michigan: A Guide to the Wolverine State* (New York: Oxford University Press, 1941), 345–46.

larger county, developed an industrial base that helped it to weather the worst of the Depression years. Saginaw County had a population of 120,717; of its residents, 9.1 percent were foreign-born, 3.9 percent were African-American, and 1.9 percent were Mexican (see table I.1). Immigrants from Germany, Poland, and Canada (French), some of whom were recruited to work in the lumber industry, helped to settle the area by the 1870s, although native-born workers continued to dominate the lumber workforce. Sugar beet farming and processing emerged by the early twentieth century as a major part of Saginaw's economy, bringing the area's first Mexicans to Saginaw as migrant laborers.[36]

Lumbering provided the economic foundation for Saginaw, and the first sawmills were built on the shores of the Saginaw River in the 1830s. Saginaw's location—just downstream from the convergence of four major tributaries of the Saginaw River—made it a logical site for storing logs and constructing sawmills.[37] The lumber industry prospered in the nineteenth century, and thus so did the city of Saginaw and the surrounding area. By the 1880s and 1890s, however, lumbering of the pine forests was on the decline, and only half of the sawmills remained in operation at the close of the nineteenth century. By the turn of the century, manufacturing began to replace lumbering as the dominant industry. Manufacturing companies, both metal and automotive, developed rapidly, including what would become the largest employers in the area: Jackson-Church and Wilcox (later to be General Motors and Saginaw Steering Gear) and Valley Grey Iron (Chevrolet Grey Iron Foundry). The auto-parts manufacturers would be major employers by World War I. By the 1920s more than ten thousand people worked in the Saginaw Steering Gear Division.[38]

Negotiating Relief is organized chronologically in the first half and topically in the latter. Chapter 1 describes pre-Depression relief in Michigan, focusing on Marquette, Saginaw, Van Buren, and Wayne counties and their social welfare systems. Michigan's welfare system was locally administered and publicly funded, even before the New Deal. Chapter 2 chronicles the efforts of both public and private agencies to meet the rising demand for unemployment relief in the early years of the Great Depression, before the Federal Emergency Relief Administration. Ultimately, all counties would face major financial crises as a result of the relief problem, but resistance to federal aid remained strong until 1932, and never entirely disappeared.

36. Germans and Canadians were the major proportion (81 percent) of Saginaw's immigrant population by 1890. Jeremy W. Kilar, *Michigan's Lumbertowns: Lumbermen and Laborers in Saginaw, Bay City, and Muskegon, 1870–1905* (Detroit: Wayne State University Press, 1990), 174, 177, 194; Jeremy W. Kilar and Sandy L. Schwan, *Saginaw's Changeable Past: An Illustrated History* (St. Louis: G. Bradley Publishing, 1994), 66, 98, 118–19.

37. Kilar, *Michigan's Lumbertowns*, 20–22.

38. Ibid., 293; Kilar and Schwan, *Saginaw's Changeable Past*, 114–15.

Chapter 3 assesses the implementation of the Federal Emergency Relief Act in 1933. The FERA years foreshadowed the deep anticentralization views regarding relief administration that would only magnify in the next five years. Local officials sought to defend home rule. Many counties resented the intrusion of the federal and state governments into what they saw as their business; they welcomed the financial help, but did not want the rules that accompanied that aid. Chapter 4 chronicles the work-relief programs of the New Deal, particularly the Civil Works Administration, Works Progress Administration, National Youth Administration, and Civilian Conservation Corps. These programs were important in bringing millions of dollars in wages to the state, and often served as a vehicle for family support until private employment became available.

Chapters 5 and 6 turn to two groups critical to relief negotiations in this period: social workers (and the profession at large) and the recipients of relief. Chapter 5 analyzes the competing professional visions for relief administration, with a focus on the effects of the Great Depression and New Deal years on social workers and the profession of social work. High demand for caseworkers created an influx of untrained relief workers who did not meet the professional-education standards, creating tension and division within the profession. The conflict culminated in the spread of social worker unions to address the labor grievances of relief workers. This chapter also examines the influence of professional social work on public welfare agencies.

Chapter 6 analyzes the relief negotiations between caseworkers and recipients, who saw federal and state officials as new allies in the administration of welfare. The recipients' narrative often contrasted sharply with that described by the caseworker. At the center of these negotiations were expectations of family responsibility, and the framing of relief around the unit of the family. Recipients were not passive participants, but agents in the administration of relief in the 1930s.

Chapter 7 turns to the statewide negotiation of relief in the welfare-reform debate after FERA's end in 1935. The ideologies of home rule and fiscal localism are central. Michigan's welfare law needed major revision to enable the state to receive federal grants under the Social Security Act. The conflicts outlined in chapter 3 only intensified as local officials sought to defend their authority against what they saw as encroachment by the federal and state governments. Debates took place during meetings and hearings of the Welfare and Relief Study Commission, appointed in 1936 to assess the state's welfare system. Local officials, and their representative associations, successfully mobilized to defeat the 1937 laws that resulted from the commission's recommendations, in a victory for home rule.

Debates about relief in Michigan in the 1930s centered on notions of expertise and power, as well as on home rule and fiscal localism. Differences between key groups, particularly local officials and advocates of professional social work, focused on beliefs about what expertise was needed for relief administration. In detailing these debates, and the competing narratives they generate, I do not aim to privilege one over the other, but seek to give voice to the complexity of those debates and to illuminate the experiences of those involved. Although associations representing specific groups often took a firm stand on welfare issues, the individuals within those groups represented a spectrum of beliefs. Some local officials advocated professional social work and centralization of relief, while some advocates of social work practices did not believe those methods were needed in public welfare. The complexities, revealed in part by the lack of a unified voice and a diversity of motives, resulted ultimately in a welfare system that represented both change and continuity.[39] The mixed nature of the 1939 Welfare Reorganization Act left few people on any side fully satisfied, and welfare administration continued to be debated in the years that followed.

---

39. Johanna Schoen, *Choice and Coercion: Birth Control, Sterilization, and Abortion in Public Health and Welfare* (Chapel Hill: University of North Carolina Press, 2005), 13–15. Schoen's introduction provides a helpful discussion of the diversity of motivations behind reproductive policy and the agency of women affected by that policy.

CHAPTER ONE

A Local Problem

SOCIAL WELFARE POLICY BEFORE THE NEW DEAL

THE ONSET OF the Great Depression precipitated an unprecedented demand for social welfare and relief services in Michigan and throughout the United States, prompting extensive debates about the most effective means to administer relief. Michigan as a whole suffered extremely high unemployment once the Depression began. State Emergency Relief administrator William Haber recalled that Michigan was extremely hard-hit by the Depression, even in a national context: "When the country has a cold, Michigan has pneumonia."[1] In 1930 agricultural unemployment was 18 percent. Unemployment at the Ford plants in Detroit reached 32 percent by early 1931. Employment dropped from more than 100,000 workers at the end of 1929 to 84,000 workers in the spring of 1931, and down to 37,000 by the end of that summer. In addition, those who were employed worked only part-time or at reduced wages.[2] Similar trends occurred in Flint, another major automobile-manufacturing town. In 1928 General Motors employed 208,981 workers; by 1932 that fell nearly 50 percent to 116,152, and the company's payroll fell 60 percent.[3]

---

1. *The William Haber Oral Biography Project: Edited Transcripts*, Bentley Historical Library, Tape X, 204.

2. Zaragosa Vargas, *Proletarians of the North: A History of Mexican Industrial Workers in Detroit and the Midwest, 1917–1933* (Berkeley: University of California Press, 1993), 172.

3. Sidney Fine, *Sit-Down: The General Motors Strike of 1936–1937* (Ann Arbor: University of Michigan Press, 1975), 21.

Between 1930 and 1933 the state overall had an unemployment rate of 34 percent, far higher than the national average of 26 percent. In October 1932, employment rates in Michigan's industries dropped to 41 percent of the rates in the mid-1920s. In 1933 unemployment reached 46 percent, with 485,000 people out of work. At one point, more than half a million people were seeking work in the state. As one historian writes, "Michigan was perilously close to economic disaster."[4]

By Black Tuesday, many workers were unable to deal with the more serious problems of the Depression. Many laborers, especially those in unskilled or low-wage occupations, had no savings or had already exhausted those funds during the uncertain 1920s. When the Depression reached its worst in 1932, public and private welfare services were strained to the point of bankruptcy. Many fund-raising drives held by private organizations fell short of their goals, and agencies were forced to cut budgets. Private agencies directed more of their funds toward unemployment relief, but could not raise enough money to meet the rising demand; as a result, more and more people turned to public agencies for help.

Public relief for poor, unemployed, or otherwise needy individuals or families was not new, but the administration of that relief changed dramatically in the 1930s. The New Deal programs often signify to many people the beginning of America's welfare state, although 1932 marked the first federal appropriations for public relief.[5] Unlike some states, Michigan had an extensive public welfare system before the 1930s. This system was almost exclusively local, funded with local tax dollars.[6] Much of Michigan's poor-relief system had existed, with only minor changes, for more than a century, and was rooted in township, city, and county governmental institutions. Local elected officials, including township supervisors and probate judges, dictated appropriations for the varied kinds of poor relief, and, if they did not administer such

4. James Lorence, *Organizing the Unemployed: Community and Union Activists in the Industrial Heartland* (Albany: State University of New York, 1996), 3–4; William Haber and Paul Stanchfield, *Unemployment and Relief in Michigan* (Lansing: Franklin DeKleine Company, 1935), 2; Haber and Stanchfield, *Unemployment, Relief, and Economic Security*, 17; Daniel Nelson, *Farm and Factory: Workers in the Midwest, 1880–1990* (Bloomington: Indiana University Press, 1995), 119–21.

5. Jeffrey Singleton, *The American Dole: Unemployment Relief and the Welfare State in the Great Depression* (Westport, CT: Greenwood Press, 2000), 6.

6. Some states and cities lacked public welfare agencies, generally because of constitutional limitations or the voluntary nature of such agencies. See Karen Ferguson, *Black Politics in New Deal Atlanta* (Chapel Hill: University of North Carolina Press, 2002), 74; Ronald L. Heinemann, *Depression and New Deal in Virginia: The Enduring Dominion* (Charlottesville: University Press of Virginia, 1983), 155–56; and Douglas L. Smith, *The New Deal in the Urban South* (Baton Rouge: Louisiana State University Press, 1988), 64–65.

relief directly, appointed the people who did. Local officials, then, wielded significant power in the distribution of that relief, and would fight to retain that power later in the decade. Public funding and local administration were the central features of Michigan's social welfare system long before the Great Depression and the New Deal.

An 1809 statute established Michigan's poor law and would continue largely unchanged for the next century. It was modeled after English law, with provisions including residency requirements of one year and disbursement of funds by local officials.[7] Many states, following the lead of Pennsylvania, organized relief through the counties. Welfare services included both institutional (usually a poorhouse or poor farm) and outdoor relief. Outdoor relief included all noninstitutional aid, usually cash or in-kind services or goods. Providing relief in most states, including Michigan, was voluntary, although most counties offered some poor relief.[8] Counties could select either the county-wide or the township system. Under the township program, found in Saginaw and Wayne counties, cities and townships within the county administered and financed their own relief programs. Township supervisors or city poor-department superintendents handled the relief responsibilities. Marquette and Van Buren counties used the county system, in which the superintendents of the poor, appointed by the county board of supervisors, administered relief.[9] Virtually all welfare needs—temporary relief needs, medical care, placement in a county or state institution, or even requests for sterilization—originated with a local official.[10]

Eligibility for relief rested on proof of residence for at least one year and evidence of need. Relief recipients in general were to own no property or other means of securing a living. Individuals who had no income or means of support, but who did own property, had to sign their property rights over to the county before receiving aid.[11] This process could be reversed once the indi-

7. Opal V. Matson, *Local Relief to Dependents* (Detroit: Detroit Bureau of Governmental Research, 1933), 9.

8. Marian Gertrude Simons, "Public Welfare Administration in Michigan" (master's thesis, University of Chicago School of Social Administration, 1931), 127; Bruce and Eickhoff, *The Michigan Poor Law*, 12, 31.

9. Matson, *Local Relief to Dependents*, 12; *Annual Abstract of the Reports of Superintendents of the Poor in the State of Michigan* (Lansing), 1891, 1895, and 1900. According to these reports, forty-seven of Michigan's eighty-three counties used the county system of organization for poor relief, while twenty-five counties used the township system.

10. Welfare and Relief Study Commission records, Box 5, Folder 10, RG 35, Archives of Michigan, Lansing, "Local Public Welfare," draft report, n.d., 33–34; Jeffrey Alan Hodges, "Euthenics, Eugenics, and Compulsory Sterilization in Michigan: 1897–1960" (master's thesis, Michigan State University, 1995).

11. Frank M. Landers and Claude R. Tharp, *Administration and Financing of Public Relief*, Michigan Pamphlets No. 17 (Bureau of Government: University of Michigan, 1942), 2–3.

vidual became self-supporting. The goal was to permit the county to recover its relief costs from an estate if a recipient died while receiving public aid.[12] In some cases, poor individuals who owned property deeded ownership to the county in exchange for regular support payments. The superintendent of the poor agreed to provide weekly relief payments and fuel, and the recipient retained a life lease on their home. Upon death, the county received the property. Mrs. Maria Lercat of Paw Paw (Van Buren County), for instance, sought county care for her property in June of 1912; she received $1.50 per week plus fuel and deeded her house and lot to the county.[13] Such cases generally involved property owners who had no family who could care for them or to whom they could leave their property in exchange for care. Mrs. Lachapelle of Marquette, on the other hand, a widow who owned property that generated some rental income, refused to sign a deed transfer and therefore did not receive aid.[14] Individuals who refused to deed property to the county generally were ineligible for poor relief, a practice that continued under the state's old-age pension law.

The responsibility of families to support their members was a cornerstone of poor relief administration. Laws mandated this implementation. Family members, including parents, grandparents, spouses, and children, were expected to contribute to, if not fully support, family members in need. The responsible-relative clause is found in the earliest poor laws and remained in force under Public Act 146 of 1925, which consolidated Michigan's poor laws. Township supervisors or superintendents of the poor enforced such support through the probate court, which could order family members to provide financial support.[15] Officials often refused relief to individuals if they believed relatives were able to support them, or reduced the poor-relief grants to applicants if family members could contribute. Anne Kokka was receiving

---

12. This was used most often for individuals committed to an institution for relief, such as the poor farm, poorhouse, or county infirmary. Such aid was considered "permanent support," while outdoor relief was seen as temporary.

13. Minutes of the Superintendent of the Poor and Poor Commission, Van Buren County, Western Michigan University Archives, entries for June 6, 1912, and October 1, 1936.

14. "Proceedings of the Board of Superintendents of the Poor," Marquette County, December 17, 1926, Marquette County Historical Society.

15. See Section 2, Chapter 1 of Public Act No. 146 of 1925, *Public Acts of the Legislature of the State of Michigan* (Lansing: Robert Smith Printers, 1925), 88. Michigan differed from some states, including Illinois, in its exclusion of brothers and sisters from the responsible-relative clause. See Isabel Campbell Bruce and Edith Eickhoff, *The Michigan Poor Law: Its Development and Administration with Special Reference to State Provision for Medical Care of the Indigent* (Chicago: University of Chicago Press, 1936), 48. Courts of domestic relations, such as those found in Chicago and New York, often were the site of family-support enforcement. See Anna R. Igra, *Wives without Husbands: Marriage, Desertion, and Welfare in New York, 1900–1935* (Chapel Hill: University of North Carolina Press, 2007), 87.

medical care from Marquette County, but an investigation found that she had several adult children, with one daughter living with her, and owned her home. The superintendents of the poor agreed that her children could provide her medical care and support her.[16] Mrs. Elliot was also cut off from aid when superintendents learned she had a daughter willing to take her in. Subsequent investigation discovered that the daughter had moved and did not save room for her mother, and aid was resumed.[17] Most poor-relief officials looked to families first for support, a practice that would continue in the New Deal programs and the reorganized welfare programs that followed.

Records documenting poor-relief practices often include only lists of bills paid and weekly or monthly totals of relief disbursed. In some cases, the administrator listed individual names and dates, as well as items or services granted. Although limited, these records do yield some insights. Outdoor relief, for example, could be in the form of grocery orders (redeemable for certain items at specific stores), fuel (wood or coal), clothing, and medical care (doctor's visits, medicine, or medical supplies). Car repairs and items such as stoves might also be provided if deemed necessary. Cash relief was a rarity not only in Michigan welfare but throughout the country before the New Deal years.

Michigan's medical system was a mix of state and local services, with significant variation throughout the state. Counties provided and investigated medical needs in different ways, and the system relied in part on the ability and willingness of the medical profession to provide services to the poor. Nathan Sinai, a public health expert who authored a 1933 report on the status of the state's medical relief, argued that it was "an outstanding example of social 'blindspot,'" one that developed "so widely and so largely and yet so haphazardly."[18] Sinai was extraordinarily critical of the system: "Under the system of relief in effect prior to the inauguration of the Emergency Relief Administration, medical relief appeared to be everybody's business in general but nobody's job in particular."[19]

Medical relief was coordinated at the local level, and its organization centered on whether the county operated relief under the county or township system, as with poor relief. Hospitalization was provided through the Univer-

16. "Proceedings of the Board of Superintendents of the Poor," Marquette County, January 18, 1924, Marquette County Historical Society.

17. "Proceedings of the Board of Superintendents of the Poor," Marquette County, October 19, 1927, January 17, 1929.

18. Nathan Sinai, Marguerite F. Hallo, V. M. Hogue, and Miriam Steep, *Medical Relief in Michigan: A Study of the Experience in Ten Counties* (Ann Arbor, MI: Edward Brothers, Inc, 1938), 2.

19. Sinai et al., 12.

sity of Michigan Hospital, created in 1875 to serve the needs of the poor in the state and to offer teaching opportunities for medical students. Once approved by the probate court, patients were cared for at the hospital, with the local unit paying the hospital costs but the state covering professional services. In 1933 the law allowed care at a local approved hospital, but local units paid all costs. Children were eligible for hospital care beginning in 1875, and adults were eligible under a 1915 law. Children's hospitalization was covered by state funds.[20]

Physician care was part of the state's outdoor-relief system and thus was both administered and financed entirely by local funds. Counties used a variety of systems to provide medical care to the poor, but virtually all reports examining the system concurred with Sinai's assessment: the medical-relief system was one of overlapping and duplicating agencies with little coordination, which resulted in higher costs and lower patient care. Some contracted with medical societies, and two counties (Wayne and Kent) operated medical clinics for the poor. Some counties employed a physician for a monthly salary, while others paid their county physicians on a fee basis. Critics argued that contracts for physician care often went to the "lowest bidder," with little attention to the quality of care.[21] Van Buren County's poor officials, for instance, received several bids from doctors in 1912 for medical care, but opted for the lowest bid. When that physician died a year later, they again chose the lowest bid among the submissions.[22] Investigation and approval for such care was the responsibility of local officials, either superintendents of the poor, township supervisors, or county agents, depending on the administrative setup in the county.

Temporary, or outdoor, relief was the dominant form of poor relief offered both in Michigan's counties and in the country as a whole. Residents sought aid from either a township supervisor or a superintendent of the poor, who decided what relief to provide. Historian Michael Katz argues that outdoor relief served far more people than did institutions in the United States, a trend true in Michigan's eighty-three counties.[23] People were much more likely to receive a grocery or fuel order, or perhaps assistance with medical treatment or rent, than they were to seek care in an infirmary. Infirmary residents

20. Sinai et al., 16–17; Isabel Campbell Bruce and Edith Eickhoff, *The Michigan Poor Law* (Chicago: University of Chicago Press, 1936), 95; and Edith Abbott, *Public Assistance: American Principles and Politics, Vol. I* (Ann Arbor, MI: Edward Brothers, Inc, 1938), 2.

21. Sinai et al., 18; Bruce and Eickhoff, 82–83.

22. Minutes, Superintendents of the Poor, Van Buren County, entries for February 12, 1912, and April 2, 1913.

23. Michael B. Katz, *In the Shadow of the Poorhouse: A Social History of Welfare in America*, Rev. Ed. (New York: Basic Books, 1996), 38.

accounted for a small portion of the care provided through local public channels—usually less than 5 or 10 percent for all counties. Statewide figures show that infirmaries served anywhere from 6 percent of all cases receiving aid (in 1895) to a high of 16.5 percent in 1920, while the remainder received noninstitutional relief.[24]

Wayne County passed Michigan's first law enabling the construction of a county infirmary in 1828. The territory followed suit the following year, passing legislation that allowed counties, townships, and cities to raise tax funds to construct such institutions to be run by appointed boards.[25] Many of these institutions developed in states across the country in the antebellum period, a part of the shift to institutional care for many groups classed as "dependents" in society.[26] Michigan had eighty-one infirmaries by 1933.[27] Superintendents of the poor or township supervisors authorized institutional care. A 1933 report on Michigan's welfare system noted that few formal requirements for the administrative positions existed, and "in a few instances the position is given to the lowest bidder." This study also found that more than half of all infirmary keepers were farmers. Such institutions usually were administered by a husband and wife, where the husband served as keeper, responsible for operating the farm, and the wife as matron, responsible for the management of the infirmary.[28] Residents receiving outdoor relief also might be required to work at the infirmary for their aid.[29]

Michigan's infirmaries housed anywhere from five thousand individuals in 1891 to thirty thousand in 1938—five years after the New Deal programs began. Residents of infirmaries represented only a fraction of those receiving relief of some form, but the infirmaries remained an important part of the relief structure. Men tended to outnumber women residents, accounting for about three-quarters of reported residents from 1891 to 1938. Children

---

24. See *Abstract of the Reports of the Superintendents of the Poor*, table II. The figures used in this section on Michigan infirmaries come from a sampling of annual reports of the superintendents of the poor. I examined figures in every fifth year available, beginning with 1891 (the 1890 report was not available) and ending with 1938, the last published report. See *Abstract of the Reports of the Superintendents of the Poor*, table I, 1891, 1895, 1900, 1905, 1910, 1915, 1920, 1925, 1930, 1935, 1938.

25. Bruce and Eickhoff, *The Michigan Poor Law*, 18–19, 74–75.

26. David J. Rothman, *The Discovery of the Asylum: Social Order and Disorder in the New Republic* (Boston: Little, Brown and Company, 1971), 181–86.

27. Matson, *Local Relief to Dependents*, 25.

28. Ibid., 25; Bruce and Eickhoff, *The Michigan Poor Law*, 42; "Local Public Welfare," WRSC, 58–59; Rothman, *The Discovery of the Asylum*, 193; and Katz, *In the Shadow of the Poorhouse*, 29.

29. St. Clair Superintendent of the Poor Records, Box 1, Folder 2, State of Michigan Archives, Lansing.

also continued to reside in infirmaries, although institutions had attempted to cease admitting children by the 1870s and 1880s, since such care was deemed damaging to children. Michigan sought to remove children from its infirmaries in 1871 with the founding of a state school for dependent children. (Small children could remain with their mothers if in a county institution.) Never a large portion of the state totals, children did comprise anywhere from 1 to 8 percent of the total poorhouse population.[30]

County infirmaries, formerly known as poorhouses, were also key institutions in the care of the aged and infirm. Originally conceived as institutions to provide for the poor, infirmaries had evolved by the twentieth century into informal nursing homes for the elderly poor, and by the 1930s had a "great proportion of mentally and physically infirm," with only a very small number of residents considered employable.[31] Medical care was the "weakest spot in the whole program of infirmary care." Just one infirmary had routine medical examinations, and just twenty scheduled regular visits by doctors. In 1933, two infirmaries even housed tubercular patients with other residents.[32] Three years later, still only seven infirmaries had hospital accommodations, and some counties transferred terminal patients to the infirmaries to die.[33]

People of color were underrepresented in infirmary populations, seldom accounting for 2 percent of the total in the years reported.[34] In Wayne County, which had the largest concentration of African-American residents in Michigan, blacks rarely were more than 4 or 5 percent of the infirmary population.[35] In part this reflects the low numbers of African-Americans in the total state population. People of color were 4.4 percent of the state's population in 1930, 2 percent in 1920, and less than 1 percent in 1910. But such figures were much higher for specific counties. Wayne County's black population, for instance, had increased from 1.1 percent in 1910, to 3.7 percent in 1920, to 7 percent in 1930; other counties with significant black populations were Cass, Lake,

30. Katz, *In the Shadow of the Poorhouse*, 107–9; Walter Trattner, *From Poor Law to Welfare State: A History of Social Welfare in America*, 4th Ed. (New York: Free Press, 1989), 107–13. The Michigan data are drawn from the *Abstracts of the Reports of the Superintendents of the Poor*, 1891, 1895, etc.

31. "Local Public Welfare," chapter III, Local Public Welfare Institutions, 62–63, WRSC Records, Box 5, Folder 10.

32. Matson, *Local Relief to Dependents*, 30.

33. "Local Public Welfare," 58.

34. Reports provide a breakdown by race (including figures for African-Americans, mulattoes, and Indians) until the turn of the century. After that year, reports included nonwhites in the "foreign-born" figure.

35. See *Annual Reports for County of Wayne*, 1895, 1900, 1905, 1910, 1915; also *Abstract of the Reports of the Superintendents of the Poor, State of Michigan*, years aforementioned in previous footnote.

and Saginaw.[36] The issue of race received little attention in surviving records, including the published reports of both the state and Wayne County. The small number of nonwhite residents in county infirmaries was likely a combination of racism and exclusion.

Infirmaries were important sources of aid for Michigan's foreign-born residents, although statistics on citizenship status were not reported. Infirmaries in nineteenth-century America tended to have high numbers of foreign-born populations in relation to reported census figures.[37] State figures show that native-born white Americans accounted for about half of county institutional residents through 1925. After that year, native-born whites accounted for slightly more than half: 54 percent in 1925, 62 percent in 1930, 53 percent in 1935, and 56 percent in 1938. The slight decline in numbers of foreign-born residents likely reflects the more restrictive immigration laws in effect, but throughout the period foreign-born whites nevertheless resided in institutions in far greater numbers than their share of the state populations.[38] Nineteenth-century critics argued that the presence of the foreign-born in infirmaries dominated because of the negative character traits attributed to many immigrants, such as laziness or ignorance, rather than circumstances or factors outside the infirmary residents' control.[39]

JUDICIAL AUTHORITY, LOCALISM, AND THE CASE OF MOTHERS' PENSIONS

Implementation of mothers' pensions in 1913 represented Michigan's first new welfare program in decades, and continued the trend that programs be funded and administered locally. Enacted at the state level and administered by local officials, mothers' pensions sought to provide poor mothers with a means to raise their children in their home and were a part of the philosophical shift from institutional child care to home care for dependent children. The term

36. See *Fifteenth Census of the United States, 1930*, table 2, 1115; table 13, 1135–40; *Thirteenth Census of the United States Taken in the Year 1910, Vol. II, Population*, 946; *Fourteenth Census of the United States Taken in the Year 1920, Vol. III, Population*, 487.

37. Katz, *In the Shadow of the Poorhouse*, 92–94.

38. *Abstract of the Reports of the Superintendents of the Poor*, years aforementioned. *Fifteenth Census of the United States: 1930, Vol. I, Population* (Washington, D.C.: U.S. Government Printing Office, 1931), table 2, 1115. As noted, the poor reports do not specify citizenship status, so it is not known how many of those classified as foreign-born were naturalized citizens. According to census figures in 1920 and 1930, 28.6 percent and 34.2 percent (respectively) of the foreign-born had not pursued citizenship at some stage.

39. Rothman, *The Discovery of the Asylum*, 290–91.

"pension" was critical; mothers were to be paid for the work of raising children. It was not to be relief or welfare, but an earned benefit much like a veteran's pension.[40] Like many such laws, Michigan's 1913 mothers' pension law did not allocate state funding, and counties had to provide money for the program from their own budgets. Michigan's law placed the program within the juvenile court, and thus probate judges, along with county agents, were its chief administrators. Disputes over whether mothers' pensions were, in fact, pensions or were instead poor relief, ambiguities in the law, as well as what David Rothman has called the "cult of judicial personality," resulted in significant variations in the program's administration across Michigan and in many other states.[41]

Juvenile court programs and mothers' pensions both grew from the Progressive Era's efforts to marshal the power and authority of the state to address social problems. Mothers' pensions emerged as part of domestic relations law, directed by what Michael Grossberg calls a "judicial patriarchy." Judges "became the buffer and the referee between the family and the state," with considerable power over the family: "Family law became their patriarchal domain."[42] Grossberg argues that, by the end of the nineteenth century, judicial patriarchy defined the role of judges in family law. In the early twentieth century, this judicial authority extended into the realm of welfare and poverty with two goals: to provide appropriate care for dependent children but also to limit financial dependency on the state.[43] Many states, including Michigan, criminalized desertion and nonsupport by fathers in an effort to force fathers to provide for their children. Without support, children could be placed either in boarding homes or institutions, or their mothers could seek a pension. Administration of welfare and juvenile justice intersected in what Michael

40. Joanne L. Goodwin, *Gender and the Politics of Welfare Reform: Mothers' Pensions in Chicago, 1911–1929* (Chicago: University of Chicago Press, 1997), 36–38; Molly Ladd-Taylor, *Mother-Work: Women, Child Welfare, and the State, 1890–1930* (Chicago: University of Illinois Press, 1994), 137, 143–48; Kriste Lindenmeyer, *"A Right to Childhood": The U.S. Children's Bureau and Child Welfare* (Urbana and Chicago: University of Illinois Press, 1997), 152–56; and Gwendolyn Mink, *The Wages of Motherhood: Inequality in the Welfare State, 1917–1942* (Ithaca: Cornell University Press, 1995), 32–34.

41. David J. Rothman, *Conscience and Convenience: The Asylum and Its Alternatives in Progressive America* (Boston: Little, Brown and Company, 1980). See chapter 7, "The Cult of Judicial Personality."

42. Michael Grossberg, *Governing the Hearth: Law and the Family in Nineteenth-Century America* (Chapel Hill and London: University of North Carolina Press, 1985), 289–91.

43. Anna Igra argues that a "dual system of family law" developed in this period, particularly in relation to antidesertion efforts. The category of deserted wives became separate from widows in the early 1900s, and deserted wives were directed to the legal system, rather than the welfare system, for support. See *Wives Without Husbands*, 43.

Willrich terms a "*mode of governance* whose object is not merely to provide a modicum of economic security to citizens but to keep legitimate claims upon the public purse to a minimum."[44] Public support was to be the last resort for financial support for children, as was the case in poor relief. The ambiguous position of mothers' pensions illustrates the tension created by competing goals: providing adequately for dependent children, recognizing the work of motherhood, and minimizing the state's welfare burden.

The first mothers' pension laws at the state level emerged in the second decade of the twentieth century, and by 1926 forty-two states had mothers' pension programs. Nearly half of those states, including Michigan, placed administration of the program in the juvenile court.[45] Some states simply placed the program under existing welfare administrators, such as superintendents of the poor, while other states created a new local agency that often was responsible for all forms of poor relief, including mothers' pensions. Administrative designations fell somewhat along regional lines; Midwestern and Western states tended to use juvenile courts more than states in the Northeast.[46] Most Michigan counties administered the program through the juvenile court staff, usually comprised of the judge, county agent, and perhaps a probation officer. Larger urban counties, such as Wayne and Kent, created separate departments and staffs for the mothers' pension program. The placement of the program in the juvenile court continued to be debated, because some judges and other officials believed it belonged in the poor-relief program.[47] But the programs were funded and administered locally in all states; the only variation was which local officials were the administrators.

The choice of the juvenile court reflected the link some experts saw between the presence of mothers in the home and the rate of juvenile delinquency: allowing mothers to remain in their home to raise their children would reduce

44. Michael Willrich, "Home Slackers: Men, the State, and Welfare in Modern America," *Journal of American History* 87.2 (September 2000): 463; See also David S. Tanenhaus, *Juvenile Justice in the Making* (New York and Oxford: Oxford University Press, 2004) and Willrich, *City of Courts: Socializing Justice in Progressive Era Chicago* (New York and Cambridge: Cambridge University Press, 2003).

45. Emma Octavia Lundberg, *Public Aid to Mothers with Dependent Children*, U.S. Children's Bureau Publication No. 162 (Washington, D.C.: U.S. Government Printing Office, 1926), 2, 10. For a discussion of Chicago, see Goodwin, *Gender and the Politics of Welfare Reform*.

46. Christopher Howard, "Sowing the Seeds of 'Welfare': The Transformation of Mothers' Pensions, 1900–1940." *Journal of Policy History* 4.2 (1992): 197.

47. The issue appears periodically in the proceedings of the National Probation Association, but it is also telling how rarely mothers' pensions are discussed at the national meetings. For an example of the argument that the court was not the appropriate site for the program, see James Hoge Ricks, "The Place of the Juvenile Court in the Care of Dependent Children," *Social Service and the Courts, the Annual Report and Proceedings of the Fourteenth Annual Conference of the National Probation Association* (Albany, NY: National Probation Association, 1920): 124–29; Matson, *Local Relief to Dependents*, 37–39.

the chances that the children would become delinquent.[48] Mothers' pensions were a means to prevent juvenile delinquency in families where the only problem was poverty due to the absence of a male breadwinner. Wayne County's Judge D. J. Healy, in fact, called the program "preventive" and argued that children under the supervision of the mothers' pension program became delinquent at a much smaller rate than children outside the program.[49] Those who, like Judge Healy, supported placement of the program in the juvenile court argued that pensions were distinct from relief and did not belong in a welfare agency. Some recipients preferred administration by the juvenile court not so much because of support for the probate judges, but rather for its separation from other welfare programs. To them and to part of the public, mothers' pensions were not stigmatized in the way that other welfare programs were. Consequently, benefits were sometimes more generous.

Michigan's 1913 mothers' pension law provided material support for needy children whose mother was a "suitable guardian" and for whom the only problem was financial need. Like many other state mothers' pension laws, Michigan's program relied solely on local tax dollars budgeted through county boards of supervisors. Probate judges, elected to four-year terms, administered the program and had an extraordinary amount of discretion, including who would receive pensions and for how much. They hired the staff—either investigators of the mothers' pensions, or county agents—who dealt with the scrutiny of pension applications, and had final say in whether a pension was awarded.[50] Their discretion was linked to Progressive Era beliefs that individual treatment was the best way to address issues related to crime, including juvenile delinquency. As a result, juvenile courts had very few guidelines, a situation that produced a "cult of judicial personality," or "a system that made the personality of the judge, his likes and dislikes, attitudes and prejudices, consistencies and caprices, the decisive element in shaping the character of his courtroom."[51] Probate courts varied considerably in their operation, including the administration of mothers' pensions, regardless of the state law.

Guidelines by the National Probation Association and the U.S. Children's Bureau recommended that a probate judge have "special qualifications for juvenile court work. He should have legal training, acquaintance with social

48. Lundberg, *Public Aid to Mothers with Dependent Children*, 10; Goodwin, *Gender and the Politics of Welfare Reform*, 101–4.

49. D. J. Healy, "Prevention of Juvenile Delinquency," in *Probation in Theory and Practice, Michigan Probation Association 1937 Yearbook*, 38.

50. Public Act 228, *Public Acts of the Legislature of the State of Michigan, 1913* (Lansing: Wynkoop Hallenbeck Crawford Co., 1913), 444–45; Arthur W. Bromage and Thomas H. Reed, *Organization and Cost of County and Township Government* (Detroit: Detroit Bureau of Governmental Research, 1933), 61–62.

51. Rothman, *Conscience and Convenience*, 238.

problems, and understanding of child psychology." But this was not always the case, according to NPA field secretary Francis Hiller, and Michigan vividly illustrates the gulf between theory and practice.[52] Probate judges were elected officials generally identified with one of the major political parties. The position had no eligibility requirements, aside from U.S. citizenship, county residence, and a successful bid for election. Neither legal training nor education was necessary, and many judges in fact were not attorneys.[53] A 1933 study of six Michigan counties found that just three judges had legal training, while three others were a civil engineer and farmer, a general store owner with an eighth-grade education, and a former lumber-company foreman.[54] A 1936 Michigan study of seventeen counties reported that some judges serving on the bench had less than an eighth-grade education. Just four judges were attorneys, and most did not have training either in law or in social work. Sitting probate judges were formerly farmers, barbers, county sheriffs, real estate salesmen, and court employees. They were an all-male, older population, with half beyond the age of fifty.[55] Few met the guidelines advocated by the NPA and the Children's Bureau.

Michigan's case also illustrates the significant variation in administrative practices, a trend rooted in the program's local administration and funding. The lack of uniformity is explained largely by the varied beliefs and practices of the probate judges. Michigan's law was among the most liberal and inclusive in the country. On its face, all mothers—unmarried, deserted, widowed and divorced, white and nonwhite, citizen and noncitizen—were eligible for pensions.[56] Michigan was also one of just three states to provide aid to unmarried mothers.[57] But a 1934 study by the State Department of Welfare found that

52. Francis H. Hiller, "The Juvenile Court as a Case-Working Agency," in *The Courts and the Prevention of Juvenile Delinquency: Annual Reports and Proceedings of the Twentieth Annual Conference of the National Probation Association* (Albany, NY: National Probation Association, 1926), 207.

53. Mabel Brown Ellis, "Juvenile Courts and Mothers' Pensions in Michigan," unpublished [1917].

54. The 1933 study included the counties of Antrim, Cass, Iron, Kent, Luce, and Roscommon. Bromage and Reed, *Organization and Cost of County and Township Government*, 25, 61.

55. "Local Public Welfare," draft of study, WRSC records, RG 35 Archives of Michigan, Lansing, Box 5, Folder 10, 81–82; "Sampling Survey" for WRSC, county notes, WRSC Records, Boxes 6 and 7.

56. Public Act No. 228 of 1913; Goodwin, *Gender and the Politics of Welfare Reform*, 160–66.

57. Theda Skocpol, *Protecting Soldiers and Mothers: The Political Origins of Social Policy in the United States* (Cambridge: Harvard University Press, 1992), 467; *Mothers' Aid, 1931*, U.S. Children's Bureau Publication No. 220 (Washington, D.C.: U.S. Government Printing Office, 1933), 12. New York's law was among the most conservative, directing nonwidows to the legal system to secure support. See Igra, *Wives Without Husbands*, 35, 107.

twenty-one counties refused aid to certain categories of mothers, despite the broad scope of the law. Seventeen counties refused pensions to divorced or unmarried mothers and four counties excluded aid to children whose fathers were in prison.[58] Widows were the overwhelming majority of recipients throughout the life of the program, often accounting for as many as three-quarters of the petitions granted.[59] Many counties would not support mothers with only one child, and some also excluded cases involving desertion, alcohol, insanity, and the physically handicapped.[60] The state attorney general also reinforced the discretion accorded to probate judges in 1938, arguing that the word *may* in the law was key; the judge had the power to grant aid, but was not required to, and any grant continued only "until the further order of the court."[61]

Although the evidence of overt discrimination is somewhat limited, the racial demographics of mothers' pension recipients further point to judicial discretion in the program's administration. Historians have documented the discriminatory nature of the program in many states, linking such discrimination to local administrative control. A 1931 U.S. Children's Bureau report found that just 3 percent of all pension recipients were black, and many of those were concentrated in just two states.[62] As Joanne Goodwin has shown, the numbers of black recipients in Chicago were not proportionate to the size of the black population, despite the city's high number of female-headed households from 1910 to 1919.[63] By contrast, the proportions of blacks in the mothers' pension program were higher in some regions of the country than the number of blacks in the population.[64] Mothers' pension programs did

58. Reba F. Harris, *Mothers' Pensions in Michigan: Report of a Study Made by the State Welfare Department* (Lansing: State Welfare Department, 1934), 1, 3–5; Memorandum of State Welfare Department, "Report on Mothers' Pensions for the Fiscal Year," 1935, WRSC Records, Research and Information Files, Box 14, Folder 5, Archives of Michigan; "Sampling Survey," Box 6, Folder 5 (Hillsdale County), and Box 7, Folder 5 (Oakland County), WRSC Records.

59. Kay Walters Ofman, "A Rural View of Mothers' Pensions: The Allegan County, Michigan, Mothers' Pension Program, 1913–1928." *Social Service Review* 70.1 (March 1996): 102, 107. See also *Biennial Reports of the Michigan State Board of Corrections and Charities, 1913–1928*.

60. Harris, *Mothers' Pensions in Michigan*, 6. Widows accounted for 61 percent of the cases analyzed in the report, with unmarried mothers accounting for just 1.25 percent. Divorced mothers were 8.8 percent of the total, and deserted mothers 16 percent.

61. *Biennial Report of the Attorney General of the State of Michigan*, Attorney General Raymond W. Starr (Lansing: Franklin DeKleine Company, 1938), 3.

62. *Mothers' Aid, 1931*, U.S. Children's Bureau publication No. 220. Washington, D.C.: U.S. Government Printing Office, 1933, 13–14, and table A-III; Howard, "Sowing the Seeds of Welfare," 200–201.

63. Goodwin, *Gender and the Politics of Welfare Reform*, 162–64.

64. Barbara J. Nelson, "The Origins of the Two-Channel Welfare State: Workmen's Compensation and Mothers' Aid," in *Women, the State, and Welfare*, ed. Linda Gordon

provide aid to immigrants and generally perceived them as able to integrate fully as Americans.[65]

Nonwhite mothers did have access to mothers' pensions in some areas of Michigan, but their numbers were relatively small. State reports in Michigan recorded only the marital status of the recipient, and later also recorded nativity, and the 1934 study included no information on the operation of race in the program.[66] A state investigation of Saginaw County's poor-relief system in 1933 revealed that mothers' pensions were extended to a somewhat diverse group of dependent mothers. This group included the foreign-born, women of color (both African-American and Mexican), and nonwidows. Five percent of Saginaw County's mothers' pension recipients in 1932 were either African-American or Mexican.[67] Yet it is difficult to determine how many other applicants were turned away or discouraged from applying in the first place.[68] Given the larger obstacles to financial stability for nonwhites (e.g., employment and housing discrimination), these numbers likely underrepresent the actual need for aid among these mothers of color. Who was granted aid remained an issue of local discretion.

Despite efforts to separate the program from welfare, administrative practices often blurred the distinction. The 1934 study by the State Department of Welfare argued that although the pensions were not intended to be poor relief, courts and probate judges used them in that way. Opal Matson, for instance, clearly placed mothers' pensions in the welfare system in her 1933

(Madison: University of Wisconsin Press, 1994), 139.

65. Linda Gordon, *Pitied but Not Entitled: Single Mothers and the History of Welfare* (New York: Knopf, 1994), 47–48, 87; Mink, *The Wages of Motherhood*, 30, 37–41; Kyle E. Ciani, "Choosing to Care: Meeting Children's Needs in Detroit and San Diego, 1880–1945," (PhD dissertation, Michigan State University, 1998), 102–3; Kyle E. Ciani, "Hidden Laborers: Female Day Workers in Detroit, 1870–1920," *Journal of the Gilded Age and Progressive Era* 4.1 (January 2005): 43–44; and Goodwin, *Gender and the Politics of Welfare Reform*, 128–29, 162.

66. Ciani, "Choosing to Care," 102–3, and "Hidden Laborers," 43–44; Victoria W. Wolcott, *Remaking Respectability: African-American Women in Interwar Detroit* (Chapel Hill: University of North Carolina Press, 2001), 43.

67. Seventy percent of recipients of mothers' pensions, according to the 1933 report, were native born. Some mothers' spouses were in institutions, and one was unmarried. *Proceedings, Saginaw County Board of Supervisors*, January 11, 1933, 54–55. Similar figures appeared in the 1936 study of Kalamazoo County's program. Sixty-five percent of recipients were widows, and 20 percent were divorced or deserted. Just 3 percent were unmarried, and 12 percent had spouses in institutions (prison, insane asylum, or tuberculosis hospital). Probate Court, Kalamazoo County, Welfare and Relief Study Commission Records, Box 7, Folder 2, Kalamazoo County.

68. State reports (Michigan Board of Corrections and Charities 1913–1920; Michigan State Welfare Commission 1921–28) indicate that many applicants were never granted aid, but the reports do not provide any information about whose applications were denied. See also Ofman, "A Rural View of Mothers' Pensions," 102.

assessment of relief programs in Michigan.[69] More than one attorney general, however, ruled that the mothers' pension program was not poor relief, and was separate and independent of poor-relief legislation for a reason: "Had the legislature intended this to be poor relief, it is reasonable to assume that it would have given supervision of such allowances to the superintendents of the poor and the township supervisors who have the charge of poor relief."[70] But not all agreed with that assessment. Seven Michigan counties had no mothers' pension programs even by 1917, not because of a lack of funds, but "due to a deliberate conviction on the part of the [probate] judge that the county poor officials are better fitted to handle relief work than the court."[71] Marquette County's probate judge and poor officials worked together to determine the most cost-effective means to provide aid. The judge referred some cases to the poor commission, believing that it could provide support more cheaply than the mothers' pension program. In one case, the judge requested poor relief instead of a mothers' pension because he didn't think a cash allowance would "be properly and judiciously spent."[72] No specifics were listed, but the judge told the board that "home conditions were such that if a Mothers Pension were granted, the children would not receive the full benefit of that aid."[73] Many counties refused to provide both mothers' aid and poor relief, regardless of the adequacy of her mothers' pension grant.[74]

The perception of mothers' pensions as poor relief depended in part on the investigative methods of the probate judge. Investigation procedures varied, and were directly linked to whether judges saw the pensions as poor relief or a "pension." Sixty-two counties used the county agent to investigate such cases, as stipulated by law. Six counties used either the probation officer or an investigator of mothers' pensions. But the report harshly criticized the seven

---

69. Matson, *Local Relief to Dependents*, 36–39.

70. *Biennial Report of the Attorney General of the State of Michigan,* Attorney General Patrick H. O'Brien (Lansing: Franklin DeKleine Company, 1934), 355; Harris, *Mothers' Pensions in Michigan,* 3.

71. Ellis, "Juvenile Courts and Mothers' Pensions," 4–5.

72. "Proceedings of the Board of Superintendents of the Poor, Marquette County," Marquette County Historical Society, January 18, 1924, and March 21, 1924, 37, 44.

73. "Proceedings, Superintendents of the Poor, Marquette County," January 22, 1931, 187. The mother received a rental allowance of ten dollars per month, and a monthly grocery order for twenty dollars.

74. Mrs. Mary Blaud of Van Buren County asked the poor commission to cease payments to her, as the probate judge refused her a mothers' pension as long as she received poor relief. Why she preferred a mothers' pension is not clear, but the reason was likely either that the funds were greater or more secure, or that she saw the mothers' pension as carrying less stigma than general poor relief. Minutes of the Van Buren County Superintendent of the Poor, April 1, 1914.

counties who used superintendents of the poor, township supervisors, or even jail officials as investigating officers. It also criticized the influence of such officials on the investigations, even if they were not conducting them.[75] To many probate judges, a mother's pension *was* poor relief, and thus they administered the law as such.

Judicial discretion, in conjunction with budget limitations, also affected the size of mothers' pension grants, which seldom reached the legal maximum level. Although by 1921 the law allowed up to $10 per week—and not less than $2 for one child—benefits averaged far below that, and also varied depending on what category the mother's situation fit. Counties paid a low of $0.40 per child per week in extreme cases to anywhere from $1.22 to $2.33. The state average was $1.75. Some probate judges would provide funds for only three or four children, regardless of the size of the family.[76] By the 1930s benefits in some counties barely covered the family's food, not to mention rent, clothing, and medical care. Variations in grant amounts point to the extremely limited funding of mothers' pensions, reinforcing Joanne Goodwin's argument that such aid was merely partial support.[77] Inadequate grants were a national problem with mothers' pensions, and Michigan actually ranked sixth in a 1931 study of average grants. But variations within the state, again because of judicial discretion and local control, rendered the averages less meaningful.[78]

Inadequate grants prompted many recipients (up to 44 percent) to seek paid work, or to have older children work. The numbers are likely low, as many mothers hid their employment in fear of losing their benefits.[79] In part, inadequacy was a function of finances, particularly during the Depression, as counties eliminated pensions or reduced grants. But variations in grants, and the inadequacy of mothers' pensions, predated the Depression, according to a 1926 study. The study pointed directly to the discretion of judges and poor investigative methods as the reasons for the varied amounts of grants: "The differences seem to be mainly due to different attitudes on the part of the

75. In many counties, the report stated, such individuals dictated the policies and administration of the mothers' pension programs, and in eight counties the local officials actually placed the mothers' pension checks in their own accounts. This point is emphasized in the 1934 study as well as the 1936 Welfare Relief and Study Commission report on Michigan's welfare system. Both criticized the program's administrative practices.

76. Harris, *Mothers' Pensions in Michigan*, 8–9; Public Act No. 16, *Michigan Public Acts, 1921,* 787.

77. Harris, 8–9; Ciani, "Choosing to Care," 99–102; Ciani, "Hidden Laborers," 45–46; and Goodwin, *The Politics of Welfare Reform,* 169–75.

78. Howard, "Sowing the Seeds of 'Welfare,'" 202.

79. Harris, *Mothers' Pensions in Michigan,* 13–14. For a study of Allegan County, Michigan, and this issue, see Ofman, "A Rural View of Mothers' Pensions," 110–11.

judges, some being more in sympathy with the system than the others."[80] The variation in grants reveals the gulf between the ideal of supporting a mother's full-time care of her children, and the views of many probate judges.

Some probate judges did not believe that mothers' pensions should be full support and administered the program deliberately using the concept of "partial support." Manistee County Probate Judge Fred Stone told the annual gathering of superintendents of the poor in 1924 that the pension was to supplement the mother's income (or income from older children). He rejected the notion that women's role was simply the home caretaker, and argued that most women had to help the family with wage work at some point. "It is very seldom that the probate court is called upon to aid those where the wife didn't help out during the husband's life time, and I don't believe that she should expect or the people should expect that she should be supported entirely by the county and do nothing for herself to earn money."[81] Stone argued that the pension was to be the supplementary income in the family—not the sole source of support. The mothers' pension was not to bring these families into the middle-class ideal of a mother whose sole focus was care of the home and family, as advocates of the pension concept argued. The Manistee County Board of Supervisors agreed with this philosophy in 1933 when it protested the minimum provision of $2 per week because it was "inadvisable, unnecessary and tends toward undue allowance under present conditions." The supervisors believed the amount of the grant should be the discretion of the probate judge.[82] Kent County Judge Clark Higbee expressed similar ideas in 1914, noting that one mother receiving a mothers' pension had "fine children; no better in Michigan." They needed "her care and attention; they require that she stay in her home and care for them." But he also noted that "she is helping too," financially.[83]

---

80. National Probation Association, *Report of a Study of Juvenile Courts and Adult Probation in Certain Counties of Michigan* (National Probation Association and Michigan State Conference of Social Work, 1926), 10. A copy is at the Harlan Hatcher Graduate Library at the University of Michigan, Ann Arbor.

81. *Proceedings of the Twenty-First Annual Convention of the State Association of the Superintendents of the Poor, Keepers and Matrons of the County Infirmaries, and City Poor Directors*, August 28, 1924, 55–56. See also "Local Public Welfare," WRSC, 96–97.

82. "Supervisors' Proceedings, Manistee County," vol. 13, April 12, 1933, 98–99. The resolution opposing the minimum allowance passed unanimously. Wayne County also supported the resolution. *Official Proceedings of the Board of Supervisors of Wayne County, 1933*, September 18, 1933, 239.

83. *Proceedings of the Eleventh Annual Convention of State Superintendents of the Poor and Keepers of County Infirmaries*, Thursday, September 24, 1914, Grand Rapids, 90.

THE 1920S: EARLY SIGNS OF STRESS

It is true that the Great Depression placed an immense strain on Michigan's poor-relief system, but the state's economic problems originated in the 1920s and went far beyond unemployed auto workers. As in many other parts of the country, the relief needs in Michigan also increased in the decade prior to the Great Depression. Michigan residents worked in agriculture, extractive industries such as lumber and mining, and, by the 1920s and 1930s, the growing industrial centers of Flint and Detroit. Agriculture was a statewide occupation, although the best land was found in the southern and middle parts of Michigan (including Van Buren County) and in what is known as the thumb area, around Saginaw Bay and the Lake Huron shoreline. Parts of the northern Lower Peninsula also yielded significant fruit production.[84] Mining was an Upper Peninsula industry, particularly in the Lake Superior regions (including Marquette County), and the lumber industry was centered in the northern Lower Peninsula and the Upper Peninsula. Counties that relied on a single industry, such as Wayne, which includes Detroit, suffered immeasurably more than counties and cities, like Saginaw, that had more diverse economies.

Michigan agriculture produced a variety of crops, including fruit, grains, beans, and sugar beets, in the late nineteenth and early twentieth centuries.[85] Michigan's total acreage in agriculture—about half of the available land in the state—peaked at more than 19 million acres in 1920. The value of the state's farmland reached a high of seventy-five dollars per acre in 1920, but fell to forty-five dollars by 1930. The value of Michigan's agricultural products reached a record high in 1920, but would not again attain that level until 1969.[86] Farming areas could weather hard times with subsistence agriculture in a way that urban workers could not, but the 1920s still proved difficult for many farmers and agricultural workers.

Mining, a Michigan industry that was in its heyday in the nineteenth century, remained a significant source of employment into the twentieth century.[87] Michigan produced half of the world's copper in the mid-nineteenth century,

---

84. *Michigan: A Guide to the Wolverine State* (New York: Oxford University Press, 1941), 7–8, 59–60.

85. Kalamazoo was a major producer of celery, and the Lake Michigan shore, stretching from southwestern Michigan north to Grand Traverse Bay, was the state's major fruit belt, producing peaches, apples, and berries. The state ranked second in the nation in sugar beet production. *Michigan*, 59–60.

86. Willis F. Dunbar and George S. May, *Michigan: A History of the Wolverine State*, 3rd Rev. Ed. (Grand Rapids: William B. Eerdmans Publishing Company, 1995), 502–3.

87. *Michigan*, 63.

and remained in third place as late as 1913.[88] World War I prompted a new boom in copper and iron-ore mining. Iron-ore production reached its peak in 1920, but fell to less than 25 percent of that level the following year. Increased mechanization also reduced the need for labor, sending many workers to the unemployment line. Employing 19,000 workers in 1909, copper mining in the Upper Peninsula employed only 12,200 workers ten years later and was down to 7,800 by 1929.[89] Between 1921 and 1925, 25,000 people left the copper-mining regions of the Upper Peninsula for opportunities in the auto industry in Detroit and Flint.[90]

Lumbering experienced a history similar to that of mining. Lumbering was at its peak in the nineteenth century, particularly in the cities of Saginaw and Muskegon, though lumber mills and camps were found throughout the northern parts of Michigan. Michigan led the nation in lumber production and employed more than 45,000 workers in 1889. By the turn of the century lumber was on the decline, but the state still had 437 sawmills in 1905. Two decades later, however, the industry was in a serious downturn, with only 12,000 workers in 1925.[91] Workers often combined part-time lumber employment with farming or other seasonal work as the industry scaled back in the early part of the twentieth century into the 1920s.[92]

Michigan's increasing reliance on industrial production worsened the effects of the economic depression. Its industrial production increased markedly in the early twentieth century, in large part because of the development of the automotive industry, as well as foundries and machine shops. Other significant industries included paper manufacturing and cereal production in the southwestern region and furniture manufacturing in the Grand Rapids area.[93] Cities hit especially hard in the 1920s included Detroit and others dependent on the automotive industry. The 1920s was a period of ups and downs for the auto industry, with layoffs occurring several times during that period. Employment fluctuations, and layoffs for retooling, contributed to what was a

---

88. Ibid., 62–64. For copper mining see Larry Lankton, *Cradle to Grave: Life, Work, and Death at the Lake Superior Copper Mines* (New York: Oxford University Press, 1991) and Arthur W. Thurner, *Strangers and Sojourners: A History of Michigan's Keweenaw Peninsula* (Detroit: Wayne State University Press, 1994).

89. Dunbar and May, *Michigan: A History of the Wolverine State*, 503–5; Lankton, *Cradle to Grave*, 244–53; Haber and Stanchfield, *Unemployment and Relief in Michigan*, 9–10.

90. Thurner, *Strangers and Sojourners*, 227.

91. *Michigan*, 61–62; William Haber and Paul L. Stanchfield, *Unemployment, Relief, and Economic Security* (Lansing, 1935), 135.

92. Haber and Stanchfield, *Unemployment, Relief, and Economic Security*, 136–38. See also Jeremy Kilar, *Michigan's Lumbertowns: Lumberman and Laborers in Saginaw, Bay City, and Muskegon, 1870–1905* (Detroit: Wayne State University Press, 1990).

93. *Michigan*, 67–68.

very unstable period for many workers, who turned to local welfare agencies, both public and private, for aid when their own resources were exhausted.[94] Racism usually resulted in quicker layoffs for both African-American and Mexican workers, but all workers, particularly the unskilled, faced uncertain times in the years before the Great Depression. By the end of 1920 about 80 percent of Detroit's auto workers were unemployed. Another production slow-down occurred just a few years later, resulting in a recession and more layoffs in 1926–1927. For workers with little experience in urban living, unemployment with no land resources on which to draw was daunting. These problems placed heavy burdens on local relief agencies. Communities such as Saginaw, which manufactured auto parts for the Detroit plants, also experienced downturns, but a more diversified industrial base lessened the magnitude of the Depression's unemployment.[95]

PUBLIC VS. PRIVATE RELIEF

Both public and private welfare services existed in most Michigan communities by the 1920s, but the two represented different approaches to social welfare. For the trained social worker, private welfare was the only likely place for employment. Few public programs were large enough to warrant full-time staff, and few areas saw a need for a professional social worker. Very few public agencies were members of the major social work organizations, including the Family Welfare Association, and most membership requirements precluded the admission of public agencies.[96] Private agencies focused on family casework, with relief as a supplemental service.[97] They sought to help families or

94. Martin Edward Sullivan, "'On the Dole': The Relief Issue in Detroit, 1929–1939" (PhD dissertation, University of Notre Dame, 1974), 36–37; Ronald Edsforth, *Class Conflict and Cultural Consensus: The Making of a Mass Consumer Society in Flint, Michigan* (New Brunswick: Rutgers University Press, 1987), 116–17.

95. Vargas, *Proletarians of the North*, 80–82; Richard W. Thomas, *Life for Us Is What We Make It: Building Black Community in Detroit, 1915–1945* (Bloomington: University of Indiana Press, 1992), 45–47.

96. Josephine Chapin Brown, *Public Relief, 1929–1939* (New York: Henry Holt, 1940), 54. The Family Service Association was a national umbrella organization for its member organizations. (It was originally chartered in 1911 as the National Association of Societies for Organizing Charity; the name was changed to the FSA in the 1930s and then the Family Welfare Association in the 1940s.) It provided a voice for social welfare professionals in the social welfare field and was largely composed of private agencies. Some public agencies did seek membership. This agency served private organizations in nine Michigan cities, including Marquette. *Social Service Organizations,* ed. Peter Romanofsky (Westport, CT: Greenwood Press, 1978), 302–6.

97. Roy Lubove, *The Professional Altruist: The Emergence of Social Work as a Career, 1880–1930* (New York: Antheneum, 1983), 18–21, 49–52; and Trattner, *From Poor Law to Welfare*

individuals solve the problems that caused their "need" for aid, which they understood to stem from other issues, including family conflict, ill health, or other situations that had caused their economic difficulties. Rather than simply providing material relief, private social workers sought to help families become self-supporting. Even in Detroit, the state's largest city, no private agency provided relief to needy individuals, who had to turn to the public agencies.[98] In contrast, public welfare was a temporary measure focusing only on the immediate material needs of the recipient. A common criticism of public welfare by the early twentieth century was the lack of record keeping and casework conducted by public officials.[99]

Private welfare encompassed a range of agencies that served a variety of constituencies. Some centered on specific religious, racial, or ethnic groups, while others were more broadly based. The development of private welfare was largely an urban phenomenon, and rural areas had far fewer private charity organizations, further highlighting the importance of public relief in the state. Each private welfare organization's focus on a specific group—serving "its own"—excluded others from receiving aid, and based many restrictions solely on citizenship or race.[100] Exclusion from public welfare programs was often part of the impetus for groups such as African-Americans, Mexican immigrants, and Mexican-Americans to establish their own social service organizations.[101] Major charities operating in Michigan included the Associated Charities (a member of the Family Welfare Association), the Salvation Army, the League of Catholic Women, the St. Vincent de Paul Society, the Detroit Urban League, and the City Rescue Mission, among others. Cities such as Detroit, Flint, and Grand Rapids had fairly extensive networks of private welfare (although not all provided material relief services), while other more rural areas, including Van Buren County, had far fewer options. Manistee County, in rural northern Michigan, had a county Social Welfare League, and Marquette County a Social Service Bureau, which coordinated social welfare efforts.[102] Most counties had

---

State, 73–103.

98. Joanna C. Colcord, *Cash Relief* (New York: Russell Sage Foundation, 1936), 86; William R. Brock, *Welfare, Democracy, and the New Deal* (Cambridge and New York: Cambridge University Press, 1988), 121.

99. Brown, *Public Relief,* 40–41, 51–55; Lubove, *The Professional Altruist,* 52–54.

100. Goodwin, *Gender and the Politics of Welfare Reform,* 59–60; Lizabeth Cohen, *Making a New Deal: Industrial Workers in Chicago, 1919–1939* (Cambridge: Cambridge University Press, 1990), 56–61.

101. Wolcott, *Remaking Respectability,* 43; Dionicio Nodin Valdes, *Barrios Nortenos: St. Paul and Midwestern Mexican Communities in the Twentieth Century* (Austin: University of Texas Press, 2000), 74–77.

102. Kathryn M. Bryan, "15th Article in the Series, 'We Too Know the People,'" *Manistee Examiner,* collection in Manistee County Historical Society.

a chapter of the American Red Cross as well. Some cities, including Detroit and Grand Rapids, coordinated their fund-raising for private charity through the local community chest, which then distributed the funds to its member organizations.[103] Van Buren County had no centralized social welfare organization. (Saginaw's private agencies were funded in part by the Saginaw Welfare League.) Some of the state's midsize cities, including Pontiac, lacked a private family welfare agency even by the 1930s.[104]

In some areas private agencies investigated cases for the public welfare system, but the funding was still public. Smaller cities and rural governments funneled their public relief funds through local private agencies, rather than having public officials distribute relief dollars. The Social Service Department of the Civic League in Bay City, which had a population of about fifty thousand in 1921, investigated cases and dispensed city funds for relief. The city also provided office space and supplies for the agency, and paid the salaries of some workers.[105] Manistee's Social Welfare League coordinated the mothers' pension program and transient relief.[106] Jackson's Welfare Bureau, a private agency, took over the city's poor-relief work when Jackson abolished the poor-relief department. Instead, it paid the Welfare Bureau's staff and provided a relief budget.[107] Flint's Social Service Bureau investigated cases for the public agency until 1930.[108] In some cases private agencies investigated relief cases, but dispensed public, not private, welfare funds.

The relief options for rural communities were more limited than those of urban areas in Michigan and throughout the nation, although rural welfare practices have received much less study than urban agencies. Few rural areas had chests or welfare leagues to coordinate fund-raising. But they did have private welfare organizations, including the American Red Cross, Salvation Army, and others often connected to local churches. Although the welfare system was less systematic and visible, it did exist. But given that even large cities

103. Lubove, *The Professional Altruist,* 187–88; Brown, *Public Relief,* 55. For information on the Detroit Associated Charities, see Oliver Zunz, *The Changing Face of Inequality: Urbanization, Industrial Development, and Immigrants in Detroit, 1880–1920* (Chicago: University of Chicago Press, 1982), 263–65.

104. Application for Membership in FWAA, Agency Correspondence, FSA Records, Pontiac, Box 58, Pontiac Folder, 1928–1935, SWHA.

105. Agency Correspondence, Reports, FSA Records, Bay City, Box 57, Folder, MI prior to 1928, and Folder 1928–1935.

106. Agency Correspondence, Reports, FSA Records, Manistee, Box 57, Folder Michigan, L–Z, 1928–1935.

107. Agency Correspondence, Reports, FSA Records, Jackson, Box 57, Folder Michigan, H–Z, MI Prior to 1928.

108. Consultation Visit, 1933, Rose Porter, Agency Correspondence, Reports, FSA Records, Box 58, Flint folder, 1928–1935, 3.

and urban areas found the needy dependent upon public relief funds, such a trend is even more likely in rural communities, where residents often had few choices but to turn to their local officials for aid when they faced unemployment or an inability to support themselves or their families.

Historically, Michigan's welfare system was local and funded with public monies. New Deal programs continued this practice, but with greater federal and state involvement. What shifted in Michigan was the level of government involved in relief. Private agencies were concentrated in more-urban areas, and even then did not provide significant relief aid. The largest new program in the pre–New Deal years was the mothers' pension program, which continued the practice of public funding and local administration. Local, public relief was critical for Michigan's unemployed, both before and during the Great Depression.

CHAPTER TWO

"The People of Michigan Will Take Care of Their Own"

THE GREAT DEPRESSION AND THE RELIEF PROBLEM

A 1931 NEWSPAPER editorial seeking support for the fund-raising campaign of Saginaw's Social Welfare League highlighted the widespread belief that solutions to the Depression's economic and relief crises rested in the private sector. The editorial stressed the tremendous need for the drive that year, and the consequences if it failed: "Whereas in other years failure to reach the campaign quota would have been merely unfortunate, this year such a failure would assume the proportions of a catastrophe." The editorial further cautioned against waiting for the government to step in, because that strategy, it argued, would simply result in paying through higher taxes: "This resolves itself into a local problem which each community must solve in its own way, using its established agencies as the basis of the whole program."[1]

The editorial's emphasis on private relief stands in stark contrast to the reality that Michigan's relief system was overwhelmingly public. By 1931 private agencies' relief expenditures accounted for just 5 percent of all relief costs in Saginaw that year, a trend true for much of the state. The newspaper's editorial illustrates the persistent belief that relief was a local, and preferably a private, responsibility. A reluctance to go into debt, the widespread antitax sentiment, and the fear of creating a class of people dependent on "the dole" prompted many government and community leaders to look to the private business sector

---

1. "Saginaw Cares—and Shares," *Saginaw Daily News,* October 4, 1931, 6.

to provide employment. Those views, which I term fiscal localism, created definite ideological barriers to the potential solutions offered. Resistance to federal aid was profound, and only when poor-relief costs threatened to bankrupt local communities did that change.

The uneven economic situation in the state in the 1920s prompted increases in relief spending, and much of the increase was in public welfare. Anne Geddes's 1937 study of relief in the early twentieth century dated the trend in rising relief costs to around 1910, nearly two decades before the Great Depression. Relief costs predictably rose during economic downturns, including the 1921–22 depression, but Geddes found that relief costs seldom returned to their predepression levels throughout the entire period. But she also found that "after each depression they again moved upward from a new and higher base."[2] Geddes reported not only that relief expenditures had grown faster than the population rate, but also that public relief increases, especially in the larger cities, were greater than most other governmental expenditures. In part this was due to the spread of mothers' pensions, but the increase also signified that public agencies were taking on a larger responsibility for welfare.[3] Historian Jeff Singleton argues that "means-tested relief was becoming the safety net for low-wage workers" before the Depression.[4] Residents in need of aid in this period turned largely to public agencies, and not private welfare organizations, for help.

Michigan funded most of its relief costs with public, and not private, funds before the infusion of federal relief dollars in 1932. Studies revealed that public funds had shouldered the relief load to a much greater degree than previously thought. In most cities and regions, private organizations funded only a fraction of relief. Even social work professionals were surprised to find that before the Depression, in 1928, 71.6 percent of relief in fifteen cities throughout the United States (including Detroit and Chicago) was funded through public agencies.[5] A study by the President's Organization on Unemployment Relief analyzed both public and private organizations' relief expenditures in the first three months of 1929 and 1931. Fifteen Michigan cities were in the study, including Saginaw, Detroit, and Grand Rapids.[6] Michigan's 1931 relief

2. Anne E. Geddes, *Trends in Relief Expenditures, 1910–1935*, WPA Research Monograph X (Washington, D.C.: U.S. Government Printing Office, 1937), 1; Singleton, *The American Dole*, 27, 44.

3. Josephine Chapin Brown, *Public Relief, 1929–1939* (New York: Henry Holt, 1940), 56–57; Geddes, *Trends in Relief Expenditures*, xiii–xiv.

4. Singleton, *The American Dole*, 27.

5. Brown, *Public Relief*, 55.

6. *Relief Expenditures by Governmental and Private Organizations, 1929 and 1931* (Washington, D.C.: U.S. Government Printing Office, 1932), 30.

expenditures were more than six times the 1929 figure for both public and private agencies in cities with populations of more than 30,000. Relief expenses increased 179 percent in cities under 30,000.[7] Wayne County's welfare costs, which included institutional care, general relief, and mothers' pensions, increased from 39 percent of the county's budget in 1925–26 to 49 percent in 1928–29.[8] Public funds provided 96.7 percent of relief dollars in Detroit in 1929.[9] The trend continued throughout the decade.[10]

What is significant is the ratio of public to private expenditures. Even in 1929, public funds accounted for far more of the relief aid in Michigan than did private monies. Michigan's larger cities aided 33,840 people per month (on average) in those first months of 1929, while private agencies assisted 9,580. In 1931 those numbers increased to 264,227 through public agencies and 37,387 for private organizations, increases of 680 and 290 percent, respectively. In Michigan private funds were not maintaining a larger share of relief aid even before the Depression, a trend shared by twelve other states in this study.[11] The same trend held true for relief funds spent by public and private agencies. All Michigan cities in the study expended far more through public agencies, even in 1929, than private (table 2.1).[12] Detroit's relief burden was financed almost entirely by public funds in the Department of Public Welfare. In 1930 and 1931 the city's share of relief funding was at 98.7 and 95.5 percent, respectively. Detroit's relief costs were among the highest in the country: "Detroit, alone, accounted for more than 25 percent of *all* the public general relief dispensed in the United States in 1930 and more than 13 percent in 1931."[13]

Michigan was not alone in its reliance on public funds for welfare before the New Deal, and the trends between public and private are not necessarily defined by region. Ten other states also relied more heavily on public agencies for relief, including Maine, Massachusetts, Rhode Island, New York, New Jersey, Illinois, Wisconsin, Minnesota, Utah, and California. Iowa and Montana

---

7. *Relief Expenditures,* 10.

8. Board of County Auditors, Wayne County, *The Cost of County Government: An Analysis of the Wayne County Budget, 1925–1929* (Detroit: Board of County Auditors, 1929), 10.

9. Sydnor H. Walker, "Privately Supported Social Work," *Recent Social Trends in the United States: Report of the President's Research Committee on Social Trends, Vol. II* (New York: McGraw-Hill, 1933), 1194.

10. Emma A. Winslow, *Trends in Different Types of Public and Private Relief in Urban Areas, 1929–1935* (Washington, D.C.: U.S. Government Printing Office, 1937), 77.

11. *Relief Expenditures,* 18–24.

12. Ibid., 30. These numbers did not include institutional care in county infirmaries, which also would be public expenditures. Few states were as consistent as Michigan, in which just one city (Kalamazoo) deviated from the statewide trend.

13. Sidney Fine, *Frank Murphy: The Detroit Years* (Ann Arbor: University of Michigan Press, 1975), 307.

TABLE 2.1
EXPENDITURES FOR PUBLIC AND PRIVATE RELIEF (%)

City	1929 Public	1929 Private	1931 Public	1931 Private	1932–35 Public	1929–35 Public
Detroit	93	7	98.8	1.2	95	5
Grand Rapids	76	24	92	8	90	10
Flint	62	38	90	10	80	20
Saginaw	84	16	95	5	86	14

Source: *Relief Expenditures by Governmental and Private Organizations, 1929 and 1931* (Washington, D.C.: U.S. Government Printing Office, 1932), 30; Emma A. Winslow, *Trends in Different Types of Public and Private Relief in Urban Areas, 1929–1935,* U.S. Children's Bureau Publication No. 237 (Washington, D.C.: U.S. Government Printing Office, 1937), 77.

shared this trend in 1929, but then reversed it in 1931. Eighteen states followed the opposite trend (private relief exceeding public): Pennsylvania, Ohio, Missouri, Virginia, South Carolina, North Carolina, Georgia, Florida, Kentucky, Tennessee, Alabama, Mississippi, Louisiana, Oklahoma, Texas, Arkansas, Arizona, and Washington. New Hampshire, Connecticut, Indiana, Kansas, and Oregon initially showed more aid from private agencies in 1929, but reversed two years later. Colorado's, Nebraska's, and South Dakota's figures were comparatively equal for both years.[14] Little uniformity existed in the reliance on either public or private welfare.

Urban areas tended to have centralized fund-raising mechanisms such as the community chests found in Marquette, Grand Rapids, Detroit, and the Saginaw Welfare League. Coordinated fund-raising organizations, like the chests, began in Cleveland in 1913, and expanded to most cities by 1929.[15] Saginaw's Welfare League organized in 1920, and Marquette's dated to 1924; Detroit's community fund arose out of World War I.[16] All faced budget problems and were forced to extend fund-raising drives and reduce budgets of member agencies to adjust for the decline in contributions in the early Depression years. Of the four counties in this study, Detroit had the largest cooperative fund-raising budget, but the city faced its own crisis of fund-raising in the early years of the Depression. Efforts to encourage greater contributions by the

14. *Relief Expenditures,* table II, 19–25; and David Joseph Maurer, "Public Relief Programs in Ohio, 1929–1939" (PhD dissertation, University of Minnesota, 1962), 7–9.

15. Judith Ann Trolander, *Settlement Houses and the Great Depression* (Detroit: Wayne State University, 1975), 26–27, 59; Brock, *Welfare, Democracy, and the New Deal,* 27–28.

16. Fine, *Frank Murphy: The Detroit Years,* 204.

wealthy yielded dismal results and fell far short of goals.[17] The spring of 1930 brought what one publication called "the most serious problem in our history." By October, the organization faced a deficit of $125,000.[18] Both Saginaw and Marquette faced difficulties meeting their goals, and eventually drastically cut budgets of their member agencies, thus reducing their annual fund-raising goals. The winter campaigns of 1932–1933 across the United States were the "supreme and final effort of the private agencies to carry a substantial share of the costs of unemployment relief."[19] Private relief expenditures reached their peak that year, but still failed to cover even 20 percent of the total cost of relief. This trend was mirrored around the state and nation. Many chests followed the path of Detroit, Marquette, and Saginaw: reducing budgets of all agencies, and shifting more funds to those organizations which provided relief to meet the rising demand.[20] Private agencies' declining budgets further limited their ability to provide relief. This shifted even more of the relief burden to local public relief.

Counties and cities responded to the economic crisis with a variety of programs to reduce the need for relief: unemployment committees and bureaus, work-relief programs, city-owned stores and fuel centers, bond proposals, and efforts to remove "unwanted" workers, including Mexicans and other foreign-born residents. Most efforts were limited in effectiveness, in part because of a lack of funds to address the severity of the unemployment problem. Fiscal localism prompted many government and community leaders to look to the private sector to provide employment. The firm belief that welfare was a local problem, demanding local solutions, is hard to overstate, despite the reality that relief had never been a private endeavor in the state. Fiscal localism narrowed the possible solutions, and solidified resistance to federal aid. Michigan was not alone in this opposition to federal and state intrusion into relief.

Emphasis on private solutions, even in states where public taxes financed welfare, can be explained in part by the widespread antitax sentiment in this period. David Beito argues that the 1929 stock market crash galvanized opposition to increased taxes, resulting in a series of laws limiting tax rates. In 1932 and 1933, sixteen states, including Michigan, enacted property tax limitations. Farmers and rural areas led the fight for a fifteen-mill tax limit that was approved through a state constitutional amendment in November 1932.

17. Irving Bernstein, *The Lean Years: A History of the American Worker, 1920–1933* (New York: Da Capo Press, 1960), 300; Richard T. Ortquist, *Depression Politics in Michigan, 1929–1933* (New York: Garland Publishing, 1982), 148, 153–54.

18. Fine, *Frank Murphy: The Detroit Years*, 204.

19. Brown, *Public Relief,* 131.

20. Ibid., 131–32.

This trend illustrates residents' resistance to higher taxes, regardless of their purpose, a resistance that made it more difficult for local and state officials to fund relief programs. Antitax sentiment was a part of the political reality of the 1930s.[21] Confronted with declining revenues and high relief costs, elected officials operated in an atmosphere very hostile to new taxes and with legal limits on what they could levy. Michael Brown argues that considering the issue of taxation and who will benefit from social programs is critical in the study of public policy: "Since policy makers must worry as much about who will feel the tax bite as who will benefit from a new social policy, they are motivated to finance the welfare state with taxes that minimize taxpayer resistance."[22]

Under the amendment approved in Michigan, the collective taxes imposed on property owners—including school, township, and county—could not exceed fifteen mills, unless approved by a majority of voters for up to a total of fifty mills. Cities and villages were exempt only if other maximum rates were established through their city charters or general laws, although some voluntarily opted to hold themselves to the fifteen-mill limit.[23] The limit, in conjunction with alarmingly high tax-delinquency rates, meant that most counties had to economize operations to keep their taxes within the constitutional limit. The decline in revenues hurt all counties, as well as the state of Michigan. Relief programs proved to be difficult to finance throughout the 1930s, regardless of the need of residents.

Another component of this resistance was a county's political affiliation. Michigan was firmly Republican, and from 1896 to 1932, with just one exception, supported the Republican presidential candidate; during the 1920s the state legislature was overwhelmingly Republican, often with no Democrats serving in either the senate or the house.[24] Just three of the state's eighty-three counties supported Democratic candidates as late as 1930.[25] The commitment to local and private welfare also remained strong at the national and state

21. David T. Beito, *Taxpayers in Revolt: Tax Resistance during the Great Depression* (Chapel Hill: University of North Carolina Press, 1989), 14–15, 141; Michael K. Brown, *Race, Money, and the American Welfare State* (Ithaca and London: Cornell University Press, 1999), 37.

22. Brown, *Race, Money, and the American Welfare State*, 6.

23. Claude R. Tharp, *A Manual of City Government in Michigan* (Ann Arbor: University of Michigan Press, 1951), 113–14; Dean L. Berry, *The Powers of Local Government in Michigan* (Ann Arbor: University of Michigan, 1961), 5, 32, 52, 77; and Fine, *Frank Murphy: The New Deal Years*, 263.

24. James K. Pollock and Samuel J. Eldersveld, *Michigan Politics in Transition: An Areal Study of Voting Trends in the Last Decade,* University of Michigan Governmental Studies No. 10 (Ann Arbor: University of Michigan Press, 1942), 4. Michigan gave its votes to Theodore Roosevelt, who ran as a Progressive, in 1912.

25. Pollock and Eldersveld, *Michigan Politics in Transition,* 14; Samuel T. McSeveney, "The Michigan Gubernatorial Campaign of 1938," *Michigan History* 45 (June 1961): 119.

levels, as well as in local communities, and was personified in President Herbert Hoover.[26] The 1932 election proved to be the turning point, with forty-seven counties supporting Democrat William Comstock for governor and Democratic majorities in both state houses; the state also voted for Franklin Roosevelt for president.[27] Although just eleven counties voted Democratic in 1934 (most supported Republican Governor Frank Fitzgerald), Republican dominance of Michigan politics was on the wane.

Van Buren County, which was the most resistant to state and federal intrusion on relief, remained fiercely Republican throughout the 1930s. A 1942 study of Michigan's politics listed Van Buren County among fourteen "safe" Republican strongholds, many of which were rural and in the Lower Peninsula.[28] Republicans also dominated local politics, even as the financial situation of the county steadily worsened in the early Depression years.[29] In contrast, Wayne County was considered a strong Democratic county, and Marquette and Saginaw were among those counties that shifted to the Democrat camp sometime in the 1930s: Saginaw in 1932 and Marquette in 1936. Marquette had one of the greatest voting shifts of any of the counties, and also the highest increase in voter participation. Marquette would remain in the Democrat column throughout the decade, although Saginaw would revert to the Republican camp in 1940.[30] The shifts would also appear in local elections.[31] All counties and cities faced serious funding constraints during these years, but Van Buren County, the most firmly Republican, was also the most resistant to federal control.

LOCAL UNEMPLOYMENT PROGRAMS

The creation of unemployment committees to assess the unemployment problem and explore solutions was the first step for many communities. Register-

26. William E. Leuchtenberg, *The Perils of Prosperity, 1914–1932* (Chicago: University of Chicago Press, 1958), 252; Bernstein, *The Lean Years*, 287–88; and Singleton, *The American Dole*, 93–96.

27. Pollock and Eldersveld, *Michigan Politics in Transition*, 10–14; McSeveney, "The Michigan Gubernatorial Campaign," 119.

28. Pollock and Eldersveld, *Michigan Politics in Transition*, 35, 70.

29. "19 County Supervisors Reelected," *Hartford Day Spring*, April 5, 1933; "Hoffman Defeats Foulkes by 8,000: Republicans Make Sweep of Van Buren County Offices," *Hartford Day Spring*, November 7, 1934; and "Republicans Victors in VB," *Hartford Day Spring*, April 3, 1935.

30. Pollock and Eldersveld, *Michigan Politics in Transition*, 14, 29, 69.

31. "Marquette County Is Republican," *Daily Mining Journal*, November 9, 1932; "Eight Offices in County Won by Republican," *Daily Mining Journal*, November 8, 1934; and "Republicans Lose," *Saginaw Daily News*, November 9, 1932.

ing the unemployed for placement on public work projects or referrals for employment thus topped the agenda of many of these committees. Committees extended beyond the local level to the regional and state levels. The Upper Peninsula coordinated its own unemployment committee, working with state and county officials, as well as with the state highway department.[32] Detroit Mayor Frank Murphy, with the help of Dr. William Haber, an economics professor who would later head the state's Emergency Relief Administration, created the Mayor's unemployment committee in the fall of 1930. As with many such committees, the Detroit group's work was limited by funding. The trend appeared again in 1931–32, when the Emergency Fund Committee sought to raise private funds for relief through the DPW. Its initial goal of $3.5 million decreased repeatedly, and the committee eventually raised about $645,000. The shortfall again points to the limited ability of the private sector to fund relief.[33]

Registering and securing jobs for the unemployed was a priority in both Wayne and Saginaw counties.[34] Saginaw's League of Women Voters organized neighborhood groups to find odd jobs for the unemployed. The program sought to get a "two-hour pledge" from as many Saginaw households as possible—to agree to provide employment for a man for two hours per week. The hope was to secure twenty to forty hours of work each week for each unemployed worker. Another project under way was to have men sell apples on the street as a means of employment, a practice also found in Detroit.[35] Detroit undertook more-extensive efforts to find jobs, although they did ask home owners to provide odd jobs.[36] Murphy pushed for a public works program, but Detroit's severe financial crisis limited his efforts. The committee established the Free Employment Bureau, which aided workers in their search for jobs, a

32. Marquette and Manistee counties also appointed unemployment committees. See "Proceedings, Board of Supervisors, Marquette County," vol. 7, November 12, 1931, 77; "Proceedings of the Board of Supervisors, Manistee County," vol. 12, October 14, 1931, 421, vol. 13, October 21, 1932, 73–74; and "Unemployment Committee to Assemble Here," *Daily Mining Journal*, November 29, 1932, 2.

33. Fine, *Frank Murphy*, 335–37.

34. *Proceedings of the Council and Boards of the City of Saginaw*, November 25, 1930, 691–692; "Mayor Calls Unemployment Conference: Group of 58 Citizens Asked to Study Plan," *Saginaw Daily News*, November 9, 1930, 1, 5; "Mayor's Committee Moves to Aid Jobless: Registration of Idle Will Be Initial Step," *Saginaw Daily News*, November 13, 1930, 1–2; "Complete Registry of Jobless Sought," *Saginaw Daily News*, November 22, 1930, 1–2; and "Board Studies Roster of Idle," *Saginaw Daily News*, November 26, 1930, 1–2.

35. Fine, *Frank Murphy: The Detroit Years*, 268–69; "Odd Job Program Launched to Provide Work for Unemployed," *Saginaw Daily News*, November 23, 1930, 4; "Apple Sale Offers Unemployment Aid," *Saginaw Daily News*, November 21, 1930, 2; and "13 Apple Salesmen Quickly Bought Out," *Saginaw Daily News*, November 22, 1930, 1–2.

36. Fine, *Frank Murphy: The Detroit Years*, 268.

practice also found in Saginaw.[37] Saginaw's committee also organized distribution of food and clothing, donated by individuals and businesses, through the city's canteen.[38]

Saginaw County's unemployment committee provided lists of eligible workers for state highway projects.[39] Under the state plan, local unemployment committees would certify the workers for the work projects—a plan again directed at men.[40] As in Detroit, though, establishing public works projects was severely hampered by a lack of funds. Tax delinquencies were running around 25 percent, and city officials believed securing voter approval for the sale of bonds was not feasible.[41] Marquette County's supervisors worked with the road commission and the poor commission to develop lists of eligible men and available projects. The supervisors then appointed the poor-commission members and road-commission representatives to the unemployment committee to continue their efforts.[42]

In retrospect, such efforts seem futile, but they underscore the entrenched fiscal localism operating behind such programs, including looking to the private sector to provide employment. Many people hoped that the unemployment problem was short-term, and that economic recovery would be soon to arrive. Most communities sought to provide work-relief programs, rather than direct relief or "the dole," and although they got the return of work on their poor-fund dollars, they still faced the reality of limited funds and taxpayer opposition.[43] Work-relief programs cost money, and many county and city governments could support such programs only for a short time.

Work-relief projects before the New Deal targeted men, particularly white male citizens, almost exclusively. The goal was to provide work for male heads

37. Ibid., 268–69; Ortquist, *Depression Politics in Michigan*, 149–54;

38. "Jobs Committee to Discontinue," *Saginaw Daily News*, May 14, 1931.

39. Joanna C. Colcord, *Emergency Work Relief* (New York: Russell Sage Foundation, 1932), 254.

40. "Meeting Called to Plan Aid for Jobless," *Saginaw Daily News*, October 17, 1931; "Group of 10 Selected for Jobs Committee," *Saginaw Daily News*, October 22, 1931. Manistee County registered 1,137 men for work relief and found jobs in the summer of 1932 for 470; expansion of the work-relief program was a key recommendation of the county's unemployment committee. See "Proceedings, Manistee County," vol. 13, October 21, 1932, 73–74.

41. "Public Works Demanded of Council," *Saginaw Daily News*, December 1, 1931, 1–2; "Money Lack Held Bar to City Job Program," *Saginaw Daily News*, December 2, 1931, 1–2; and "No Job Relief, Council Holds," *Saginaw Daily News*, December 8 1931, 1–2.

42. "Reach Peak Employment on County Roads," *Daily Mining Journal*, November 12, 1931; "Board Names Committee on Unemployment," *Daily Mining Journal*, November 13, 1931; and "Proceedings, Marquette County," vol. 7, May 18, 1932, 87–88. Van Buren County also provided lists of unemployed, through the township supervisors, for road projects. "Proceedings of the Board of Supervisors, Van Buren County," January 5, 1932, 63.

43. Ortquist, *Depression Politics in Michigan*, 149–52.

of household who could work on public works projects repairing roads and bridges, digging new sewer lines, and woodcutting. Men of color faced limited opportunities on the early road projects, and thus had to rely on odd jobs or relief from a public or private welfare agency. Women had no work-relief possibilities in these communities before 1933. Government officials viewed their communities through the lens of the family wage, whether such a reality existed or not in all households. Such an ideology also permeated New Deal work projects, which have since been criticized for their lack of attention to women workers in need of jobs. But New Deal programs, although limited by ideas about gender, race, and class, did offer some opportunities for women, unlike the local work-relief programs before 1933.[44]

ESCALATING RELIEF COSTS

Because work-relief projects were mostly small-scale, Michigan's counties and cities faced their growing unemployment problem in the context of dramatically rising relief costs. In all four counties, the expenditures of the poor fund and of mothers' pensions wreaked havoc on county and city budgets. Property taxes funded the bulk of local government, and the combination of rising relief costs, high tax-delinquency rates, and thus decreased revenues, prompted local governments to examine their own poor-relief practices and programs, resulting in budget cuts in other areas, including reductions in wages and services. Detroit's rising relief costs compounded an already dismal debt problem, exacerbated by tax-delinquency rates as high as 25 percent. Wayne County also faced increasing welfare costs, largely related to its institutional programs. Marquette and Saginaw both turned to bond proposals to raise funds for work and direct relief, but Van Buren—the most fiscally conservative of the four counties—resisted increased debt, instead seeking to further discourage relief applications and to force the state to pay tax monies owed to the county. All counties faced an uphill battle as the Depression worsened and more and more people sought relief.

Detroit confronted the starkest financial crisis, both in unemployment rates and relief costs. As noted earlier, the city funded its relief almost exclusively with public funds, and its unemployment rates were high because of its

44. Martha Swain argues, in *Ellen S. Woodward: New Deal Advocate for Women* (Jackson: University Press of Mississippi, 1995), that although Woodward was criticized for the limited nature of work programs for women, it is amazing what Woodward was able to accomplish. See also Susan Ware, *Holding Their Own: American Women in the 1930s* (Boston: Twayne Publishers, 1982), especially chapter 3 on women and work.

dependence on the auto industry. The city's dismal financial situation resulted in efforts to economize its operations. Rooted in the large percentage of its tax levy that went to debt service, the city's budget underwent severe cuts in the early Depression years. In the 1931–32 budget, city workers suffered significant pay cuts, up to 10 percent and higher, and layoffs were widespread. Several thousand city employees lost jobs, adding to the existing unemployment problem in the city, and virtually every part of Detroit government was affected, including the Department of Public Welfare.[45]

The city's DPW was crumbling under the escalating caseloads. A caseload of about 15,000 in August 1930 jumped to more than 50,000 families by the following February. Caseworkers could not keep up with the increasing numbers, and investigations became cursory at best; most semblance of professional social work practice was gone.[46] Reversing the caseload's relentless increase was the only feasible way to contain the escalating costs. Members of the Public Welfare Commission sought the removal of 15,000 families from the relief rolls in July 1931. By July 17, the department successfully eliminated more than 6,000 families, including those who had some income, even if it was only $2 for domestic work. Relief supervisors told the commission that more than 2,600 of the cuts were arbitrary. Some of the families cut had children, and few had resources, but they had been dropped to meet the quota. District superintendents protested the cuts, and opposed further reductions in the caseload: "Feeling that the Commission will ask us to make further reduction we want to go on record here that we feel we have reached absolute bed rock as far as reducing families with intelligence, justice, or consideration . . . We naturally oppose this earnestly and wish to advise you that we will not accept further responsibility or the consequences." But cuts continued, and by the end of the month more than 18,000 families had been removed from the caseload.[47]

By early 1931, poor-fund costs in Saginaw and Marquette counties also reached a critical point, although on a smaller scale than Detroit. The city of Saginaw's budget deficits prompted suggestions of staff cuts and 20 percent wage cuts for city employees.[48] Few departments survived with their budgets intact, and the poor-fund appropriation went from $121,000 to $109,000,

45. Fine, *Frank Murphy: The Detroit Years,* 317–25.
46. Ibid., 303–4.
47. Minutes, Detroit Public Welfare Commission, vol. 7, July 17, 1931, 61, Burton Historical Collection (hereafter cited as BHC); Fine, *Frank Murphy: The Detroit Years,* 326–27.
48. "20% Wage Cuts Urged as Council Attacks Budget," *Saginaw Daily News,* April 13, 1931, 1–2.

despite having spent far more than that the previous year.[49] Marquette County did pass a bond proposal to fund relief. Relief costs began to rise in early 1930 in Marquette County, and county overdrafts on the poor fund in October 1930 necessitated increased appropriations.[50] The county set a new record high for poor relief in January 1931. Relief county-wide was running more than $10,000 per month, with expectations that it would increase.[51]

Van Buren County, the county that best illustrates the power of fiscal localism, ultimately ceased financing both poor relief and mothers' pensions. Poor-relief funds accounted for the largest line item in Van Buren County's 1931 budget, with the poor fund at $50,000 and mothers' pensions at $20,000—after the board reduced the requested appropriation for poor relief by $10,000.[52] Poor-relief costs reached a record level by May 1, 1932.[53] The deficit grew at a rate of $8,000 to $10,000 per month.[54] Van Buren County supervisors refused to go further into debt to address the financial problems. Its board of supervisors was also committed to reducing taxes, as were other counties, in light of the fifteen-mill tax limitation and the economic burden its residents faced; economy and tax relief provided the basis of most of the board's actions. Tax relief for property owners was an entitlement, while poor relief was most certainly not, in the eyes of Van Buren's supervisors.[55]

Rising relief costs prompted virtually all public relief officials to ensure that only those who needed and deserved relief received it. Some counties reorganized programs; others sought ways to discourage relief or, in the case of Van Buren County, simply eliminated poor relief altogether. After yet another need to transfer $36,450 to the poor department in May 1931, Saginaw Mayor

---

49. "1931 City Budget Climbs near Taxation Limit," *Saginaw Daily News*, April 14, 1931, 1; "Estimators' Axe Cuts $82,800 from Budget," *Saginaw Daily News*, May 5, 1931, 1, 10.

50. "$63,000 Boost in County Tax Budget Voted," *Daily Mining Journal*, October 14, 1930, 2; "Proceedings, Marquette County," vol. 7, October 13, 1930, 24.

51. "County's Poor Relief Fund Is Fading Rapidly," *Daily Mining Journal*, February 20, 1931, 3; "Proceedings of the Board of Superintendents of the Poor, Marquette County," October 22, 1931; and "County's Tax Bill Is Reduced $37,000: Budget Cut Is Made despite Heavy Demands," *Daily Mining Journal*, October 6, 1931, 1.

52. "Proceedings of the Board of Supervisors, Van Buren County, Michigan," October 26, 1931, 46–47; "County Solons Cut $28,727.49 off the Budget," *Hartford Day Spring*, October 28, 1931, 1, 8.

53. "Supervisors Order Audit of County Books," *Hartford Day Spring*, January 18, 1933, 1.

54. "County Solons Meet to Face Money Tangle," *Hartford Day Spring*, April 12, 1933, 1–2.

55. Karen Miller argues that taxpaying became a central component of citizenship, intersecting with race, in Detroit in the 1930s. Her argument resonates throughout the state, although race was not the central factor in other areas, including Van Buren County. Karen R. Miller, "The Color of Citizenship: Race and Politics in Detroit, 1916–1940" (PhD dissertation, University of Michigan, 2003), 200–201.

George Phoenix launched efforts to reexamine the department.[56] Phoenix visited Grand Rapids, among other cities, to study its programs before drafting his own. Grand Rapids implemented a controversial program to address its poor-relief problem, and other Michigan cities and counties, including Saginaw, looked to the city as a model of how to address the rising costs of poor relief.[57]

Grand Rapids' financial problems reached a crisis months before the stock market crash, following a slump in the furniture industry. The numbers of people seeking aid from the city's relief program in 1929 jumped drastically, from about two hundred to thousands.[58] After severely cutting the city budget and foregoing his own salary, city manager George Welsh balanced the city's budget by September 1929. Like many, Welsh also opposed the practice of "the dole," or giving aid to able-bodied workers. Instead, he instituted a work-relief system, targeted almost exclusively at male workers.[59] The controversy centered on the use of scrip, redeemable for groceries at the local commissary, to pay workers. The commissary, which bought food in bulk, could offer better prices for food than local grocers, and thus save scrip workers money on their food budgets. Welsh expanded the program over the next two years to include many major city projects, including city sewer work, and again invited the anger of some business owners, who argued that such programs denied their employees work.[60] The system prompted a large debate, with criticism coming from all political fronts in the city. The scrip system eventually disappeared, and the city switched to cash payments in November 1932.[61]

Other Michigan counties implemented various programs to address the rising relief problem. Saginaw Mayor Phoenix advocated requiring all relief recipients to work for their aid. Workers were paid with grocery orders, redeem-

56. "Mayor Will Ask Transfer of Funds," *Saginaw Daily News,* May 12, 1931, 1; "Better Inquiry Asked by Board," *Saginaw Daily News,* May 14, 1931, 1–2; and *Proceedings, City of Saginaw,* May 12, 1931, 335–36; June 16, 1931, 375–76.

57. Ann Arbor also instituted a scrip payment program for work-relief recipients. Other communities followed the work-relief model, but few incorporated scrip payments into their systems. David Katzman, "Ann Arbor: Depression City," *Michigan History* 50 (December 1966): 314–17. Joanna Colcord criticized the Grand Rapids program in her guide to work-relief programs. See Colcord, *Emergency Work Relief,* 85–90, 245–46.

58. Richard H. Harms, "Paid in Scrip," *Michigan History* 75 (January/February 1991): 38–39.

59. Workers removed snow from sidewalks and roads, and more than 650 men applied at the first call for workers. Other projects included highway work for the state, city sewer work, and running the commissary itself. Harms, "Paid in Scrip," 39.

60. Lorence, *Organizing the Unemployed,* 60–61; Harms, "Paid in Scrip," 38–41; and Julius H. Amberg, "Scrip-Wise and Pound Foolish," *Survey,* November 15, 1932, 596, copy in National Social Workers' Association Records, SWHA, Box 5, Folder 42.

61. Amberg, "Scrip-Wise and Pound Foolish," 596–97; Harms, "Paid in Scrip," 42–43.

able at local grocery stores, rather than with scrip. Phoenix's plan sought to achieve the same dual purpose as in Grand Rapids: providing material help for those in need while also completing necessary work projects in the city.[62] Again, the project clearly targeted men with families.[63] By mid-August, 160 men were employed on the work projects, including water main work, ditch cleaning, and woodcutting.[64]

Rising relief costs prompted Marquette County to seek ways to economize all areas of its operations. Criticisms of the poor commission's practices prompted supervisors to improve investigative methods to ensure that all who received relief needed it. The committee recommended reinvestigation of all cases of mothers' pensions to ensure that recipients who received cash relief in this form were spending it well. About 20 percent of the cases were either transferred to poor relief or had their grants reduced.[65] Supervisors, in a move that would reappear throughout the state in the coming years, hired a business executive from the Cleveland Cliffs Iron Company, rather than a social worker, to administer the poor department, hoping that such an investment would help stretch the county's shrinking poor fund. They also rejected the idea of a county store or commissary, because of the stigma attached to a commissary.[66]

Van Buren County supervisors, who ultimately eliminated poor relief, sought to discourage people from seeking relief. Some supervisors warned residents that relief could not be relied upon during the upcoming winter, urging people to "work now to eat next winter." The warning, posted in the supervisors' districts and published in the *Hartford Day Spring,* stated that aside from care in the county infirmary and outdoor relief for "a few old people outside the infirmary," poor relief was not available. Supervisors advised frugality and industry; they suggested raising large gardens and canning all surpluses, rather than selling them for immediate cash. They also encouraged

62. "Phoenix to Inspect Poor Departments," *Saginaw Daily News,* June 4, 1931, 1; "Mayor Launches Plan to End Dole System," *Saginaw Daily News,* June 17, 1931, 1, 5.

63. "Mayor Launches Plan to End Dole System," *Saginaw Daily News,* June 17, 1931, 1, 5; "Estimators Hold Up Poor Fund Proposal," *Saginaw Daily News,* July 7, 1931, 1–2; and "Board Allows Half of Poor Relief Fund," *Saginaw Daily News,* July 9, 1931, 1–2.

64. "Dole List Workers Now Number 160," *Saginaw Daily News,* August 20, 1931, 9.

65. "Supervisors Okeh [sic] Report of Special Budget Committee," *Daily Mining Journal,* July 28, 1932, 1, 7; "Supervisors Okeh [sic] Final Report of Budget Committee," *Daily Mining Journal,* October 11, 1932; and "Proceedings, Marquette County," 7, May 18, 1932, 86–87; July 27, 1932, 94–99.

66. "Supervisors Okeh [sic] Report of Special Budget Committee" and "Text of Committee's Report to Supervisors on Tax Investigation," *Daily Mining Journal,* July 28, 1932, 1, 7; "Wood-Chopping and Gardening Are Essential," *Daily Mining Journal,* April 20, 1933, 2; and "Proceedings, Marquette County," vol. 7, July 27, 1932, 96–97, 104–5; October 10, 1932, 122.

paying for winter coal before the snow flew "instead of joyriding or going to shows."[67] The supervisors believed that some poor-relief recipients were not doing all they could to prevent their need for relief.

The Hartford newspaper supported the supervisors' efforts to provide tax relief to residents as early as 1931, although cost increases limited their ability to do so. Taxes were a product of the residents' demands, the editorial continued, and thus residents had to share the blame for the escalating costs.[68] Eighteen months later the newspaper's editorial page reiterated its position when it identified the poor-relief situation as the problem, noting that "the county is the beneficent stepdaddy to more unfortunate families than ever before."[69] The idea that relief recipients were somehow deficient, in part because of their dependency, operated in this county and others, despite the extent of the economic crisis.

Fiscal localism was the key ideology evident in Van Buren County's actions. Its budget cuts were a financial necessity in the supervisors' eyes, but they left area residents in need of aid with few options. With poor-relief funds virtually gone, residents had to look to township supervisors, who probably had little to offer, or to private agencies, such as the county's Social Service Bureau or the American Red Cross. These agencies likely had little left to give, either. If family members were unable to help, then, the needy had nowhere else to turn. Verifying need among recipients was a strategy employed by all four counties in their efforts to reduce relief costs, but Van Buren was the only one to cut off relief funds. Van Buren County officials would return to this position in the ensuing years, resisting any and all efforts to sacrifice fiscal economy to the relief needs of their residents. Poor relief was not an entitlement but a service provided only when the county could afford to do so.

MOTHERS' PENSIONS

Mothers' pension programs were a casualty of budget cuts in many Michigan counties during the Depression, but not all local officials agreed to such cuts quietly. In some cases, debates over mothers' pensions proved to be a contest between local officials, with judicial authority again playing a key role. By

---

67. "Editorial: Idle Warned to Work Now to Eat Next Winter," *Hartford Day Spring*, May 10, 1933, 1.

68. "Supervisors Made Honest Effort to Cut Taxes," *Hartford Day Spring*, November 4, 1931.

69. "County Solons Meet to Face Money Tangle," *Hartford Day Spring*, April 12, 1933, 1–2.

1934, thirty-four of the state's eighty-three counties had eliminated mothers' pensions.[70] Saginaw County engaged in a vigorous debate over the funding of mothers' pensions in the early Depression years. The city of Saginaw operated a poor department separate from the county, but Saginaw County administered mothers' pensions for all county residents. Saginaw County faced its own poor-fund problems, which began to appear by mid-1931, as well as difficulties financing mothers' pensions. By 1933 funding for mothers' pensions was in serious jeopardy, prompting a heated power struggle between supervisors and the local probate judge. Saginaw County's experience highlights the funding disputes between local officials, and the operation of judicial authority. It also illustrates the continued debate over whether mothers' pensions were, in fact, poor relief.

Probate Judge John Murphy used his judicial authority to defend and save the program. Already short of funds by October of 1933, Murphy requested an additional $25,000 to fund pensions until the end of the year.[71] But two weeks later, the board voted unanimously to deny the request, and told Murphy to cease taking applications for mothers' pensions. The question of whether the state law regarding mothers' pensions was voluntary or mandatory was crucial in this conflict.[72] The county's prosecuting attorney issued a legal opinion that "the matter of mothers' pensions is wholly within the discretion of the probate court, over which the county board of supervisors and the board of county auditors have no control." In response, Murphy announced that he would continue to issue orders to recipients who, after investigation, were found eligible for the pensions. If the county refused to pay, he stated, he would not initiate any legal action, but recipients certainly could do so.[73] When the final vote came for the budget two days later, the entire appropriation for mothers' pensions was nearly cut; Charles Bois, Birch Run Township supervisor and longtime opponent of mothers' pensions, advocated eliminating the program and adding $50,000 to the poor fund; recipients of mothers' aid could seek poor-relief aid. Bois' motion to eliminate the appropriation from the budget

70. Harris, *Mothers' Pensions in Michigan*, 1.

71. "Mothers Fund Plea before Supervisors," *Saginaw Daily News*, October 9, 1933, 1, 8; "Supervisors Waver on Demand for Fund," *Saginaw Daily News*, October 10, 1933, 1–2; *Official Proceedings of the Board of Supervisors, Saginaw County*, October 9, 1933, 2–3.

72. "Deny Mothers Pension Fund Plea: Supervisors Flout Provisions of Law," *Saginaw Daily News*, October 24, 1933, 1–2; *Proceedings, Saginaw County*, October 23, 1933, 105. Marquette County's supervisors also believed that the law required counties to fund mothers' pensions if funds were available and thus continued to do so well into the Depression. See "Officials Say Aid to Mothers Is Mandatory," *Daily Mining Journal*, October 25, 1933, 3.

73. "Mothers Aid Will Continue," *Saginaw Daily News*, October 25, 1933, 1–2; *Proceedings, Saginaw County*, October 25, 1933, 115.

failed by just one vote; even still, the board ignored Murphy's request for an additional $25,000.[74] Thus mothers' pensions ceased and did not resume again until February of 1934.[75]

Murphy continued to advocate for the program, arguing that it was a legal and moral duty to provide for all needy children in the county.[76] In the meantime, recipients of mothers' pensions received letters explaining the fund problem and instructing them to seek aid from their city or township.[77] Two local attorneys donated their services in a court challenge to the supervisors' decision, arguing that mothers' pensions were mandatory.[78] The county supervisors argued in response that the funds were not there, and that the court had no authority over the board of supervisors.[79] Proponents of mothers' pensions lost the fight when the court ruled that the county lacked the funds to provide further for mothers' pensions that year; the responsibility rested with the townships and the city, or with the newly formed welfare-relief commission under the Federal Emergency Relief Act, to provide aid until the 1934 appropriation began.[80]

Not all counties had probate judges who exerted this effort on behalf of the mothers' pension program, but the situation in Saginaw shows that, under the law, they could. The "cult of judicial personality" worked in favor of recipients of mothers' pensions in Saginaw County. In this case, Murphy was able to preserve much-needed aid for Saginaw's poor mothers for the following year, although pensions ceased for the rest of 1933.[81] Van Buren County was one of the thirty-four counties to end mothers' pensions, as well as poor relief, before the New Deal. The only welfare funds in the budget were for institutional care,

74. "$522,319 Tax Total Voted by Supervisors: Approve 1934 Budget, Slash General Fund," *Saginaw Daily News,* October 27, 1933, 1–2; "Mothers Pension Fund Put in Budget," *Saginaw Daily News,* October 27, 1933, 1, 10; and *Proceedings, Saginaw County,* October 26, 1933, 131–32.

75. "Resumes Paying Mother Pensions," *Saginaw Daily News,* February 1, 1934. The prosecuting attorney's duties under Michigan law included providing legal advice and opinions to county officials. Bromage and Reed, *Organization and Cost of County and Township Government,* 63.

76. "To Ask Judge Explain Views," *Saginaw Daily News,* November 3, 1933; "Mother Fund $10,000 in Red," *Saginaw Daily News,* November 4, 1933; and *Proceedings, Saginaw County,* November 3, 1933, 159.

77. "Mothers Apply to City for Help," *Saginaw Daily News,* November 6, 1933; "City to Aid Needy Widows," *Saginaw Daily News,* November 9, 1933.

78. "Suit May Force Mothers' Pension Payments," *Saginaw Daily News,* November 7, 1933; "Pension Case Order Signed," *Saginaw Daily News,* November 8, 1933.

79. "Defend Position on Mothers' Pensions," *Saginaw Daily News,* November 13, 1933; "Pension Mandamus Denial Likely," *Saginaw Daily News,* November 17, 1933.

80. "Points Way to Relief for Needy Mothers," *Saginaw Daily News,* November 18, 1933.

81. Rothman, *Conscience and Convenience;* see chapter 7, "The Cult of Judicial Personality."

hospitalization costs, and soldiers' and sailors' relief. Supervisors ordered Probate Judge Merle Young to pay any remaining outstanding pensions, but then stop once these had been paid. Supervisors had already reduced the program from twenty-two thousand dollars to twelve thousand dollars in 1932.[82] Young did not publicly protest the cuts, as Saginaw's Murphy did, and Van Buren officials did not see mothers' pensions as mandatory under the law. Again, the funds were not there and thus they could not provide aid, a position Young apparently agreed with, as he undertook no public efforts to reinstate the pensions. Probate judges could either serve as advocates for the program, and defend it during difficult budget times, or let supervisors eliminate it. Again, local authority was important, and fiscal localism often served as a key limiting factor in efforts to advocate for the poor.

REPATRIATION

Economic hard times often reinforce already existing hierarchies and discrimination, and the Depression years were no exception. People of color and noncitizens were among the first fired from jobs as unemployment rose, and they faced much higher rates of unemployment than white native-born workers. In their efforts to control relief costs, some public agencies, in conjunction with the state welfare department and the Michigan legislature, denied aid and employment to noncitizens. This trend culminated in repatriation programs funded by the state welfare department and local governments. Although repatriation was often defined as "voluntary," historians have criticized taking the term at face value. Coercive methods often encouraged noncitizens to return to their native countries as a means to reduce unemployment and relief costs.[83] Mexicans and Mexican-Americans are the most well-known targets of repatriation efforts, but Michigan's program returned noncitizens from many countries to their homeland. In contrast to other regions of the country, repatriation in Michigan and the Midwest was a function of social welfare, rather than immigration, policy.[84] In the 1930s, economic conditions combined with racism and nativist views to render citizenship a defining category in the administration of social welfare.

82. "Supervisors End October Session: Look for Spots to Further Cut County Budget," *Hartford Day Spring*, October 25, 1933, 1, 8; "Proceedings of the Board of Supervisors, Van Buren County," October 19, 1933, 58–59; October 20, 1933, 60.

83. Abraham Hoffman, *Unwanted Mexican Americans in the Great Depression: Repatriation Pressures, 1929–1939* (Tucson: University of Arizona Press, 1974), 24–25.

84. Valdes, *Barrios Nortenos*, 125–26.

Western states, in particular California, are much more known for these programs, but the Midwestern states also instituted repatriation programs. Michigan, Illinois, and Indiana had just 3.6 percent of the nation's Mexican population, but accounted for about 10 percent of repatriated Mexicans.[85] Sixty-four percent of all Mexicans in the Midwest were repatriated, and populations in all major cities, including Detroit and Chicago, declined significantly.[86] Michigan's commitment to repatriation began in 1932, under Governor Wilber Brucker, and continued throughout the decade. The state welfare department worked with the Immigration and Naturalization Service, in addition to Mexican consular officials, to institute the later repatriation program. The state legislature appropriated twenty-five thousand dollars in the fiscal years 1935–36 and 1936–37 to pay transportation costs, with the expectation that far more would be saved in relief costs.[87]

Shifting racial categories in the U.S. Bureau of the Census have made it difficult to gauge exact population growths for some foreign-born populations in the United States, a trend that is particularly true for Mexicans. The 1920 census, for instance, included Mexicans in the white population. In 1930 a separate category was created, but in 1940 Mexicans were again defined as white.[88] According to the 1930 census, Mexicans accounted for just 0.3 percent of Michigan's total population.[89] More than half of the state's 13,336 Mexicans counted in the 1930 census resided in Wayne County (most in the city of Detroit); Saginaw County had the next highest portion at 17 percent of the overall Mexican population in the state.[90]

85. By the end of 1932, between 1,100 and 1,500 Mexicans had left Michigan to return to Mexico under the repatriation program. Norman D. Humphrey, "The Migration and Settlement of Detroit Mexicans," *Economic Geography* 19 (October 1943): 360; Hoffman, *Unwanted Mexican Americans,* 121; and Juan R. Garcia, *Mexicans in the Midwest, 1900–1932* (Tucson: University of Arizona Press, 1996), 230. The *Saginaw Daily News* reported that 1,156 had left Michigan by mid-December of 1932. "More Mexicans Leave Tu [sic]," *Saginaw Daily News,* December 18, 1932, 5.

86. Garcia, *Mexicans in the Midwest, 1900–1932,* 238.

87. Lynn G. Kellogg, *Repatriation in Michigan* (Lansing, MI: State Welfare Department 1936), 2; Norman D. Humphrey, "Mexican Repatriation from Michigan: Public Assistance in Historical Perspective," *Social Service Review* 15 (September 1941): 498; and Valdes, *Barrios Nortenos,* 94–100.

88. Sharon M. Lee, "Racial Classifications in the US Census: 1890–1990," *Ethnic and Racial Studies* 16.1 (January 1993): 77–79; and Mark Reisler, *By the Sweat of Their Brow: Mexican Immigrant Labor in the United States, 1900–1940* (Westport, CT: Greenwood Press, 1976), 56.

89. Hoffman, *Unwanted Mexican Americans,* 14; and *Fifteenth Census of the United States: 1930, Vol. I, Population* (Washington, D.C.: U.S. Government Printing Office, 1931), 1115.

90. One estimate places the population of Mexicans in Detroit at 8,000 in 1920, but their numbers fluctuated with the availability of jobs. Although Wayne County had a higher number of Mexicans than Saginaw County, Mexicans in the latter comprised a larger percentage (2

The fluidity of racial categories reflects larger debates over race and citizenship. Immigration restrictions in the 1920s legislated beliefs about which groups were white and able to become full American citizens, and a significant component of the debate centered on moral character linked to racial "fitness." Mexican immigration actually received little public attention before the 1921 and 1924 immigration laws, which did not include Mexicans or Canadians in immigration quotas.[91] But those who supported more relaxed Mexican immigration laws did so because they valued Mexicans as cheap laborers, not because they saw them as a desirable group for American citizenship. Mexicans remained outside the category of "white" while other immigrants, including those from European countries, gained the legal status of white citizens.[92]

Mexicans and other foreign-born populations faced limited job opportunities even before the Depression. Mexicans tended to be concentrated in the unskilled, least desirable jobs, and enjoyed little upward mobility. Before the Great Depression, they were recruited to fill U.S. labor needs. Faced with reduced European immigration because of restrictions during World War I and the restrictive National Origins Act of 1924, agricultural employers sought a new, unrestricted labor pool.[93] The sugar beet industry had shifted to a predominantly Mexican labor force around World War I, when labor agents began to recruit Mexicans and Mexican-Americans from Texas to work in the sugar beet fields of mid-Michigan as well as in Minnesota, Wisconsin, Iowa, and Ohio.[94] The seasonal work prompted some Mexicans to return to Texas, but many more went to the cities, including Detroit and Saginaw, to seek work

---

percent) of its overall population in 1930. *Fifteenth Census of the United States: 1930, Vol. I, Population,* 1152. Genesee County (particularly the city of Flint) and St. Clair County north of Wayne County had the next largest numbers of Mexicans, but they were only a fraction of those in Wayne and Saginaw. Wayne had 7,104; Saginaw had 2,270; Genesee had 649; and St. Clair had 535. See also Humphrey, "Mexican Repatriation," 500.

91. Clare Sheridan, "Contested Citizenship: National Identity and the Mexican Immigration Debates of the 1920s," *Journal of American Ethnic History* 21 (Spring 2002): 4–5; Desmond King, *Making Americans: Immigration, Race, and the Origins of the Diverse Democracy* (Cambridge: Harvard University Press, 2000), 233; and Roger Daniels, *Coming to America: A History of Immigration and Ethnicity in American Life* (New York: HarperCollins, 2002), 291–92.

92. James Barrett and David Roediger, "Inbetween Peoples: Race, Nationality, and the 'New Immigrant' Working Class," *Journal of American Ethnic History* 16.3 (1997): 9–10; King, *Making Americans,* 20; and Sheridan, "Contested Citizenship," 4–5. See also David R. Roediger, *Working toward Whiteness: How America's Immigrants Became White* (New York: Basic Books, 2005).

93. Vargas, *Proletarians of the North,* 24–28; Garcia, *Mexicans in the Midwest, 1900–1932,* 10–17.

94. The Michigan Sugar Beet Company recruited its first Mexican workers in 1915, beginning an annual migration of about two thousand workers for the next fourteen years. By 1922 Mexicans were 33 percent of the state's beet-worker population, and that figure rose to 75 percent by 1929. Garcia, *Mexicans in the Midwest, 1900–1932,* 14.

in the growing factories. By the 1920s, historians document a major shift to factory employment among Mexicans and Mexican-Americans.[95]

Mexican workers in the United States faced two major obstacles to continued employment in the 1920s and 1930s: their race and their Mexican citizenship.[96] Even during the 1920s, auto workers, and particularly Mexicans, did not enjoy full-time, year-round work, but as companies experienced economic downturns and layoffs, Mexicans, Mexican-Americans, African-Americans, and noncitizens were among the first targets. Between 1929 and 1931, 1,027 Mexicans, or 40 percent of those employed by Ford, lost their jobs. Restrictive hiring practices also increased, as signs stating "Only White Labor Employed" became more common, even in the sugar beet industry. Companies, encouraged by government officials at all levels, replaced Mexican workers with whites, particularly with whites who were American citizens.[97] Restrictive hiring practices soon extended to all noncitizens. Wayne County instituted a policy in 1930 that all workers on county projects must have been citizens and residents of Detroit for at least two years.[98] In 1931 Michigan passed the short-lived Spolansky Act, which required all noncitizens to register and verify their legal immigration status before they could "reside, sojourn, engage in business, or work in Michigan."[99] Many work projects under the New Deal, including the Works Progress Administration, hired only citizens, and industries were slow to reverse their hiring practices even after defense work began in 1941.[100] Such action was a combination of American nativism and racism, targeting those not seen as American by virtue of either their birth or skin color, or both in the case of Mexicans.

Mexicans were often among those who did not seek citizenship, or did not want to renounce their native citizenship. In 1930 about 28.6 percent of the foreign-born population in Michigan had not sought citizenship status.[101]

95. Vargas, *Proletarians of the North,* 50–52; Garcia, *Mexicans in the Midwest, 1900–1932,* 33–34; Valdes, *Barrios Nortenos,* 27, 42, 45–46; Reisler, *By the Sweat of Their Brow,* 100; Robert N. McLean, "A Dike against Mexicans," *The New Republic* 49 (August 14, 1929): 335; Garcia, *Mexicans in the Midwest, 1900–1932,* 65.

96. Barrett and Roediger, "Inbetween Peoples," 9–10, 16–17; and Sheridan, "Contested Citizenship," 5–8.

97. Garcia, *Mexicans in the Midwest, 1900–1932,* 224–25.

98. *Official Proceedings of the Board of Supervisors of Wayne County, 1930,* October 3, 1930, 713.

99. An immediate court challenge rendered the law moot within a week of its passage in May 1931. Thomas A. Klug, "Labor Market Politics in Detroit: The Curious Case of the 'Spolansky Act' of 1931," *Michigan Historical Review* 14 (Spring 1988): 1, 31.

100. Valdes, *Barrios Nortenos,* 101–2.

101. *Fifteenth Census of the United States: 1930, Vol. I, Population* (Washington, D.C.: U.S. Government Printing Office, 1931), 1115.

Much of the discrimination and racism Mexicans faced before the Depression was connected to their race, and not their citizenship status. They faced segregation in housing and general derision because of stereotypes about Mexicans.[102] Prior to the Depression, citizenship affected their ability to find employment of some kind only minimally, as most were recruited to the area for their labor. Many Mexicans saw racism, not their foreign-born status, as the key reason for their limited opportunities and choices. Many Mexicans hoped to return to Mexico eventually. The Mexican consulate also worked to limit the Americanization of Mexicans, including discouraging their adoption of U.S. citizenship.[103]

As employment opportunities became more and more linked to citizenship in the 1930s, and thus more Mexican immigrants likely considered citizenship for themselves, particularly if their children were American-born, the process of obtaining U.S. citizenship became much more difficult. Changes in the immigration law in 1929 created new obstacles to naturalization, including a 300 percent increase in fees to become a citizen. Social workers in both Saginaw and Wayne counties often helped Mexicans and other noncitizens navigate the naturalization process, but public funds for fees were not available. During a time of economic hardship, such an increase made citizenship effectively impossible for many immigrants, Mexican or otherwise. Education requirements, with English literacy rates low among Mexican immigrants, also proved an impediment to citizenship.[104] Just as the motivation for citizenship likely increased with the link between naturalization and employment, the barriers to obtain citizenship also strengthened.

Discrimination against noncitizens culminated in efforts to return them to their native countries. The first efforts to remove Mexicans from the Michigan population actually occurred in the 1920–21 depression, when Mexican workers appeared to threaten American jobs.[105] The city of Detroit and Wayne County reported all Mexican relief applicants to the Immigration Bureau,

---

102. Valdes, *Barrios Nortenos,* 44–46; Sheridan, "Contested Citizenship," 4.

103. Valdes, *Barrios Nortenos,* 73; Norman D. Humphrey, "The Detroit Mexican Immigrant and Naturalization," *Social Forces* 22 (March 1944): 334. Roger Daniels argues that a similar trend existed among later Mexican immigrants. Daniels, *Coming to America,* 317–18.

104. Humphrey, "The Detroit Mexican," 334; and Adrena Miller Rich, "Case Work in the Repatriation of Immigrants," *Social Service Review* 10 (December 1936): 570. Attaining citizenship involved formally declaring one's intent to become a citizen of the United States, which could be done anytime after the immigrant arrived in the United States. The alien then could petition a court for citizenship after two years, providing she or he had been in the country for five years total. The federal court judge then decided whether to grant citizenship. Avery M. Guest, "The Old-New Distinction and Naturalization: 1900," *International Migration Review* 14.4 (1980): 494–95.

105. Sheridan, "Contested Citizenship," 5–6.

making them targets for deportation. Saginaw officials refused aid to Mexican workers outright, arguing that they had come to the area voluntarily or at the instigation of the beet companies, and were not the government's responsibility. The city repatriated two hundred Mexican beet workers to Mexico in February 1921.[106] Inaction by the federal government prompted local officials to use repatriation to alleviate local unemployment and relief problems even before the Great Depression, yet another manifestation of fiscal localism.

Saginaw, Flint, Port Huron, Mount Pleasant, and Detroit all participated in the repatriation efforts of the 1930s. Michigan newspapers carried reports of Mexicans returning to Mexico in 1931 and 1932. The first in Saginaw occurred in September 1931, when the *Saginaw Daily News* reported that "the first combined voluntary and involuntary deportation ever undertaken in the United States for a large group of aliens" began with sixty-eight Mexicans, thirty-seven of whom had entered the country illegally and thus were being deported. The rest of the group comprised family members or other Mexicans who had been on poor relief and were returning voluntarily to their native country. State welfare department supervisor Earl White worked with local officials to coordinate the deportation, and told those gathered that all but five of the people leaving had been on the city poor lists; the cost of moving them was far less than continuing to support them in Saginaw.[107] The group then went to Detroit, where it was joined by a group of Hindus, Chinese, and Mexicans also leaving the United States.[108] Three such trainloads left Saginaw and other cities that fall, and another round took place the following year.

State welfare official Arthur Webster approached the Saginaw City Council in October of 1932 for five thousand dollars to cover the transportation costs of ninety-eight Mexican families who were willing to return to Mexico. Webster argued that although these families were not yet on poor relief, they likely soon would be. If they were employed, he continued, their jobs should go to Saginaw citizens.[109] The council eventually appropriated the five thousand dollars.[110] Detroit Mexican Consul Ignaxio Batiza warned Mexicans in Saginaw that conditions in the United States would only worsen, with few job opportunities, and thus they should return to Mexico "and become good citi-

---

106. Vargas, *Proletarians of the North,* 83; and Valdes, *Barrios Nortenos,* 94–95.

107. "Mexican Journey to Border Begins," *Saginaw Daily News,* September 24, 1931, 1, 10; "Mexican Population Here Believed Reduced by 300," *Saginaw Daily News,* September 3, 1931, 10; and Hoffman, *Unwanted Mexican Americans,* 38–39.

108. "Mexicans to Start Journey to Border," *Saginaw Daily News,* September 23, 1931, 1, 9.

109. "Move to Send Mexicans Back," *Saginaw Daily News,* October 8, 1932, 1–2.

110. "Mexican Colony's Exodus Discussed," *Saginaw Daily News,* October 10, 1932, 1, 10; "Council Debates Moving Mexicans," *Saginaw Daily News,* October 11, 1932, 7.

zens there."[111] About four thousand Mexicans in the state were repatriated in 1932, including several trainloads from Saginaw.[112] Most newspaper accounts in Saginaw presented a picture of Mexicans happy to be returning home, and described them as a "merry throng" and a "happy lot." The accounts clearly depicted the Mexicans as foreigners, not as Americans, portraying them as "dusky skinned fathers and mothers, black-haired babies" who were joined by Mexicans of other areas, their "compatriots," who were heading to "the land below the Rio Grande."[113] The travelers were always represented as voluntary participants, and were promised land upon their arrival in Mexico, but one article noted that ten potential travelers changed their minds at the last minute. They left the train, abandoning their baggage, to remain in Saginaw, rather than return to Mexico.[114]

By the Depression, Michigan's welfare department began to work for the repatriation of other foreign-born residents as well. Repatriation efforts extended to European and African immigrants, both in Michigan and the rest of the nation. In 1934 Mexicans comprised the largest group of those repatriated nationally but were just 16 percent of the total number of people repatriated that year.[115] In 1933 about 330 families had left Detroit for "various British possessions," and the Department of Public Welfare planned to return a large number of Turkish people to their homeland as well.[116] In a 1936 report, the Michigan State Welfare Department argued that immigrants had few resources and little family to turn to in times of need, while in their native country they could find both.[117] The report did not acknowledge that noncitizens were excluded from many kinds of employment, and usually were the first fired if they did obtain work. It also ignored the exclusion of noncitizens from work-relief programs.[118]

Transports to Europe were scheduled approximately every four weeks, and repatriates traveled by rail and then steamship to their homeland. During the

111. "Urges Mexicans to Return Home," *Saginaw Daily News,* October 21, 1932, 1, 10.

112. Detroit's Department of Public Welfare financed the return of about six hundred Mexicans that November. Valdes, *Barrios Nortenos,* 95; "Proceedings of the Detroit Public Welfare Commission," Nov. 1, 1932, 37.

113. "Train Carries 430 Mexicans," *Saginaw Daily News,* November 23, 1932, 1, 7.

114. "432 Mexicans Quit Detroit for Home," *Saginaw Daily News,* November 16, 1932; "Mexicans' Exodus Cost City $3,565.16," *Saginaw Daily News,* December 7, 1932.

115. Rich, "Case Work," 572. Of the total, 6,384 were Mexicans, followed closely by natives of England at 4,841.

116. "Proceedings of the Detroit Public Welfare Commission," August 15, 1933, 161.

117. Kellogg, *Repatriation in Michigan,* 1.

118. See Harold Fields, "Where Shall the Alien Work," *Social Forces* 12 (December 1933): 213–21; Hoffman, *Unwanted Mexican Americans,* 18; Vargas, *Proletarians of the North,* 109–12; and Reisler, *By the Sweat of Their Brow,* 228–29.

eighteen-month period of the study, 219 applications were received; of these 130 were completed, involving 232 people.[119] According to the report, 20 were residents of institutions, and 56 families had received relief for more than two years. The repatriates headed for numerous countries in this period. The largest number (51) returned to England; the next largest group (40), to Mexico. Other countries of destination were Bulgaria, Germany, Romania, Holland, and Yugoslavia.[120] These efforts occurred after the largest number of repatriations took place. Repatriation declined after states began to receive federal aid for relief in 1932 and 1933. Federal funds could not be used for repatriation programs, thus reducing the incentive to return noncitizens to their native countries.[121]

Historian Juan Garcia disputes the argument that Mexicans posed a significant relief burden, arguing that "a substantial body of evidence contradicts this premise."[122] Mexican workers were reluctant to seek public assistance for a variety of reasons, according to Garcia. For many, accepting public aid was too humiliating; instead, they sought aid from community mutual-aid societies.[123] Those Mexicans who entered the United States illegally, at a time when labor demands relaxed immigration practices on the southern border, feared deportation if they sought public aid. Some public agencies would aid only those Mexicans who agreed to repatriation, or would have agency officials use coercive methods to prompt Mexicans to "choose" repatriation. Detroit officials in the Department of Public Welfare encouraged Mexicans to leave the city by requiring them to take their meals in the department "restaurants," rather than issuing a grocery order or cash relief. The food was poor and did not follow Mexican cooking habits, and the program carried a significant stigma in the community. One caseworker noted that a "'family is contemplating returning to Mexico and the caseworker feels they might return more quickly if they are kept on a cafeteria list rather than be given a grocery order.'"[124] Agencies also sometimes refused aid altogether or withdrew aid, including rent support, if

119. Of the 232 people, 61 were citizens or the children of immigrants. Just eight had been in the United States less than five years, and 47 had resided in the United States between five and nine years. Nearly half—109 people—had lived in the United States more than ten years, and 24 of those for more than twenty-five years. Kellogg, *Repatriation in Michigan*, 4, 8.

120. Other nations included South Africa, Albania, and several European countries. Kellogg, *Repatriation in Michigan*, 8. Canadians make up none of the noncitizens repatriated in this report, despite their high numbers among immigrants to the United States after the legal restrictions were passed in 1921 and 1924.

121. Hoffman, *Unwanted Mexican Americans*, 113.

122. Garcia, *Mexicans in the Midwest, 1900–1932*, 226.

123. Detroit had about fourteen nationality-based organizations in the 1920s, and groups also existed in Saginaw. Such groups provided charitable help and served as social organizations. See Valdes, *Barrios Nortenos*, 46, 74–75.

124. Garcia, *Mexicans in the Midwest, 1900–1932*, 227–28.

a family would not accept repatriation.[125] The practice extended to Mexican-Americans, as well as to Mexicans with children born in the United States. Garcia argues that the relief problem did not decline significantly after repatriation, lending little credence to the argument that the Mexican population had constituted a large portion of the relief problem in the Midwest.

The numbers in Michigan validate Garcia's argument. While repatriations represented a significant movement, particularly in the Mexican communities of Detroit and Saginaw, numerically they were not a sizeable portion of the overall relief situation. In 1936, 5,018 noncitizens were on the relief rolls, a small part of the state total.[126] But the context in which the repatriations occurred is noteworthy. Detroit's Department of Public Welfare underwent its most extreme budget crisis in 1931, and a considerable part of its expenditures went for relief. Caseloads reached more than 50,000 in February and dropped to 32,000 in June. The city spent more than $14 million on relief in that fiscal year, and saw deep and brutal cuts in relief rolls to accommodate the declining budget. The department was forced to cut its rolls in half, from 32,000 to 16,000.[127] About 4,000 Mexican nationals left Detroit in 1932. The number was a minor fraction of the relief load for the city, and there is no evidence that a substantial number of those who left Detroit were receiving relief. Officials, however, assumed they were, and believed their departure to be a means of reducing welfare costs. In Detroit, officials were desperate to reduce relief costs (or to appear to), and noncitizens, especially Mexicans, were politically popular targets.

THE STATE OF MICHIGAN

Michigan, like many states, was slow to participate financially in the relief crisis. Commissions and committees were the first step, but few states followed those efforts with any funds to help local governments; the concept that relief was a local issue demanding local solutions was widespread.[128]

125. Ibid., 232.

126. State Emergency Welfare Relief Commission Minutes, May 8, 1936, Box 2, Folder 5; Archives of Michigan, RG 58-12. The number of cases in 1936 ranged from a high of 82,912 to a low of 60,073. Those cases included as few as 193,414 people to as many as 276,689. George F. Granger and Lawrence R. Klein, *Emergency Relief in Michigan, 1933–1939* (Lansing: May, 1939), 31.

127. Fine, *Frank Murphy: The Detroit Years,* 307, 325–27; "Proceedings of the Public Welfare Commission," July 8, 14, and 17, 1931, 42–64.

128. David Joseph Maurer, "Public Relief Programs in Ohio, 1929–1939" (PhD dissertation, Ohio State University, 1962), 2–3, 9–10, 22–25, 46–47; Dwayne Charles Cole, "The Relief Crisis in Illinois during the Depression, 1930–1940" (PhD dissertation, St. Louis University, 1973),

Michigan Governor Wilber Brucker appointed a state unemployment commission in 1931 to coordinate all relief activities in the state and to work with local committees to develop work-relief projects. Comprised of 105 members and led by a 15-member executive committee, the commission coordinated with churches, labor unions, and other local organizations to avoid duplication of relief services. It was a central clearinghouse for local and county relief information, but encouraged local control and decentralization. The state commission also attempted to encourage people and the economy with cheerful advice and witty slogans, although historian Richard Ortquist argues that it accomplished little and soon found that "words and catchy phrases would not win the war against want." He maintains that the committee was different from those of other states, such as New York and Illinois, in that it did little to address the relief problem in any practical way.[129]

Part of the reason for the lack of financial help was that the state government had little money to allocate. A majority of the state's revenues came from property taxes, but as with the counties, the state faced the fifteen-mill limitation and rising tax-delinquency rates; too many people simply were unable to pay their property taxes. State legislators sought to alleviate the property tax burden, given the high rates of tax delinquency. They postponed the sales tax and canceled many tax penalties. The passage of the fifteen-mill limit in 1932 had prompted the state to enact its first sales tax in 1933. The 3 percent tax was to replace the property tax revenues, which now funded local governments.[130] But sales tax revenues were difficult to project and unstable, dependent upon the status of the state's economy. The state had no income tax, as voters had repeatedly rejected constitutional amendments on that issue.[131] The state released twelve million dollars in highway funds to be used by local agencies for relief in 1931. County and city unemployment commissions used the funds in part for local work-relief projects. The state also received four million dollars from the U.S. Bureau of Public Roads. In 1932 Michigan authorized the distribution of a portion of the gasoline-tax revenues, amounting to about nine million dollars annually. Although they were not direct relief funds, the money did help local budget problems. But none of the appropriations represented additional expenditures and only advanced the distribution date of the funds.[132]

24–26, 38, 42–45; and Raymond L. Koch, "The Development of Public Relief Programs in Minnesota, 1929–1941" (PhD dissertation, University of Minnesota, 1967), 22.

129. Ortquist, *Depression Politics in Michigan*, 144–45.

130. Wilson and Dunbar, *Michigan: A Wolverine State*, 523.

131. Fine, *Frank Murphy: The New Deal Years*, 263–64. Income tax amendments failed in 1922 and 1924, and again in 1934 and 1936.

132. Haber and Stanchfield, *Unemployment and Relief in Michigan*, 34–35; Ortquist, *Depression Politics in Michigan*, 145.

Many states, including Michigan, did not immediately push for federal funds for relief, seeking every alternative before relinquishing the concept of localism in relief administration.[133] Michigan's governor and state legislature adopted a "do it ourselves" approach until as late as 1932. Indeed, many states were optimistic that they could handle the relief and unemployment problems in their states, despite evidence to the contrary, and preferred not to invite federal intervention.[134] Michigan Governor Fred Green opposed the creation of an unemployment commission in late 1930 because he thought that "such a move would only emphasize the problem." Green did attempt to secure early release of highway funds so that the state could extend its highway projects, but was not successful.[135] His successor, Governor Brucker, also opposed federal aid for relief. Brucker telegraphed President Hoover on August 21, 1931, stating that "the people of Michigan will take care of their own problem." In his view, one shared by many officials, relief was the arena of private charity and local government, which had not yet been proven incapable of handling the load.[136] The reluctance of Michigan, and other states, to provide funds for relief also was linked both to the resistance to taxes and to fiscal conservatism.

Not all officials in Michigan shared Brucker's assessment. Just one month before, Detroit Mayor Frank Murphy, along with representatives from numerous other municipalities and labor organizations, had petitioned Hoover to call a special session to approve loans to the states for relief purposes. Murphy, who would be elected Michigan's governor in 1936, told Hoover that Detroit had already expended large sums on relief, and could not do more: "The imminence of another winter of unprecedented deprivation through unemployment finds Detroit as determined as ever that no man, woman or child shall lack the elemental needs of food, clothing and shelter, but also finds the City less able than before to provide these necessities."[137] He and other Michigan municipal leaders had already sought state aid for unemployment relief, but

133. Maurer, "Public Relief Programs in Ohio, 1929–1939," 9, 25; Cole, "The Relief Crisis in Illinois," 103–6; Blanche D. Coll, *Safety Net: Welfare and Social Security, 1929–1979* (New Brunswick: Rutgers University Press, 1995), 9; Cecelia Bucki, *Bridgeport's Socialist New Deal, 1915–1936* (Urbana and Chicago: University of Illinois Press, 2001), 138–39; and Ferguson, *Black Politics in New Deal Atlanta,* 73–76.

134. James T. Patterson, *The New Deal and the States: Federalism in Transition* (Princeton: Princeton University Press, 1969), 28–31.

135. Ortquist, *Depression Politics in Michigan,* 140–41.

136. Brock, *Welfare, Democracy, and the New Deal,* 118–19; Ortquist, *Depression Politics in Michigan,* 141–42.

137. Ortquist, *Depression Politics in Michigan,* 154–55; Harry L. Hopkins, *Spending to Save: The Complete Story of Relief* (New York: Norton, 1936), 48, 50; and Sullivan, "On the Dole," 51–60, 66–67.

with little success, thus prompting them to turn to Washington DC.[138] Murphy galvanized the state's mayors in a special conference in 1932 to seek federal aid for relief. The seventeen mayors and city managers in attendance unanimously endorsed the bid for more federal aid on behalf of the unemployed.[139] By the fall of 1932, according to historian Irving Bernstein, "municipal relief . . . was bankrupt in virtually every city in the United States."[140]

Michigan did enact an old-age pension law in 1933, two years before the federal Social Security Act, to aid the state's elderly poor. The Depression's severity fueled approval for old-age pensions in Michigan and elsewhere in the country, but the initial old-age pension laws resulted in few pensions. More Americans began to support the idea of old-age pensions as the Depression worsened. By 1930, ten states had old-age pension programs and the issue was becoming a hot political issue in elections.[141] Michigan's law created an old-age pension bureau in the state welfare department. County agents, also responsible for the investigations for the probate court, were designated as the investigating officials. Administration was again local, through county old-age pension boards comprised of the county agent, probate judge, and "one woman" appointed by the county board of supervisors.[142] In contrast to mothers' pensions, the law provided state funding for the old-age pension program. Legislators finally agreed to a two-dollar head tax on all persons more than twenty-one years of age, to be placed in the old-age pension fund; failure to pay the tax was a misdemeanor punishable by a fine of one hundred dollars or ninety days in the county jail.[143]

To be eligible for an old-age pension, one had to be seventy years old and a continuous resident of Michigan for the past ten years. Anyone guilty of deserting a spouse or failing to support a child was ineligible. The law specifically excluded noncitizens and required at least fifteen years of citizenship.

---

138. Ortquist, *Depression Politics in Michigan,* 155–56. For a detailed analysis of Murphy's role in seeking help for Detroit's relief crisis, see Fine, *Frank Murphy: The New Deal Years,* 340–46.

139. Fine, *Frank Murphy: The Detroit Years,* 346–48. The city of Jackson was one municipality that did not share Murphy's goal of federal aid. Brock, *Welfare, Democracy, and the New Deal,* 120–21.

140. Bernstein, *The Lean Years,* 300–301; Ortquist, *Depression Politics in Michigan,* 149–50.

141. Jill Quadagno, *The Transformation of Old Age Security: Class and Politics in the American Welfare State* (Chicago: University of Chicago Press, 1988), 67–72; Bernstein, *The Lean Years,* 485–87; Ortquist, *Depression Politics in Michigan, 1929–1933,*134–36; and Patterson, *The New Deal and The States,* 12.

142. See Sections 4 and 5, Public Act No. 237 of 1933, *Public and Local Acts of the Legislature of the State of Michigan* (Lansing: Franklin DeKleine Company, 1933), 378–79; *Old Age Assistance in Michigan, 1933–1937* (Lansing, 1938), 4.

143. Sections 33–36 of Public Act No. 237 of 1933, *Public and Local Acts,* 383–84.

This effectively excluded all immigrants who had not secured naturalization papers by 1918. Under the poor laws of Michigan, it also excluded anyone with family who was legally responsible for his or her care and support.[144] Although called a pension, the law provided assistance for the aged based on need. As with mothers' pensions, framers of the law sought to reduce the stigma of public aid. The legislative language would cause much confusion for both this law and the Old Age Assistance law later passed in conformity with the federal Social Security Act of 1935.

A key difference from mothers' pensions was the inclusion of state funding, however flawed it would prove to be. The state sought to raise funds through the head tax specifically for old-age pensions. Governor William Comstock said in 1933 that old-age pension laws, then in existence in twenty-eight states, had "'proved themselves the most economical and self-respecting method of caring for the aged.'"[145] In fact, some people hoped that a full system of old-age pensions would eliminate the need for county infirmaries, except for the very ill. Other elderly people, still able to care for themselves, would be able to remain in their homes, living off an old-age pension, which would be much less costly for the state than supporting them in a public institution. By 1934, twenty-eight states had old-age pension laws, but also faced criticism. Many of the main problems were also found in Michigan's 1933 law: the age requirement restricted aid only to those at least seventy years of age, and the pension grants were entirely inadequate. Critics also disliked the controversial head tax and the citizenship requirement.[146]

Furthermore, the law paid few actual pensions in its first years. It did not include any mechanism for collecting the head tax, and only $5,500 had been collected by August of 1933, far short of the cost of pensions, estimated at $60,000. Many counties had a collection rate of just 3 percent, and the collection during the program's life was a mere 7 percent.[147] The state received 42,000 applications from October 1933 to December 1934, but only 2,660 elderly received grants in that time. Another 6,575 applications were approved, and the rest were awaiting investigation.[148] The Hartford newspaper questioned

144. Section 10, Public Act No. 237 of 1933, *Public and Local Acts,* 379–80. Lengthy residence requirements and ages between sixty-five and seventy were common. See Coll, *Safety Net,* 42.

145. *Unemployable Persons on the Emergency Relief Rolls in Michigan,* A Report of the State Emergency Welfare Relief Commission (Lansing, 1935), 18.

146. *Unemployable Persons on the Emergency Relief Rolls in Michigan,* 18–19; and Coll, *Safety Net,* 41–42.

147. "Old Age Pension Law Not to Take Effect in October," *Hartford Day Spring,* August 16, 1933, 1; *Old Age Assistance in Michigan,* 5–6.

148. Coll, *Safety Net,* 42.

whether the law was a "hoax," and criticized legislators for raising the hopes of needy elderly people. The newspaper also charged that the entire process was merely a "vote-getting" campaign.[149] Investigations did not keep pace with applications, and in October 1935, Van Buren County was still investigating applications from 1933 and 1934.[150] Delays often meant that applicants, who often were ill in addition to being elderly, died before their cases were ever investigated. Cindy Early, for instance, applied for a grant November 27, 1933, but died the following March before her case was investigated, and her example is not unique.[151] Sarah Goodman, a widow living in Detroit, applied for an old-age grant in late 1933, but her case was never investigated until 1936. Her grant was finally approved in February 1936.[152] Before 1935, old-age pensions remained a rarity in Michigan. Old-age assistance did not reach a significant number of Michigan's elderly citizens until the state became eligible for federal grants under the Social Security Act in 1936.

Requirements within the law also slowed the investigation process, or prompted some to withdraw their applications. A number of applicants believed the program was a pension, and not public assistance—an entitlement to them in their old age regardless of their financial circumstances. Some immediately withdrew their applications when they realized it was "welfare," or when their children assumed their care. A requirement of the 1933 program was that recipients sign their property to the state in return for assistance. Many were reluctant to do so, as they wanted their homes or property to go to their children (and some adult children also resisted this requirement). Others opposed the responsible-relative part of the law; either parents refused to provide information that would allow their children's ability to help to be investigated, or children themselves refused to cooperate. About 10 percent of all applications reviewed in Wayne County fell under the latter two categories.[153]

Efforts to address the unemployment and relief problems of the Depression occurred at all levels of government, as well as in the private sector. The problem was too extensive for most communities, private organizations, and even the state government; it required the participation of the federal government. Calls for private solutions, particularly in the funding of welfare, did not

149. "Pensions for Aged Are Not Available Now," *Hartford Day Spring*, August 2, 1933, 4; "Is Old Age Pension Law a Hoax?" *Hartford Day Spring*, August 16, 1933, 4.

150. "Supervisors Hear Report on Old Age Pensions," *Hartford Day Spring*, October 23, 1935, 8.

151. Case #A8204385, Reel 4059, Wayne County OAA Cases, RG 57-30, Archives of Michigan.

152. Case #A8207430, Reel 4072, Wayne County OAA cases.

153. The dynamics of these conflicts will be examined in chapter 6.

mesh with the reality that Michigan's welfare system was locally administered and publicly funded, both before and during the Great Depression and New Deal years. The resistance to state and federal intrusion into the administration of relief foreshadowed the conflicts that would erupt with the New Deal programs, and the backlash that followed these conflicts. Local officials welcomed the federal funds, but also rejected the requirements attached to the money they so desperately needed. They continued to want "to take care of their own problem" as they saw fit.

CHAPTER THREE

A Contest for Home Rule

THE NEW DEAL FEDERALIZES SOCIAL WELFARE

VAN BUREN COUNTY'S supervisors were less than enthusiastic about the Federal Emergency Relief Administration, despite the county's acute financial crisis. The minutes of the Van Buren County Board of Supervisors reveal a pattern of inattention, if not contempt, for the new program. They approved the use of office equipment by the Welfare Relief Commission, but tabled "until some future time" a request to use highway funds for a work-relief project, likely because the project fell under WRC supervision.[1] Numerous other communications regarding the WRC were also tabled, with no discussion or description in the minutes, including a letter from Governor William Comstock.[2] Comstock's letter requested that the supervisors contribute the county's share of gasoline-tax money (eleven thousand dollars) to emergency relief. Although the minutes record no formal action, the *Hartford Day Spring* reported that the supervisors refused to comply with the request. One supervisor called the governor's proposal an "insult to every board of supervisors in the state."[3]

Van Buren County, although among the most resistant to FERA, was not

1. "Proceedings of the Board of Supervisors, Van Buren County," October 10, 1933, 34–35.

2. "Proceedings of the Board of Supervisors, Van Buren County," October 10, 1933, 34; January 8, 1934, 74.

3. "Solons Refuse Cash to Governor: County Not to Yield Gas Tax to Relief Fund," *Hartford Day Spring*, January 10, 1934, 1.

alone. Franklin Roosevelt's administration greatly expanded federal intervention with the New Deal. FERA prompted the creation of a mass of state and local agencies to administer the new programs. Success demanded cooperation between local, state, and federal governments. The state's extreme financial need clashed with the ideologies of many local officials. Federal intervention in relief threatened the long tradition of local control of relief programs. Home rule, fiscal localism, and the role of professional social work were the core issues of conflict in the early days of FERA.

Fiscal localism, coupled with home rule—minimizing expenditures and maximizing tax relief, and the belief that local administrative control was best, regardless of who provided funding—was at the center of the conflicts over FERA. But while local officials defended home rule, political scientists and policy makers criticized the organization of local government and the state's cumbersome structure of the township system. Local government was often comprised of multiple and, at times, overlapping units. Tax revenues in many cases were not enough to provide for basic services, including poor relief.[4] The authors of a 1933 study pointed to the cost and inefficiency of the township system, and recommended consolidation in the counties and reorganization of county government.[5] The stress of the Depression, and its escalating relief costs, eventually strained and, in some cases, broke the local system in place. A key problem was that while American society and its economy had changed profoundly since the eighteenth century, poor law had not.[6] Resistance to change was significant, but given the conditions of the 1930s, "Confrontation with the idea of local responsibility as understood in America was inevitable."[7]

The increasingly desperate financial situation of most local governments fueled support for federal aid from some governors, state legislators, municipal leaders, and social work professionals.[8] A survey of local Michigan agencies conducted by the American Association of Public Welfare Officials found that areas around Detroit, Grand Rapids, and the Upper Peninsula were in need of either state or federal help. The report noted that Upper Peninsula counties faced "much distress and practically no financial resources."[9] Some

4. Brock, *Welfare, Democracy, and the New Deal,* 51–56.

5. Bromage and Reed, *Organization and Cost of County and Township Government,* 75, 125–26.

6. Brock, *Welfare, Democracy, and the New Deal,* 76–77.

7. Ibid., 83.

8. Brown, *Public Relief,* 107–8.

9. Report of Steering Committee, "A Social Work Study of Federal Aid for Unemployment Relief," January 1932, 10; National Association of Social Work Records, Box 18, Folder 195, SWHA; and Bernstein, *The Lean Years,* 462–63.

social workers supported federal aid by the spring of 1932, although the American Association of Social Workers did not endorse federal aid until January 1933.[10]

The growing demands resulted in the passage, in July 1932, of the Emergency Relief and Construction Act, which authorized the distribution of $300 million through the Reconstruction Finance Corporation. Federal funds were to be loans paid off by a state's federal highway funds. RFC funds became grants-in-aid to the states, but government officials did not know that in 1932.[11] Eventually about 60 percent of the total appropriation went to seven states, including Michigan, California, Illinois, New York, Ohio, Pennsylvania, and Wisconsin.[12] Michigan received $21.8 million, a portion of which was spent on highway construction. The remainder was distributed to local public welfare agencies through the state unemployment commission. But RFC funds were not enough to alleviate the extreme financial problems facing local governments. Fiscal localism again emerged, as both state and local officials balked at the "loans," fearing to commit themselves to further debt when their coffers were so empty.

Roosevelt's administration greatly expanded the federal government's role in social welfare. The most critical New Deal relief programs were the Federal Emergency Relief Act, the Civil Works Administration, and, later, the Works Progress Administration. All three dealt with relief in some form, and FERA and WPA also used investigative social work methods to determine eligibility. FERA included an appropriation of $500 million and had a two-year limit. FERA provided grants-in-aid to the states for both direct and work relief, with the amount received by the state related to the amount the state expended for relief and work relief.[13] The goal of the grants was to stimulate states to appropriate funds that could then be supplemented with federal monies; FERA was to establish a federal-state partnership to address the relief problem.[14]

FERA provided aid in two major forms: work relief and direct relief. The plan was for local governments and schools to create work-relief projects in their communities to employ local residents. Local funds provided the materi-

---

10. Resolution in favor of federal aid for relief, American Association of Social Workers, NASW Records, Box 18, Folder 196.

11. Hopkins, *Spending to Save*, 90–91; Brown, *Public Relief,* 124–25; Coll, *Safety Net,* 10–11; and Haber and Stanchfield, *Unemployment and Relief in Michigan,* 36.

12. Brown, *Public Relief,* 126.

13. Dorothy Carothers, *Chronology of the Federal Emergency Relief Administration, May 12, 1933, to December 31, 1935,* WPA Research Monograph VI (Washington, D.C.: U.S. Government Printing Office, 1937), 1–3; Nancy Rose, *Put to Work: Relief Programs of the Great Depression* (New York: Monthly Review Press, 1994), 29–30.

14. Coll, *Safety Net,* 25.

als, and federal funds furnished the payroll. Direct relief, or "the dole" in its derogatory terminology, was for those people and families who had no one employable to work on a project, or for whom no work was available. Direct relief was actually cheaper to provide than work relief, which required funds for project materials in addition to payroll, but public opinion, as well as most policy makers, favored work relief. Work relief reduced the stigma of welfare for recipients and provided some concrete product in return—either improved roads, buildings, or other public improvement, or else goods to be distributed to relief recipients: clothing, canned goods, or bedding.[15]

The federal programs targeted *employable* people, or those who could work but were unable to find work. *Unemployable* individuals, unable to work because of age, health, disability, or family responsibilities, were confined to the local relief programs. Regulations specified that federal funds were not to finance mothers' or old-age pensions, hospital care, or institutional (including infirmary) care; local governments were to continue to fund those services.[16] Nationally, unemployables made up 20 percent of relief recipients, and in Michigan that number ranged from 17 to 24 percent in FERA's second year.[17] The distinction between employable and unemployable was made along gender lines, and also considered age as a factor. Many women, for instance, able to work but with children to care for, were classified as unemployable. Mothers' pensions were meant to care for those women and their families, but more than thirty counties discontinued mothers' pensions by 1934. Both Saginaw and Van Buren counties halted mothers' pensions in October 1933 because of budget constraints.[18] Furthermore, Michigan's flawed old-age pension law of 1933 proved woefully inadequate and did little to alleviate the poverty of older Michigan residents. Thus FERA, through the local welfare-relief commission, often cared for unemployables prior to the Social Security Act in 1935. In states with no public welfare program before the New Deal, FERA instituted the creation of one.[19]

15. Brown, *Public Relief,* 150–51, 158; Haber and Stanchfield, *Unemployment, Relief, and Economic Security,* 241–42; and Rose, *Put to Work,* 30, 37–38.

16. Carothers, *Chronology,* 8; and Brown, *Public Relief,* 237.

17. Rose, *Put to Work,* 32; Haber and Stanchfield, *Unemployment, Relief, and Economic Security,* 57–58.

18. "Report on Mothers' Pensions for the Fiscal Year July 1, 1934 to June 30, 1935," Michigan State Welfare Department, WRSC Records, RG 35 Archives of Michigan, Lansing Box 14, Folder 5, 2; "Michigan, December 1933 Report of Counties Now Paying Mothers' Pension Grants," 1, Children's Fund of Michigan Papers, State Emergency Relief 1934 Folder, Bentley Historical Library.

19. The New Deal's federal funds prompted both states and municipalities to create welfare agencies, usually the local emergency-relief commission. See Jo Ann E. Argersinger, *Toward a New Deal in Baltimore: People and Government in the Great Depression* (Chapel Hill: University

FERA's funds, and later the Works Progress Administration, came with strings attached; states were allowed to set up their own commissions and emergency-relief administrations to administer the federal program, but had to operate within federal guidelines. The federal authority extended to funds contributed by local and state governments: "When these powers of control are considered, it is clear that the FERA constituted not only a source of financial aid to the state, but also a very definite and powerful authority over relief activities in each state which received Federal funds."[20] States that refused to conform to federal rules and regulations over grants—including Kentucky and Ohio—faced federal officials assuming control of their state emergency-relief programs. Although Michigan governors and legislatures certainly had conflicts with FERA officials during this period, they never lost control of the state emergency-relief administration.[21] The state's reluctance and some local governments' unwillingness to allocate funds for relief frustrated federal officials, but such conflicts never reached the crises found in other states.[22]

Michigan enacted enabling legislation for FERA on June 28, 1933, and appropriated twelve million dollars for relief. No funds were distributed, however, until August 3.[23] The law established a State Emergency Welfare Relief Commission (SEWRC) to set policy for the State Emergency Relief Administration (SERA), and also established a welfare-relief commission (WRC) in each county. State-commission members were appointed by the governor, and county commissions, comprised of three county residents, were appointed by the state commission and approved by the governor. All communications with FERA went through the state administration, which also distributed federal funds to the counties.[24] It was the state commission's responsibility to ensure

of North Carolina Press), 30–32; Ronald L. Heinemann, *Depression and New Deal in Virginia: The Enduring Dominion* (Charlottesville: University Press of Virginia, 1983), 155–56; and Smith, *The New Deal in the Urban South,* 62–64.

20. Haber and Stanchfield, *Unemployment and Relief in Michigan,* 39.

21. Ibid., 4. Federal officials stepped in to administer federal relief in Georgia, Louisiana, Massachusetts, North Dakota, Ohio, and Oklahoma. See Brown, *Public Relief,* 209; Edward Ainsworth Williams, *Federal Aid for Relief* (New York: Columbia University Press, 1939), 176–78; Patterson, *The New Deal and the States,* 65–73; Brock, *Welfare, Democracy, and the New Deal,* 184; and George T. Blakey, *Hard Times and New Deal in Kentucky, 1929–1939* (Lexington: University Press of Kentucky, 1986), 51–52. Blanche Coll argues that in states which did face federal takeovers, such as in Ohio, FERA "left a legacy ranging from discontent to resentment of the heavy federal hand" (Coll, *Safety Net,* 29).

22. Patterson, *The New Deal and the States,* 66–67; Michigan report by Howard Hunter, December 1933, FERA-WPA Narrative Field Reports, Michigan, Box 58, Harry Hopkins Papers, FDR Library.

23. Russell H. Kurtz, "On the Governor's Doorstep," *Survey* 69 (October 1933): 344; Sullivan, "On the Dole," 131.

24. Public Act 201 of 1933, *Public and Local Acts of the Legislature of the State of Michigan* (Lansing: Franklin DeKleine Company, 1933), 303–7; Haber and Stanchfield, *Unemployment*

that county personnel were qualified under federal regulations, and that the operation of the emergency-relief administration remained nonpartisan and free from the interference of local government officials.[25]

The inclusion of a commission member and administrators with social work backgrounds contributed to the state commission's willingness to accept FERA policies. Michigan's commission appointed Fred Johnson of Detroit, who was secretary of the Michigan's Children's Aid Society and a recognized social work professional, as administrator of SERA. William Haber, an associate professor of economics at the University of Michigan who would succeed Johnson as administrator one year later, was appointed a field supervisor.[26] State-commission members included Will Norton of Detroit. Norton headed the Children's Fund of Michigan and also led the Detroit Community Fund (later the United Way) from 1917 to 1930.[27] Johnson, Haber, and Norton shared the social work philosophy behind FERA, and sought to enforce FERA policies at the local level, rather than allowing local officials free rein. Although staffing and distance limited the state's ability to enforce federal guidelines, they were willing to do so. FERA officials often complimented Michigan's state commission, which appointed able commissions and administrators, and enforced federal policies. Howard Hunter, a FERA field representative, reported in 1934 that Michigan was "one of the best operated State Commissions in the country."[28]

William Haber, who served as administrator from 1934 until he resigned in 1937, was a critical force in SERA. He also served as deputy director of the state's WPA program. Haber, who had been born in Romania and had come to the United States at the age of ten, served on the Mayor's unemployment committee in Detroit and the state unemployment commission in the early years

---

and Relief in Michigan, 44–48.

25. Haber and Stanchfield, *Unemployment and Relief in Michigan*, 44.

26. Minutes of the State Emergency Welfare Relief Commission, Box 2, Folder 1: July 7, 1933; "State Organization for Public Welfare in Michigan," WRSC Report, WRSC Records, Box 5, Folder 4, 184. Haber's successor, George Granger, shared his social work background. He had a bachelor's degree from the University of Syracuse, had taken graduate courses in social work at the University of Michigan, and was a member of the National Association of Social Workers. NASW Records, Box 6, Folder 56, Membership Listing, 1936.

27. Norton also was chair of Detroit's Emergency Relief Committee in 1931. Other commission members were Charles Bender, a banker from Grand Rapids, and Earnest Brooks, who worked in insurance, of Holland. Sullivan, "On the Dole," 87; Ortquist, *Depression Politics in Michigan*, 153. See SEWRC Minutes, July 7, 1933; *The William Haber Oral Biography Project: Edited Transcripts*, Tape X, "Michigan in the Thirties," 201; *Holland City Directory* (Detroit: R. C. Polk & Co., 1936), 68.

28. Michigan reports by Howard Hunter, March 25, 1935, 1; August 13, 1934, 1; February 12, 1934, 1; FERA-WPA Narrative Field Reports, Michigan, Box 58, Harry Hopkins Papers, FDR Library.

of the Depression. Besides teaching economics at the University of Michigan, he also taught in the university's Institute of the Health and Social Sciences, which housed its first social work curriculum.[29] He published widely on relief and unemployment issues, and his articles appeared in a range of publications, including social work journals. He earned a national reputation for his administrative abilities. The *New York Times* called Haber an "uncrackable nut" when it came to contests with local officials over relief.[30] Federal officials admired his willingness to tackle difficult problems, and he became to many the face of FERA in the state.[31] He would become a central target during the reorganization debates.

SERA's power to appoint county welfare-relief commission members and relief administrators would take center stage in the conflicts with local officials over relief that followed, but also would earn the praise of federal officials. Home rule ideology was at the heart of these debates. County WRCs were comprised of three residents of the county, and no supervisor could serve either as a commission member or as administrator.[32] FERA officials hoped to remove politics from relief by requiring trained workers, if possible, or at least supervision over the workers by professional social workers. They also sought to minimize the granting of jobs as political gifts and to ensure that relief cases were adequately investigated by professionals. The exclusion of supervisors from this process alienated many supervisors from the WRC even before it began work. Long responsible for relief, many supervisors greatly resented the loss of administrative control. Although caseworkers often consulted supervisors on recipients in their townships or cities, supervisors were on the outside looking in and most did not like it.[33]

The state commission also approved the appointments of county administrators, who were to handle the daily administration of the programs, including the hiring of staff, with the county WRC providing guidance and

29. *Who's Who in Michigan,* ed. Herbert S. Case (Munising, MI: 1936), 158; Sam Howe Verhover, "William Haber, Who Directed Aid to Jewish Refugees, Is Dead at 89," *New York Times,* January 3, 1989, D17.

30. "Spoilsmen Foiled by Relief Head," *New York Times,* August 15, 1937, 38.

31. Michigan report by Howard Hunter, June 1, 1934, FERA Michigan Field Reports, Box 138, Folder 2, National Archives.

32. By October, sixty-nine of Michigan's eighty-three counties had established welfare-relief commissions. Minutes of the State Emergency Welfare Relief Commission, Box 2, Folder 1: July 17, July 28, August 11, and October 13, 1933. Studies of both Illinois and Ohio reveal similar views; both states adhered to the concept that local officials, and not social workers, should administer relief. See Maurer, "Public Relief Programs in Ohio, 1929–1939," 77; Cole, "The Relief Crisis in Illinois during the Depression, 1930–1940," 285–91.

33. Brown, *Public Relief,* 274–76; Brock, *Welfare, Democracy, and the New Deal,* 184.

supervision.[34] Each county agency had to have one "trained and experienced investigator" and also at least one supervisor who was "trained and experienced in the essential elements of family case work and relief administration."[35] Administrators were not always social workers, but investigators were to be, if possible.[36]

The establishment of the county WRC did not entirely exclude township supervisors and superintendents of the poor from the relief process. In many counties, township supervisors continued to be consulted on most cases, particularly those in rural areas. WRC workers in Van Buren County often consulted local township supervisors as one of three required reference checks on new applications, and usually followed their lead. WRC workers also sought suggestions from township supervisors on long-term cases, and informed officials regarding who was on relief in their county. Both WRC staff and township supervisors in Marquette County saw the supervisor as a part of the investigation process.[37] Township supervisors were consulted on a less systematic basis in Saginaw County, although they were permitted to write relief orders on cases approved by the ERA.[38] Such attitudes are less overt in records after the Social Security Act was implemented in Michigan, but remained a part of the case-file records in the earlier days of the New Deal.

The size of relief grants varied from county to county, and most increased during the second year of FERA. The average grant in the state for the first fiscal year of FERA (ending June 30, 1934) was $5.18 per month for an individual, and $21.22 for a family. That average increased to $9.14 per person the following year (ending June 30, 1935) and $32.79 per family.[39] The average grant per family nationally in May 1933, two months before FERA was implemented, was $15.15; that figure rose to $24.53 one year later—slightly more than Michigan's average grant. By May 1935, the national average was $29.33, less than Michigan's average grant.[40]

34. Haber and Stanchfield, *Unemployment and Relief in Michigan*, 44–46.

35. Carothers, *Chronology*, FERA Rules and Regulations No. 3, 7.

36. Brown, *Public Relief*, 274–76.

37. "Welfare Activities in Counties—Survey Report," Van Buren County, October 15, 1936, WRSC Records, Box 15, Folder 3, 1; "Proceedings, Marquette County Supervisors," November 13, 1935, 335. ERA case files clearly document the consultation by ERA workers with township officials on the worthiness of applicants' requests for aid.

38. "Sampling Survey of Local Relief Agencies," Saginaw County, WRSC Records, Box 7, Folder 7. Wayne County did not permit its rural supervisors to write emergency-relief orders. Report dated November 18, 1936, WRSC Records, Box 15, Folder 3.

39. Haber and Stanchfield, *Unemployment and Relief in Michigan*, Appendix, table 3; Haber and Stanchfield, *Unemployment, Relief, and Economic Security*, figure 11, 42; table 16, 84; and Appendix, table VIII.

40. Brown, *Public Relief*, 249.

Despite nondiscrimination requirements, studies found racial disparities in grant amounts, and such variations were not confined to the South. Relief grants in Detroit in 1935 averaged $39.42 for all family recipients, but the average for whites was $40.90 while grants to black families averaged $35.13. Such disparities were found in numerous cities throughout the United States, with average grants for blacks at $24.18, while whites received $29.05. Explanations for the differential included smaller case sizes or the lack of an employable household member in black cases. In the latter instance, blacks would then be ineligible for work relief, which paid higher benefits.[41] Many historians have documented the effects of local administration under federal guidelines in New Deal programs, and in areas with minimal state and federal interference, administration of the programs often replicated discriminatory practices already in place. In some cases, different budget formulas were used for the two groups. Most studies find that minorities gained much greater access to public relief programs, particularly in the South, but such access was by no means equal.[42]

Breakdowns by counties reveal greater variation in the amounts of grants. Although the average grants in all counties increased from the first year to the next, significant differences between counties remained. Van Buren and Saginaw had the lowest average grants, while Wayne County's remained the highest in the state for both years (see table 3.1). Many of the counties paying the lowest grants were in Michigan's southern agricultural region, including Van Buren.[43]

Variations in grants stemmed from numerous factors, including the cost of living and poor-relief traditions; areas that had formerly paid low relief rates tended to continue that trend. The climate and the availability of work, including seasonal agricultural work, also affected the size of grants. Fuel costs were much higher in Marquette County than in Van Buren County, and the ability of a family to raise food in a garden or to earn supplemental income in the agricultural season was much higher in the latter county.[44] Gardens were

41. Enid Baird, *Average General Relief Benefits, 1933–1938* (Washington, D.C.: U.S. Government Printing Office, 1940), 31–32.

42. Ira Katznelson, *When Affirmative Action Was White* (New York: Norton, 2005), 37–38; Karen Ferguson, *Black Politics in New Deal Atlanta* (Chapel Hill: University of North Carolina Press, 2002), 74–80; Jack Irby Hayes Jr., *South Carolina and the New Deal* (Columbia: University of South Carolina Press, 2001), 47–50; and Richard Lowitt, *The New Deal and the West* (Bloomington: Indiana University Press, 1984), 22–24.

43. Haber and Stanchfield, *Unemployment, Relief, and Economic Security,* figure 11, 42–43.

44. Similar arguments can be made about variations in grants among states. Contributions by states to relief funds were a major reason for discrepancies in grants. See Patterson, *The New Deal and the States,* 54–55.

TABLE 3.1
AVERAGE MONTHLY GRANTS FOR 1934 AND 1935

County	1934			1935		
	Average Family Grant	Average Individual Grant	Ranking in State	Average Family Grant	Average Individual Grant	Ranking in State
Kent	$20.57	$4.87	11	$29.43	$8.23	17
Marquette	$21.01	$4.43	7	$31.62	$8.56	10
Saginaw	$13.85	$3.71	48	$26.14	$6.06	33
Van Buren	$10.17	$2.62	79	$16.86	$6.36	79
Wayne	$28.64	$6.69	1	$43.47	$11.72	1
State of Michigan	$21.22	$5.18	6	$32.79	$9.14	10

Source: Haber and Stanchfield, *Unemployment and Relief in Michigan*, Appendix, table 3 and figure 19; Haber and Stanchfield, *Unemployment, Relief and Economic Security*, figure 11, p. 43, table 16, p. 84, and Appendix, table VIII. Grants listed under 1934 refer to average grants for the fiscal year ending June 30, 1934, and grants from 1935 refer to average grants for the fiscal year ending June 30, 1935.

expected of people in areas with suitable soil and climate, and relief could be refused if space was available and applicants failed to attempt to raise a garden.[45] Agricultural areas, like Van Buren County, also reduced relief rolls during the planting and harvest seasons, as officials believed ample work was available with local farmers.[46]

Rural parts of Saginaw also had agricultural employment available, particularly in the sugar beet industry. Relief clients were expected to accept work if it was available, but only at a "living wage." When sugar beet company officials asked the State Emergency Welfare Relief Commission to deny aid to those families who refused employment in the sugar beet fields, the commission would not, "as the amount of wages is not such as will enable [relief clients] to provide for themselves without the aid of relief agencies." It is not clear whether cases received supplementation from the WRC or if relief recipients were empowered to refuse sugar beet employment altogether. The SEWRC

45. Carothers, *Chronology*, 41, 51; SERA Letter #7, 1934, Michigan State Emergency Welfare Relief Commission Papers, 1934–1939, Box 1, Folder January to June 1934; and "Ask Relief Clients for 1,000 Gardens," *Hartford Day Spring*, April 24, 1935, 1.

46. State Emergency Relief Administration Letters #353 dated May 1, 1935, and #579, dated May 18, 1936, reminded county administrators to review relief cases for those who could take temporary work. See SERA Letters #353 and #579, SEWRC Records, Box 1; see also Devra Weber, *Dark Sweat, White Gold: California Farm Workers, Cotton, and the New Deal* (Berkeley: University of California Press, 1994), 130.

did rule that "where a living wage is offered for an honest day's work," families refusing such employment should be removed from the relief rolls.[47] When sugar beet representatives renewed their request just two weeks later, the commission reiterated its earlier stand, noting "that they deemed it their duty in the interest of humanity to see that labor is decently paid," and asked administrator Fred Johnson to inform people "that the Commission was not going to be an instrument in forcing labor into the sugar beet fields at a starvation wage."[48] Farmers in Manistee County also complained of an inability to secure workers for their fields, but WRC administrator Louise Armstrong argued that they paid "disgracefully low wages, if they paid cash wages at all." Some farmers paid their workers only with goods, and sometimes at prices far inflated above the market value. Some workers also received no wages until the farmer sold the crop.[49]

Conflict over relief grants and the availability of low-wage labor occurred throughout the country in the implementation of New Deal relief programs. Local demographics determined what groups were the targets of efforts to preserve low-wage workers. Critics charged that relief grants encouraged workers to reject low-wage employment, including agricultural work in Michigan. The issue was particularly significant in the South, where local and state officials resisted attempts to disrupt the low-wage labor supply, thus explaining in part the lack of access blacks had to direct and work relief. When access to relief was granted to blacks, it was granted partially to ensure that they did not leave the area, which would preserve their availability to work during planting and harvesting seasons. Devra Weber found a similar trend in California, where growers protested the granting of relief to migrant workers, either through direct relief or the transient program, arguing that it cost them workers. As in Michigan's sugar beet fields, California's growers found that their wages were far less than relief grants, which were already meager enough. The availability of relief instituted a "de facto minimum wage," Weber contends, and enabled agricultural workers to bargain for better wages.[50]

The SEWRC ruled that wages for agricultural work had to equal minimum

47. Minutes of the State Emergency Welfare Relief Commission, Box 2, Folder 1: May 23, 1934.

48. Minutes of the State Emergency Welfare Relief Commission, Box 2, Folder 1: June 6, 1934.

49. Louise Armstrong, *We Too Are the People* (Boston: Little, Brown and Company, 1938), 130–31.

50. Hayes, *South Carolina and the New Deal,* 165–66; Katznelson, *When Affirmative Action Was White,* 39–41; Heinemann, *Depression and New Deal in Virginia,* 82–84; Lowitt, *The New Deal and the West,* 16–17; and Devra Weber, *Dark Sweat, White Gold,* 127–28.

relief grants.[51] The SEWRC rulings, however, did not preclude local agencies from implementing different policies until state or federal officials became aware of them. Other local discriminatory practices certainly existed, despite federal regulations, including the denial of benefits to people of color and to noncitizens. As with other regulations, federal supervision was not thorough enough to prevent suffering by specific groups. The problem occurred throughout the country, although its specifics varied with local demographics and practices. Ultimately, supervision of WRC policies, including relief for migrant and agricultural workers, diminished with the demise of FERA.

CONFLICTS OVER LOCAL CONTRIBUTIONS

A key factor in the size of grants was the amount of federal and state funds available. Estimated ahead of time, grants could prove inadequate if relief rolls increased more than anticipated, thus causing the reduction of all grants because of fund shortages.[52] Often the problem stemmed from a lack of local contribution to emergency-relief funds; once federal funds were exhausted, the expected share of local monies was intended to fund relief. But in counties that rarely provided funds, such as Van Buren and Manistee counties, grants were reduced and sometimes eliminated. This was especially true by late 1935, when SERA and FERA officials began to withdraw state and federal funds from counties that refused to provide local matching funds. The conflicts centered not only on whether the county could pay, but also on who (often state-appointed social workers) was administering the funds; county officials were often reluctant to provide money over which they had no administrative control.

During the first year of FERA, Michigan counties contributed varied amounts to the local county WRC, with the state average at a low 6.18 percent. The availability of funds was a key reason, but the county officials' attitude toward SERA and the relief program also played a role. Counties like Van Buren and Manistee, which had major conflicts with SERA, contributed the least. Saginaw and Marquette, whose relationships with SERA were more amiable, were among those counties contributing the highest percentage of relief funds statewide (see table 3.2).[53] Overall for the fiscal year ending June 30,

---

51. The Commission also agreed that relief clients refusing agricultural work at a living wage would be refused relief. Minutes of the State Emergency Welfare Relief Commission, Box 2, Folder 1: May 23, 1934. For California, see Weber, *Dark Sweat, White Gold*, 127–28.

52. Brown, *Public Relief*, 233, 249–51.

53. Haber and Stanchfield, *Unemployment and Relief in Michigan*, figure 12.

TABLE 3.2
PERCENTAGE OF RELIEF FUNDS FROM COUNTIES

County	1934		1935	
	Percent of Local Funds for Emergency Relief, FY	Ranking in State	Percent of Local Funds for Emergency Relief, FY	Ranking in State
Kent	1.69	64	9.06	70
Manistee	0.03	78	3.19	82
Marquette	23.64	8	23.35	15
Saginaw	27.86	3	27.05	9
Van Buren	4.96	45	3.65	80
Wayne	3.96	50	11.32	56
State average	6.18	43	13.42	50

Source: Haber and Stanchfield, *Unemployment and Relief in Michigan,* figure 12, Appendix, table 3; Haber and Stanchfield, *Unemployment, Relief and Economic Security,* figure 8, p. 35.

1934, local funds accounted for slightly more than 10 percent of all relief funds expended, while state dollars contributed 22 percent and the rest—more than two-thirds—came from federal dollars.[54] No county was able to contribute more than 38 percent of relief costs in the program's first year, in part because few counties had the money available.[55] Contributions from most counties increased in the second year, but Van Buren was one of the few counties to actually contribute a smaller share the second year, when just three counties provided a smaller percentage of relief funds than Van Buren.[56]

Contributions varied depending on the economies of the counties involved; the major industrial counties tended to contribute much higher amounts to relief than agricultural, mining, or lumbering counties. Wayne County and the other ten largest industrial counties contributed 90 percent of all local relief dollars in the state in 1937–38.[57] Michigan's problem of changing economics—and the decline of mining and timber industries with no viable replacement industries—translated into the inability of some counties to finance their

54. Ibid., figure 9.
55. Haber and Stanchfield, *Unemployment and Relief in Michigan,* 54.
56. Ibid., figure 12; Haber and Stanchfield, *Unemployment, Relief, and Economic Security,* figure 8, 35.
57. George F. Granger and Lawrence R. Klein, *Emergency Relief in Michigan, 1933–1939* (Lansing: State of Michigan, 1939), 53.

share of relief. As industrial counties increased their contributions, other areas decreased. Counties with high relief rates tended to have the lowest contributions.[58] In a report to Harry Hopkins, Howard Hunter expressed frustration with Michigan's refusal to appropriate funds for relief: "These people have been mollycoddled by the Federal government for over a year." Hunter did not fault the state commission, but rather local and state officials, who "believe that Santa Claus will keep on coming down the chimney no matter how bad they are."[59] But all three state reports on emergency relief recognized the inability of some counties to finance even a small portion of relief. Conflicts arose with counties that the state believed could do more, including Van Buren County.

Local governments contributed more to work-relief projects. Contributions tended to center on materials for the projects; local units, for instance, provided more than 60 percent of all materials and equipment on the projects. Overall, a 1935 report showed that local funds provided about 24 percent of the costs of projects, while nearly 71 percent was from federal ERA monies.[60] Counties were more likely to contribute to work relief than direct relief; this was particularly true after the WPA began in 1935. A 1939 report states that contributions to the WPA came at the expense of emergency relief. By 1937–38, counties were contributing $4 million more dollars to WPA than to emergency relief, with local contributions for direct relief at about $11.7 million, as opposed to $15.5 million for the WPA.[61]

Conflict in the projects centered on administrative control and on determining who would work on the projects, rather than on the contributions themselves. Under the FERA and WPA programs, all workers were certified through the relief agencies, thus eliminating local county and city officials from the process. (Under the Civil Works Administration, the predecessor of FERA, workers did not apply through relief agencies, nor did they have to prove need. About half of Michigan's workers in the first year came from the relief rolls; others were simply unemployed.)[62] Home rule again appears. Van Buren County supervisors were among the most opposed to federal work-relief programs. Federal supervision left local officials little say in who was hired on those projects. Before the New Deal, supervisors had recommended

---

58. Granger and Klein, *Emergency Relief in Michigan, 1933–1939*, 53–54.

59. Michigan report by Howard Hunter, December 1933, Box 58, FERA-WPA Narrative Reports.

60. *50,000 Men: Report of the Work Division of the Michigan Emergency Welfare Relief Commission* (Lansing: 1935), 29.

61. Klein, *Emergency Relief in Michigan, 1933–1939* (Lansing: 1939), 56–58.

62. Bonnie Fox Schwartz, *The Civil Works Administration, 1933–1934: The Business of Emergency Employment in the New Deal* (Princeton: Princeton University Press, 1984), 42–43; Haber and Stanchfield, *Unemployment and Relief in Michigan*, 130–31.

men from their own townships to work programs using county funds or state highway funds. Work projects now fell under the county WRC, which coordinated work assignments. Some supervisors resented the loss of that authority, again believing they knew best who needed and deserved aid.[63] They also disliked the project application process, arguing that "CWA projects were obtained only by pilgrimages to Lansing."[64]

County administrators and WRC members played a crucial role in the negotiations for local contributions, and in relations between SERA and local officials. They were expected to provide detailed information about the relief efforts, including costs, caseload information, and the status of work projects. They were told to use the threat of withdrawal of federal and state funds as leverage in the negotiations of local-fund contributions. But they also were allowed to use their judgments in situations where counties or cities could not afford the expected one-third. County administrators were told not to wait for local officials to come to them, but to initiate contact before annual budget meetings, usually held in October.[65] By the second year of FERA, they also were expected to help "sell" the ERA structure, and to persuade local officials that a professionally run social work agency was preferable to, and more efficient than, the old poor-relief system.[66] This effort to promote the ERA structure became particularly important as Michigan entered its welfare-reorganization debates following passage of the Social Security Act in 1935. Van Buren County's WRC had six different administrators in three years, an indication of the county's rocky relationship with SERA.[67] In recalling those years, Haber remembered the conflicts with state and local officials over the relief administration under FERA, and the need to persuade them of its merits. "It was not well received, because even in those days there was still a prevailing, a widely held point of view, that people on relief didn't want to work," he recalled forty years later.[68]

63. "Hartford Will Have Share in Road 'Relief,'" *Hartford Day Spring,* November 4, 1931, 1, 6; "Solons Refuse Cash to Governor," *Hartford Day Spring,* January 10, 1934, 1.

64. "Solons Refuse Cash to Governor," *Hartford Day Spring,* January 10, 1934, 1.

65. SERA Letter #173, October 5, 1934, SEWRC Records, Box 1, Folder October–December 1934; SERA Letter #360, May 10, 1935, Folder April–June 1935; and Letter from SERA Administrator William Haber to all county boards of supervisors, dated October 1, 1935, Folder October–December 1935.

66. SERA Letter #468, October 7, 1935, and SERA Letter, November 11, 1935, SEWRC Records, Box 1, Folder October to December 1935; and SERA Letter #544, March 31, 1936, Folder January–March 1936.

67. Ernest B. Harper and Duane L. Gibson, *Reorganization of Public Welfare in Michigan: A Study of Transformation of a Social Institution* (East Lansing: Michigan State College, 1942), 27.

68. *William Haber Oral Biography Project,* transcripts, 205.

Conflicts often revolved around how much counties could contribute to relief. Fiscal localism and home rule are interconnected in this issue; local officials were reluctant to expend funds over which they had little control. The *Hartford Day Spring* reported "murmurs of dissatisfaction with the manner in which county welfare relief is to be administered" under the new program. A key criticism was that the new administrative setup would not provide much financial relief for the county or its taxpayers. Supervisors argued that not only were they required to fund one-third of the new relief program, under federal law, but also they retained financial responsibility for mothers' pensions, the county infirmary, and hospitalization costs. Van Buren County believed those obligations should be considered relief contributions, while state and federal policies did not include them.[69]

Fiscal localism was central in Van Buren County. County officials were unwilling to provide the one-third requested by state officials in January 1934 when federal funds ran out; relief recipients faced large cuts in grants. Supervisors eventually agreed to a contribution of $1,568.45. Given that SERA expended more than $311,000 in the first year in the county, the amount offered was hardly enough to solve the relief-fund crisis.[70] The state again requested a one-third contribution from the county in October. The supervisors did adopt a resolution agreeing to partial payment of the funds it owed "insofar as funds are available," but only after the year's tax rolls were collected.[71] The county would not commit funds to relief until other obligations were met and its revenues were collected.

Inextricably linked to the issue of local contributions was home rule: who would administer those funds and what expertise was needed in that administration. Van Buren officials agreed to contribute their share, but only if the "county 'dads' would handle [the] relief funds."[72] This paternalistic attitude was directed not only at the relief recipients but also at those involved in the state relief administration. The county supervisors extended this offer to the state:

> Resolved, that the board of supervisors of Van Buren county offered their services to the state welfare commission as so-called case workers in their respective townships at no expense to the commission, displacing present

69. "Supervisors End October Session: Look for Spots to Further Cut County Budget," *Hartford Day Spring*, October 25, 1933, 1.

70. "Proceedings of the Board of Supervisors, Van Buren County," February 16, 1934, 92; "County Welfare Costs $311,502.17," *Hartford Day Spring*, October 17, 1934, 1.

71. "County Budget Totals $136,793.76," *Hartford Day Spring*, October 24, 1934, 1.

72. "County 'Dads' Would Handle Relief Funds," *Hartford Day Spring*, February 21, 1934, 1, 5; "Proceedings of the Board of Supervisors, Van Buren County," February 16, 1934, 92.

case workers, and that the county pledges itself to contribute one-third of the total expense of the class of relief handled by the county commission, provided above offer is accepted and complied with, and in case this county receives its full quota of relief from state and federal funds.[73]

Supervisors sought to regain control of relief administration, suggesting that they replace "so-called case workers," which they clearly did not see as better able to administer poor relief. Van Buren's supervisors argued that supervisors would perform their relief duties as part of the job of supervisor, thus saving the county the cost of professional social workers. The supervisors believed that they were more qualified to administer relief, an argument that would recur in the 1937 and 1938 debates.

Some counties used their existing poor-fund allocations, if any were left, to provide their share of WRC costs. Both Saginaw and Marquette counties contributed a fair proportion of funds, but the effort came at a cost to services and salaries. There was little opposition to participating in the federal program, and initially local control was not an issue vocalized a great deal. In Saginaw, city officials opposed a county-wide tax because city residents already paid taxes for the poor commission, whose funds had been previously pledged, in large measure, to the county WRC.[74] The county had stopped funding mothers' pensions the month before, forcing those women to seek aid from the poor commission or their township supervisors. Instead, the county voted to contribute ten thousand dollars of the county's poor fund, to be placed in reserve with the county treasurer for the WRC to draw upon for administrative costs.[75] Marquette County also used its poor-fund budget to contribute to the WRC. Marquette County's supervisors' main conflict with SERA stemmed from their belief that while they had shouldered their share—and more—of the relief problem, other counties had not: "It might also be pointed out," the Marquette County board writes, "that there are only three counties in northern Michigan that have apparently played ball with the state ERA." Marquette was one of them.[76]

73. "County 'Dads' Would Handle Relief Funds," *Hartford Day Spring*, February 21, 1934.

74. "Supervisors Debate Relief Fund Request," *Saginaw Daily News*, October 14, 1933, 1, 3; "Welfare Fund Need Explained," *Saginaw Daily News*, October 16, 1933, 1–2; "Pledge Relief Cooperation," *Saginaw Daily News*, October 17, 1933, 1, 9; and *Official Proceedings of the Board of Supervisors of Saginaw County, Michigan*, October 13, 1933, 82–83; October 14, 1933, 87.

75. "Relief Board Asks $10,000," *Saginaw Daily News*, October 18, 1933, 1–2; "Favor Relief Fund Request," *Saginaw Daily News*, October 21, 1933, 1; and *Official Proceedings of the Board of Supervisors of Saginaw County, Michigan*, October 18, 1933, 95–96; October 23, 1933, 107.

76. "Proceedings of the Board of Supervisors, Marquette County," vol. 8, February 15, 1939, 59.

Marquette officials saw the creation of the WRC as a way to share the work and financial burden of relief. Although the surviving records are not clear on the relationship between the WRC and the county's decision to create, and then eliminate, the office of poor director, the two events seem connected. The county supervisors unanimously voted to eliminate the position just a few months after hiring a mining executive in August of 1933.[77] It seems likely that the supervisors believed that the newly created WRC could coordinate the relief programs in the county, thus eliminating the need for the four-thousand-dollar appropriation for the director position.[78] The WRC took over investigating cases of emergency and work relief, but the poor commission continued to investigate requests for medical care and unemployable cases. They also worked with the WRC on a work-relief project to repair the county infirmary, with the cost of materials for the project taken from the poor-fund budget.[79]

The cost of staff and administration was a widespread criticism of the SERA. SERA issued a report in 1935 to counter those charges, and reported that 91.4 cents of each dollar went for relief, with just 8.6 cents spent on administration. Van Buren County administrative costs were about 8.29 percent of the total amount spent on relief. The greater amount of the cost rested in the salaries of staff, including caseworkers. The report defended these costs, despite the fact that they were much higher than pre-Depression days, and argued that in some areas, staffs were not adequate to fully investigate their cases. Careful investigations resulted in fewer people being able to "cheat" the system, the report argued.[80]

State officials eventually took a more punitive stance toward counties unwilling to pay their share. Manistee County's relief program closed briefly in 1934 over disagreements about the county's contribution.[81] Allegan County, immediately north of Van Buren County, experienced this in December 1935, when the state ERA cut off state and federal funds to the county because its board refused to appropriate twenty-four thousand dollars for relief needs. The county offices were closed, and at the same time state officials announced the

77. "Proceedings of the Board of Supervisors, Marquette County," August 30, 1933; "Proceedings of the Board of the Superintendents of the Poor, Marquette County," April 21, 1933.

78. "Making Progress Backward," *Daily Mining Journal*, September 6, 1933, 4.

79. "Proceedings of the Board of Supervisors, Marquette County," October 8, 1934, 229.

80. Michigan State Emergency Welfare Relief Commission, *Cost of Administration in the Emergency Relief Program* (Lansing, 1935), 3, 7.

81. Armstrong, *We Too Are the People*, 284–86; "Demand Appropriation for Welfare Purposes," *Manistee Examiner*, November 1, 1934, clipping in Armstrong papers, Box 1, Reviews Folder 3; "$5,000 Welfare Fund Turned Down," *Manistee News-Advocate*, November 6, 1934; and "Relief Is Ordered Resumed," *Manistee News-Advocate*, November 26, 1934.

start of an investigation into Van Buren County, which also had not contributed relief dollars to its budget. Van Buren officials argued that their share was
covered through hospitalization costs, as well as through poor relief administered through the county poor commission, which still operated.[82] The board
of supervisors voted fifteen to five to provide for relief at the rate of two thousand dollars per month until the April elections, when the new board could
tackle the issue that had perplexed local officials for more than five years.[83] No
county appropriation was forthcoming after April 1, and funds were exhausted
by mid-June. County administrator Harold Humphrey reported in June that
despite reductions in the relief load, funds would be gone before more state
funds were forthcoming on July 1, 1936. And a shortage of funds had already
resulted in reduced budgets and denials of aid, further resulting in "insuffi-
cient relief and suffering."[84]

Recipients approved for emergency relief had to seek out their local supervisor for assistance when the WRC ran out of funds. Jerry Brewster, a thirty-
year-old farmer afflicted with inflammatory rheumatism, was approved for aid
in April 1936. He and his wife, Lillian, sought a few grocery orders to carry
them until he had recovered enough to resume farming. They were readily
approved, and the caseworker approved aid for a longer period of time, as
she believed he would need longer to recover. The WRC covered the grocery
orders until mid-May, but then Brewster had to seek help from the township
supervisor because the WRC offices were not able to extend aid until June 1.[85]
The records do not indicate whether he was successful. Other recipients faced
similar problems, at a time when townships had little money and mothers'
pensions were no longer funded. Options for relief were few when the WRC
could not help.

The rural character of a county played a role in its relationship with
SERA, even within counties such as Saginaw, which was both urban and
rural. Saginaw County operated under the township system; townships were
charged individually for their share of relief costs, and the county allocated no
direct funds for emergency relief.[86] Opposition to the WRC allocation of ten

82. Allegan County was also a rural, agricultural county and one that remained loyal to
the Republican Party throughout the 1930s. "State Probes County's ERA Funds," *Hartford Day
Spring,* Dec. 11, 1935.

83. "Solons Vote $2,000 Month Relief Fund," *Hartford Day Spring,* January 15, 1936, 1; "Pro-
ceedings of the Board of Supervisors, Van Buren County," January 10, 1936, 84.

84. "Administrator Gives Figures on Van Buren County Relief," *Hartford Day Spring,* June
17, 1936, 1; "Proceedings of the Board of Supervisors, Van Buren County," April 14, 1936, 4.

85. Case #5217, Van Buren County ERA Records (hereafter VB ERA), Box 1, Folder B.

86. *Proceedings of the Council and Boards of the City of Saginaw,* October 31, 1933;
November 7, 1933.

thousand dollars in Saginaw County came from sixteen supervisors, many representing the rural townships.[87] The core of the opposition centered on the equitable distribution of the relief burden among townships, as well as on the issue of home rule. As with Van Buren County, some Saginaw County supervisors believed they could more efficiently administer relief than the WRC. Although the administrative costs were funded by the county, the local shares of relief costs were to be paid individually by the townships and the city of Saginaw. The WRC paid the bills and then charged the local costs back to the township, while the city provided its poor-relief funds and then was later reimbursed by the WRC. The townships eventually paid the share not covered by the state ERA.[88] Over the next three years, twenty-four of Saginaw's twenty-seven townships opted to participate with the WRC. The three townships that did not declined because their officials believed they were "able to look after [their] own." Saginaw Township initially participated, but was cut off for six months until it paid the eleven hundred dollars it owed the WRC.[89] Rural opposition was rooted in a desire for control over the administration of those funds, and a desire to minimize the taxes imposed on county residents. The antitax sentiments of the period fueled ideas about home rule and fiscal localism.

Wayne County, and the city of Detroit, faced such serious financial difficulties over relief funding that conflict with SERA was not an issue. DPW head John Ballenger had a friendly relationship with Fred Johnson, the first administrator.[90] State officials did order an investigation into the disbursement of relief checks in 1934, and a state auditor handled the relief payrolls during that investigation.[91] SERA prompted the department to improve its accounting and administrative practices, and Howard Hunter was particularly critical of the administration in Detroit. He believed that Ballenger was spread too thin and that the commission was susceptible to political influence.[92] Conflicts

87. *Official Proceedings of the Board of Supervisors of Saginaw County, Michigan,* October 23, 1933, 107.

88. The city of Saginaw's poor department investigated emergency-relief cases for the WRC and was reimbursed by the county for two-thirds of the funds expended. The other third was their share of the relief burden. WRSC Records, Sampling Survey of Local Relief Agencies, 1936, Box 7, Folder 6; "Relief Board Asks $10,000," *Saginaw Daily News,* October 18, 1933, 1–2; and *Proceedings of the Council and Boards of the City of Saginaw,* October 31, 1933, 367.

89. WRSC Records, Sampling Survey of Local Relief Agencies, 1936, Box 7, Folder 7, Saginaw County.

90. "Proceedings of the Public Welfare Commission," Detroit, July 18, 1933, 150–51.

91. SEWRC Minutes, April 18, 1934.

92. Joanna C. Colcord, *Cash Relief* (New York: Russell Sage Foundation, 1936), 87; Sullivan, "On the Dole," 131–34, 139; and Report from Howard Hunter to Harry Hopkins, dated August 13, 1934, 1–2; June 1, 1934, 3–4; Harry Hopkins Papers, Box 58, Folder Michigan.

between Wayne County and SERA would escalate in the latter part of the decade, but remained cooperative in the early years of the program.

Fiscal localism and home rule worked in tandem in the early negotiations between officials in the administration of relief. While the issues were more muted in some counties, such as Saginaw and Wayne, in the early years, they emerged as strong from the start in Van Buren County. The difficulties of this era highlight the issues that came to the forefront in the debates over welfare reorganization. But the New Deal programs played a significant role in alleviating the hardship of the Depression, as well as in enabling local communities to improve public facilities and the state to improve its infrastructure. The next chapter turns to that story.

CHAPTER FOUR

"We Need Help at Once for These Poor People"

THE NEW DEAL AND MICHIGAN FAMILIES

"**WHAT WE NEED** in Hillsdale is a federal officer to investigate the condition of the unemployed," wrote Pearl Gibbon to Franklin Roosevelt in July 1933. "We have families who are starving. The fathers are willing to work, but they have no work and no help from the welfare. When they ask for help, the county officers reply, 'there are no funds, the county is broke.' Can you help us out? We need help at once for these poor people."[1] Jack Tatro of Marine City also wrote Roosevelt about the poor-relief situation in his city at about the same time. Tatro noted that relief orders were inadequate to feed the families, clothing was impossible to procure, and "consequently children are practically naked as are their parents in some cases." Efforts to gain clothing or shoes meant being "sent from Supervisor to Supt of Poor and each refers them to one another, without results from either." As in Gibbon's case, county officials told Tatro that there was no money for help.[2] Tatro wrote that he was not complaining, but simply stating the facts: "The people of this county are true

1. Letter from Pearl Gibbon of Hillsdale, dated July 29, 1933, to FDR, FERA State Series, Michigan Complaints, RG 69, Box 141, Folder G–H. Hillsdale is a small town located in Hillsdale County in the southern agricultural section of Michigan.
2. Letter from Jack Tatro of Marine City to Franklin Roosevelt, dated July 31, 1933, FERA State Series, Michigan Complaints, RG 69, Box 141, Folder T–Z. Marine City, located in St. Clair County, is on the eastern shore of Michigan north of Detroit.

Americans and are not wont to complain."[3] Both letters show a very different perspective from that of local officials. The Federal Emergency Relief Act had become law less than two months earlier and was in the formative administration stages in most Michigan counties. FERA, in conjunction with other programs such as the Works Progress Administration, the Civilian Conservation Corps, and the National Youth Administration, brought significant help to Michigan residents.

Both direct- and work-relief programs injected millions of dollars into Michigan's economy, providing invaluable aid to residents in desperate need. During the six years of emergency relief, nearly $242 million was spent on all relief programs, with the state contributing more than $84 million (34.7 percent) and local governments nearly $47 million (19.4 percent).[4] Michigan and the federal government endeavored to provide work, rather than simply direct relief, for as many of the unemployed as possible. Work relief, as well as programs such as the CCC and NYA, provided wages for the unemployed. First, through the Civil Works Administration, the programs channeled millions of dollars in wages to families and thus to their communities. The key problem with the work programs was that they discriminated by race, citizenship, gender, and age, providing employment largely for white men. Many groups had limited work options under those programs, and family remained at the center of administration. Policies were predicated on the idea of a family as a unit for relief, and virtually all programs viewed recipients through that lens.

DIRECT RELIEF

Direct relief served more residents than work relief in the Depression years, and Michigan's economic problems led to high demand for relief. The percentage of Michigan families receiving relief during the first year of FERA ranged from a high of 16.8 percent to a low of 9.6 percent. By 1933 the worst of the relief problem was concentrated in the Upper Peninsula, including Marquette County, rather than in the industrial cities, which faced their most difficult times in the first years of the Depression (see table 4.1). The continued decline of the lumbering and mining industries, which in turn affected the railroad and retail industries, was the biggest factor in high relief rates in the Lower Peninsula. Poor-quality farmland, in addition to a pool of inexperienced farmers, also contributed to the problem. Saginaw and Van Buren counties were

---

3. Letter from Tatro to Roosevelt, July 31, 1933.
4. Granger and Klein, *Emergency Relief in Michigan, 1933–1939*, 50–51.

TABLE 4.1
PERCENTAGE OF RESIDENTS ON RELIEF

County	% Relief Recipients in Highest Month, 1934	% Relief Recipients in Highest Month, 1935	Monthly Average, 1934	Monthly Average, 1935
Marquette	57.4 (July)	32.9 (Dec.)	34.1	29.3
Saginaw	11.9 (Dec.)	12.6 (Feb.)	8.4	10.3
Van Buren	13.2 (Dec.)	17.7 (Feb.)	7.1	13.3
Wayne	16.0 (Dec.)	15.3 (Dec.)	10.9	11.1
State of Michigan	16.8 (Nov.)	17.8 (Dec.)	12.9	14.6

Source: Years in the table refer to the first two fiscal years of FERA. Thus 1934 refers to July 1933 to June 1934, and 1935 refers to July 1934 to June 1935. Haber and Stanchfield, *Unemployment and Relief in Michigan*, Appendix, table 7; Haber and Stanchfield, *Unemployment, Relief and Economic Security*, 304–5.

among those with the lightest relief load; both were in areas—the "thumb area," on the east side of the state, near Saginaw Bay and the southern agricultural counties—that tended to be the lowest in relief numbers. Agricultural counties in southern Michigan generally had lower relief rates than other areas, as residents could rely on subsistence farming even if they could not produce a cash crop. The state's industrial counties often had lower percentages of relief rates but, given their higher populations, had the greater number of people receiving relief.[5]

Relief generally was extended to families, rather than individuals, although the types of families varied. The average monthly caseload of families receiving relief during FERA's first year included about 13 percent of Michigan's population, and that number rose to 14.6 percent during the second year.[6] The largest age group receiving relief was made up of children under sixteen. In the first year of FERA, 41 percent of all relief recipients were children, or about one-sixth of the state's population in that age group. About 15 percent of recipients were ages sixteen to twenty-four, and about a quarter were ages twenty-five to forty-four. Cases that involved single persons comprised

5. William Haber and Paul L. Stanchfield, *Unemployment and Relief in Michigan* (Lansing: Franklin DeKleine Company, 1935), figure 3, 9, 11–12; Appendix, table 7; Michigan reports by Howard Hunter, August 13, 1934, 3; FERA-WPA Narrative Field Reports, Michigan, Box 58, Harry Hopkins Papers, FDR Library.
6. Haber and Stanchfield, *Unemployment and Relief in Michigan*, 65; Haber and Stanchfield, *Unemployment, Relief, and Economic Security*, 19.

just 12.6 percent of all cases the first year, and increased to 14.6 the second year.[7]

Case-file analysis confirms that most recipients were in families, although that is less true for OAA recipients. Eighteen percent of Marquette County's OAA recipients, about 20 percent of Saginaw County's OAA recipients, and 23 percent of those in Wayne County had no children. Many did not live with their children, even if they had them. The absence of children eliminated a major source of support for older people, and the numbers of recipients with no children on the relief rolls is not surprising. Needless to say, all ADC recipients had children, although about 12 percent of Saginaw's recipients and 5 percent of Wayne County's recipients received aid for relatives, including nieces, nephews, siblings, and grandchildren. Just 15 percent of Van Buren County's emergency-relief recipients had no children.

Race also affected who received relief, although opinions on why varied.[8] In general, the percentage of African-Americans receiving relief was larger than their share of the population in Michigan. Most African-Americans who received relief were in urban areas with populations of more than 2,500. Blacks accounted for 8 percent of all relief recipients, but about 29 percent of all blacks in the state received relief. Whites comprised 91.4 percent of relief recipients, which was about 12 percent of the total white population in 1930; other nonwhite people, including Mexicans, accounted for the remaining 0.6 percent. Overall, about 15 percent of the state's 1930 nonwhite population received relief.[9] Both Marquette and Van Buren counties were almost entirely white; Van Buren County's 1930 census, for instance, listed just 1.4 percent of the population as black, and Marquette had no nonwhite relief recipients among the case files analyzed. Just one of Van Buren County's cases before 1940 involved an African-American family. In Saginaw County, blacks accounted for 70 percent of the minorities in the sample, while Mexicans or Mexican-Americans comprised 23 percent. The remainder were Native Americans.[10]

---

7. Haber and Stanchfield, *Unemployment and Relief in Michigan*, 66; Haber and Stanchfield, *Unemployment, Relief, and Economic Security*, 77.

8. Harvard Sitkoff argues that decentralized administration of many of the New Deal programs translated into severe discriminatory practices, particularly in the South. Harvard Sitkoff, *A New Deal for Blacks: The Emergence of Civil Rights as a National Issue* (New York and Oxford: Oxford University Press, 1978), 46–52; Jacqueline Jones, *Labor of Love, Labor of Sorrow: Black Women, Work, and the Family, from Slavery to the Present* (New York: Vintage, 1985), 217, 223–24.

9. Haber and Stanchfield, *Unemployment, Relief, and Economic Security*, 77–80.

10. In Saginaw County, people of color were 10 percent of the case files analyzed for both ADC and OAA ($N = 593$). They comprised a larger share of the ADC files (13.5 percent) as compared to the OAA files (3.5 percent). In Wayne County, people of color comprised 185 of the cases sampled ($N = 605$). They also comprised a larger share of the ADC files (29 percent)

TABLE 4.2
PERCENTAGE OF NONWHITE RELIEF RECIPIENTS

County	% Nonwhite, 1930 Census	% Nonwhite Case-File Samples
Marquette	0.4	0.0
Saginaw	5.8	10
Van Buren	1.4	0.0
Wayne	7.37	21
State of Michigan	3.8	NA

Wayne County's nonwhite recipients were almost entirely black; just one of the cases involved a Mexican family. Nonwhites were not represented in two of the counties (Marquette and Van Buren), but likely had greater need than demonstrated by those numbers (see table 4.2). People of color had fewer job opportunities in the labor market and thus were concentrated in low-wage, unskilled occupations. They were among the first laid off or fired during economic downturns and were therefore among the first to suffer unemployment when the Depression began. Caseworkers themselves commented on the limited employment opportunities available both to people of color and to noncitizens.[11]

Foreign-born residents, both citizens and noncitizens, also tended to receive relief in greater numbers than their share of the population. A SERA study of Detroit relief rolls found that foreign-born whites comprised 43 percent of the heads of families receiving relief, although the 1930 census reported 39 percent of family heads as foreign-born. Native-born whites, by way of comparison, represented 31 percent of all heads of families receiving relief, but were 53 percent of family heads in the 1930 census.[12] Although statewide figures are not available, similar trends can be seen in Marquette, Saginaw, Van Buren, and Wayne counties (see table 4.3). Figures for the foreign-born among the case-file recipients demonstrate that non-native-born residents sought relief in larger numbers than their population.[13] Foreign-born residents may have faced more discrimination in hiring, particularly if they were not citizens, as

as compared to the OAA files (12.3 percent).

11. SERA reports acknowledged that unequal job opportunities were a large reason for the racial differences among relief numbers in Michigan. Haber and Stanchfield, *Unemployment, Relief, and Economic Security*, 77–80.

12. Ibid., 80–81. The Detroit study, based on one month of relief in 1934, is the only statistic available on citizenship and nativity on Michigan relief rolls.

13. *Fifteenth Census of the United States: 1930, Vol. III* (Washington, D.C.: U.S. Government Printing Office, 1931), 1138–40.

TABLE 4.3
PERCENTAGE OF FOREIGN-BORN RECIPIENTS

County	% Foreign-Born, 1930 Census	% Foreign-Born, 1940 Census	% Foreign-Born, Case File Sample	% Foreign-Born Who Were U.S. Citizens
Marquette	22.8	15.8	59	81
Saginaw	9.1	9.7	27	68.5
Van Buren	10	9.1	13	68
Wayne	25.3	18.6	35	62.7

Source: *Fifteenth Census of the United States: 1930, Vol. III* (Washington, D.C.: U.S. Government Printing Office, 1931), 1138–40; *Sixteenth Census of the United States: 1940, Vol. II, Population* (Washington, D.C.: U.S. Government Printing Office, 1943), 787–88.

described in chapter 2. They also may have had fewer family members to turn to in need, and thus may have sought relief more often.

WORK RELIEF

Work relief proved a more politically popular solution to the Depression's unemployment problems, and the numbers show the critical importance of these programs in the state's economy and in the larger relief effort. By June 31, 1934, nearly $19 million had been spent on work relief in the state. About 30 percent of families on relief were on work relief, and nearly 40 percent of all relief expenditures went to work relief.[14] In the second year, the state spent almost $34 million on work-relief projects, of which more than $27 million was for wages. Those numbers accounted for 44 percent of all expenditures for work and general relief, and 34 percent of all relief costs, including administration, in the state.[15] Through the six years of emergency relief, work relief accounted for 16.5 percent of all cases in an average month in 1933–34, 50.1 percent in 1936–37, and 43.8 percent in 1937–38.[16] In total, the WPA expended more than $441 million until its demise in 1943.[17] The goal, following Michigan's responsible-relative laws, was to provide aid for families

14. Haber and Stanchfield, *Unemployment and Relief in Michigan*, 92–93.
15. Haber and Stanchfield, *Unemployment, Relief, and Economic Security*, 238.
16. Granger and Klein, *Emergency Relief in Michigan, 1933–1939*, 41.
17. *Final Report on the WPA Program* (Washington, D.C.: U.S. Government Printing Office, 1948), 120.

through employable household members. Male heads of household were the first choice.

Early works programs originated through the Public Works Administration and FERA, and then through the Civil Works Administration. The early FERA projects were largely continuations of locally funded projects, but with federal money.[18] The need for a more expansive works program prompted the creation of the Civil Works Administration in November 1933. A part of the National Recovery Act, the CWA had a crucial difference from FERA work projects, and later from the Works Progress Administration: proving need was not a requirement for employment. Any unemployed worker was eligible (see figure 4.1). Applicants did not have to undergo the intrusive investigation that relief recipients experienced; unemployment demonstrated need. While some CWA workers were approved relief cases, not all were, nor did they need to be. They also were under different wage rates than FERA workers and thus earned higher wages and were not limited in the hours they worked. CWA did not carry the stigma or the intrusion that FERA and, later, the WPA did, but it also operated for less than six months.[19] Certification for virtually all works programs, except the CWA, was through the county welfare-relief commission.

The Works Progress Administration (later the Works Projects Administration) was intended to provide work relief for employable residents, and thus remove those individuals from direct relief. It was a reaction against "the dole," and its inauguration coincided with the demise of FERA and the passage of the Social Security Act in 1935. The WPA would provide employment for those able to work, and the SSA would provide help for the unemployable. Direct relief would no longer be the center of the federal relief program. The National Youth Administration, a part of the WPA, provided jobs for young people to enable them to continue their educations.[20]

Work-relief projects improved roads and bridges, and also built or repaired buildings and schools. The majority of projects focused on repairs and construction, including sewers, airports, and bridges. In FERA's first year, 26 percent of projects highlighted building and school repairs and new constructions, and another 13.7 percent went to street and road repairs (figure 4.2).[21] Thousands of miles of roads were built or improved, and crews constructed

18. Rose, *Put to Work,* 38.
19. Rose, *Put to Work,* 45–47; Swain, *Ellen S. Woodward,* 45–46.
20. Rose, *Put to Work,* 94–95; Granger and Klein, *Emergency Relief in Michigan, 1933–1939,* 5–6.
21. *50,000 Men: Report of the Work Division of the Michigan Emergency Welfare Relief Commission* (Lansing: 1935), 30.

Figure 4.1 Participants in an aviation ground-school program offered through FERA and held at the REO Car Company Club house in Lansing. Photo courtesy Archives of Michigan.

thirty-seven new schools and repaired more than eighteen hundred others. They erected fifty-five municipal garages and twenty-three county and city halls, and built or repaired eighty-two bridges. Other projects spotlighted conservation programs and improvements to recreational facilities. Projects also employed white-collar workers in its educational and recreational programs. Workers also produced goods, from canned food to mattresses and clothing, which were distributed to relief families.[22] Work relief not only brought wages to families and injected money into local economies, but also resulted in visible improvements to local communities.

While racial discrimination did exist on job assignments, despite federal regulations to the contrary, historian Harvard Sitkoff argues that federal programs, in spite of their shortcomings, made a real difference in the lives of blacks, especially by 1936. Regulations against discrimination became more stringent, although never totally effective, but the numbers of blacks employed

22. Haber and Stanchfield, *Unemployment, Relief, and Economic Security,* 229–238; *WPA Projects* (Works Progress Administration, 1937), 55; and *Employment on Projects in March 1936, WPA Including NYA* (Works Progress Administration, 1936), 59.

Figure 4.2 Workers on a Manistee County skidway project. Photo from Louise Armstrong Collection, courtesy of Bentley Historical Library, University of Michigan, Box 1, Photographs Folder.

by New Deal work-relief agencies increased significantly by President Roosevelt's second term. African-Americans were able to secure jobs through the CWA, CCC, WPA, and NYA, and some were reluctant to accept employment in private industry because of the lack of discrimination on work projects.[23] A 1937 report on the projects of Michigan's National Youth Administration lauded the number (ninety-three total) of projects that included black youth. The projects, the report continued, included a variety of training opportunities, especially in Detroit, although whites benefited from training programs more than blacks. In August 1939, the majority of projects for blacks were in

23. Sitkoff, *A New Deal for Blacks,* 51, 69–72, 74–75.

recreation, library, gardening, clerical, health and hospitals, and construction and wood shops. They existed in nineteen counties, including Genesee, Kent, Saginaw, and Wayne, and employed 648 blacks among 5,093 total young people.[24] But the larger problem, according to the report, was that "after receiving this wonderful training, there are very few outlets for this training." Few places would hire blacks, despite their skills, leaving the youth no better off in terms of employment.[25]

Nonwhites did obtain work relief in Michigan. In Wayne County's sample, 18 percent of all nonwhite ADC recipients had at least one family member assigned to a WPA job, compared to 15 percent among whites. In Saginaw County more than 20 percent of all nonwhite ADC recipients had a family assignment to WPA, compared to nearly 14 percent for whites. Rates for the National Youth Administration were highest for nonwhites in Wayne County, where nearly 10 percent of all ADC cases had a student assigned to NYA, compared to 3 percent for whites. Saginaw's rate for whites and nonwhites was 3 and 2 percent, respectively.[26]

The Civilian Conservation Corps provided employment for young men, most between the ages of seventeen and twenty-three. The program's goal was to provide training and education for young men who could help support their families through CCC work. Although segregated, the CCC did offer some opportunities for nonwhites. Men worked in camps on a variety of conservation projects in forests, parks, and other public areas.[27] Michigan had more than 102,000 men in fifty-seven camps. The programs also reduced relief expenses for states and local governments. Enrollees sent more than twenty million dollars in wages to families, thus reducing their need for relief.[28] The assignments were predicated on aid for the family; the WPA, CCC and NYA wages were intended to help support the individual's family, whether the individual was the parent, sibling, or child.

Michigan's CCC program's first priority was to combat the threat of forest fires. In the first two years, crews constructed 3,050 miles of truck trails

24. "Work Report by Districts and Counties," August 16, 1939, NYA, from John B. Kirby, ed., *The New Deal and Black America* (Frederick, MD: University Publications of America, 1984, microfilm), reel 6. This collection (hereafter cited as NDBA) contains twenty-five reels of microfilmed documents related to African-Americans and the New Deal agencies.

25. Letter dated August 27, 1937, from C. R. Bradshaw, acting director of the NYA in Michigan, to Richard Brown, deputy executive director of the NYA, NYA (Record Group 119), NDBA, reel 4, 1–2.

26. Virtually no OAA cases in any county had work-relief assignments, due to the unemployability of the recipients. Few also had family to support them.

27. John A. Salmond, *The Civilian Conservation Corps, 1933–1942* (Durham: Duke University Press, 1967), 30.

28. Roger Rosentreter, "Roosevelt's Tree Army: Michigan's Civilian Conservation Corps," *Michigan History* 70.3 (May/June 1986): 22–23.

and 600 miles of firebreaks, as well as new fire towers. Men also worked on fish hatcheries and dams, and conducted lake surveys.[29] Bridges spanning the Muskegon and Manistique rivers (103 and 170 feet long, respectively) were completed, and crews improved miles of streams and planted more than seventy-five million fish into the state's waterways. They also established the Seney National Wildlife Refuge and Isle Royale National Park in the Upper Peninsula. In addition, the CCC was also a key part of firefighting efforts in the state, including stopping a fire on Isle Royale that burned 35,000 of the island's 132,000 acres.[30] The CCC left a significant legacy in the state's recreational and conservation systems.

Although many of the camps were segregated, they did provide black youth with employment (see figure 4.3). By 1940 the South contained ninety-three segregated camps and another sixty-eight were found throughout the country. Three camps were in Michigan, one of which was in the Manistee National Forest.[31] The state also included a camp for Native Americans in the eastern Upper Peninsula.[32] Blacks comprised about 3.5 percent of the state's population, but by 1941 held about 7.2 percent of the placements. Clearly black young men sought these positions, and at one point the Detroit Department of Public Welfare found itself with an inadequate number of places for blacks. Openings did exist for whites, but segregation prevented assigning blacks to those slots. Efforts to secure another Michigan camp for blacks failed, as federal officials believed that other states were in greater need of additional camps for blacks.[33] Assignment rates for the Civilian Conservation Corps were comparable for both whites and nonwhites in the Wayne County case sample: about 3 percent. But nonwhites in Saginaw County had more than 9 percent in the CCC, while whites had about 4 percent. As with other programs, the goal was to provide aid for the family. Enrollees were paid thirty dollars, twenty-two to twenty-five of which had to be sent home to dependents.[34] About ninety-two million dollars was spent on the CCC in the state during the program's history, and more

29. G. A. Young, "Michigan State Civilian Conservation Corps, July 1, 1933, to July 1, 1939," CCC Records, Department of Conservation, Box 1, 5, 7–10, State Archives of Michigan.

30. Rosentreter, "Roosevelt's Tree Army," 17–18.

31. Sitkoff, *A New Deal for Blacks,* 51, 74–75; Rosentreter, "Roosevelt's Tree Army," 21; "The CCC and Colored Youth," CCC (Record Group 35), Division of Planning and Public Relations, reel 8, 2; and "Negro CCC Camps," April 1940, NDBA, reel 8.

32. Rosentreter, "Roosevelt's Tree Army," 21.

33. Letter from Charles Taylor, Asst. Director, CCC, to G. R. Harris, Director of Detroit DPW, April 21, 1941, NDBA, reel 9. Harris argued that one reason for the decrease in white applicants was the renewal of industrial employment, which was open to whites but not blacks. See letter from Harris to H. J. Rigterink, CCC Selection, State Welfare Commission, March 9, 1941, NDBA, reel 9.

34. Salmond, *The Civilian Conservation Corps,* 30.

Figure 4.3 Enrollees in the CCC camp library in Bitely. Photo courtesy Archives of Michigan.

than twenty-one million of that was sent home to a camp enrollee's family.[35] While the benefits of the program were many, not all young men wanted to work in remote areas supporting their families, a trend explored more fully in chapter 6.

While the benefits of the projects were visible and many, the WPA and other work-relief programs were not without conflict. Local officials criticized the programs, but work-relief recipients also had complaints. Michigan was the site of significant organizing of the unemployed, including WPA workers, during the 1930s. Such activism was found throughout the state, including the Upper Peninsula. In the WPA, workers formed the WPA Project Workers' Union. Allied initially with the American Federation of Labor, the WPA union suffered from accusations of Communism, but even though such red-baiting hurt the alliance with the AFL, the union still expanded.[36] The state saw

35. *Second Biennial Report, Michigan Social Welfare Commission, July 1940–June 1942* (Lansing: December 1942), 20.

36. James J. Lorence, *Organizing the Unemployed: Community and Union Activists in the Industrial Heartland* (Albany: State University of New York Press, 1996), 108–9. Lorence provides the most in-depth analysis of the organizing efforts of the unemployed throughout the 1930s.

thirty-four strikes between 1935 and 1937, and issues ranged from wages and basic working conditions to union recognition, hours, and the quality of the projects created under the WPA. WPA administrators, including State Director A. D. Hall, largely dismissed workers' complaints, blaming the discontent on a handful of agitators. Historian James Lorence argues that the workers did have legitimate issues that warranted attention. Despite the lackluster administrative reaction, at both the state and local levels, the unions achieved some success, including increased wages in 1936. Such successes only fueled workers to join the union. The union also sought expanded projects and employment in 1938.[37]

Most work projects, including those in the pre–New Deal years as well as the CCC, the WPA, the CWA, and most FERA projects, were directed at male heads of household or older sons. In fact, the CWA included primarily construction work, which eliminated employment for women. In response to demands for employment for women, Harry Hopkins, whose lack of concern for women's employment has been documented, created the Civil Works Service.[38] The CWS included some white-collar work projects and also production-for-use programs, which employed women in canning, sewing, and other projects (see figure 4.4). But the CWS fell under FERA, and thus included both the means test and lower-wage rates and hours in contrast to the CWA program.[39] Work programs for women also employed only a fraction—perhaps 10 percent—of the total numbers of relief workers in Michigan. The number of women employed on the CWA, CWS, and education programs seldom surpassed 5,000 in the state in early 1934, and decreased further when the CWA ended.[40] In contrast, monthly numbers of workers peaked at more than 60,000 in November 1933, and again surpassed that figure in June 1934. A total of 475,669 relief workers were tallied from July 1933 to June 1934; women comprised only a small fraction of that total.[41] Expenditures for women's work projects totaled $1.8 million—just a small part of the $27 million spent in the second year of the work programs.[42]

The trend continued under the WPA, with its emphasis on construction and public works improvement projects. Employment was not restricted to men only, but the goal was to employ male heads of household, if possible, to protect their authority in the family. This included putting "some brake upon

37. Ibid., 109–12, 117–20, 180.
38. Rose, *Put to Work*, 94–98; and Rose, *Workfare or Fair Work*, 39–41.
39. Rose, *Put to Work*, 47–48; Swain, *Ellen S. Woodward*, 44–45.
40. Haber and Stanchfield, *Unemployment and Relief in Michigan*, 119.
41. Ibid., 97.
42. Haber and Stanchfield, *Unemployment, Relief, and Economic Security*, 244; *50,000 Men*, 42.

Figure 4.4 Women working on a WPA sewing project in Manistee County. Photo courtesy Archives of Michigan.

women's eagerness to be the family breadwinner, wage recipient, and controller of the family pocketbook."[43] Married women were given WPA assignments, as in the case of Mabel Stevenson, who previously had worked as a domestic worker and as a packer at a celery plant. She and her husband, Henry, were both employable, but she was assigned to a Van Buren County recreation project in June of 1938. Henry, a day laborer, was having difficulty finding work, and apparently no appropriate assignment was available for him, and caseworkers accepted Mabel's request for employment. That ended eighteen months later, when Mabel was to be recertified. She was rejected "on the basis that the logical head of the family is not being certified."[44] The caseworker had bent the rules apparently, but the WPA supervisor rejected the certification.

Women with small children were also not perceived as "eligible" for WPA employment, although regulations did not directly exclude them. SERA's policy relating to women who received mothers' pensions and also supplemental relief from the WRC permitted certifying a son or daughter, if old enough, for WPA, in order to support the family. The policy specifically advised not certifying the mother for WPA unless there was another older person able to care for the children: "We do not want to defeat the purpose of the pension

---

43. Quoted in Rose, *Workfare or Fair Work,* 40.

44. Letter dated January 25, 1940, from Earl Scott, chief, intake and certification, Case #18155, VB ERA Records, Box 3, Folder 4.

law by stimulating those mothers to work outside the home."[45] WPA redefined "eligible worker" in its manual and included all women who were able to work, and did not specifically exclude mothers with home responsibilities. In the bulletin alerting county administrators to this change, SERA administrator Haber cautioned about applying the new rule to mothers: "It is not the intent to stimulate employment outside the home of women who have not previously sought such employment."[46] Some confusion seemingly followed, as Haber clarified the ruling a few weeks later, firmly stating that the new ruling did not mean that all women, "particularly those with small children," were required to be certified for WPA, unless they requested it and were willing to accept full-time work.[47]

In practice, caseworkers went further than simply not encouraging women with children to seek employment; eligibility for ADC could exclude women from certification for a WPA project, or eventually cause them to be removed from their assignment. Mary Linderson, a divorced mother of two children, ages fourteen and sixteen, was a supervisor for a WPA sewing project in Saginaw. She began receiving ADC in mid-1937, and supplemented her grant with income from boarders. In 1938 she asked to be recertified for WPA, but caseworkers told her that they could not because she was eligible for ADC.[48]

Women who were eligible for ADC but employed on WPA projects lost their assignments as the decade waned. Although some wanted to work rather than receive ADC, they had no choice. Hannah Justin lived with her two sons, ages eight and fifteen, in Saginaw. She also was employed on WPA but was removed in January 1939 because she was eligible for ADC. She applied for ADC that month. Justin faced difficulty finding private employment because she was separated from her husband but not divorced. She told her caseworker that she had been supporting and caring for her family on WPA before this, but had been given no choice in the change: "She feels that it is up to us to take care of her," wrote her caseworker, "and in a way that is true."[49] Even the caseworker acknowledged the agency's responsibility in this woman's unemployment problem. Justin eventually borrowed the money for a divorce and secured a factory job in December 1940. Gertrude Schneider faced a similar situation; a WPA employee from 1936 to 1939, she lost her assignment because

45. SERA Letter #445, August 30, 1935, SEWRC Records, Box 1, Folder July–September 1935.

46. SERA Letter #472, October 11, 1935, SEWRC Records, Box 1, Folder October–December 1935.

47. SERA Letter #485, November 1, 1935, SEWRC Records, Box 1, Folder October–December 1935.

48. Case C7300203, reel 4534, Saginaw ADC, case history, October 27, 1938.

49. Case C7300100, reel 4532, Saginaw ADC records, case history, April 19, 1939.

of her eligibility for ADC. She had seven children, four of whom still lived at home, ranging in age from six to fifteen. Divorced in 1938, Schneider faced the foreclosure of her home because she could not keep up the house payments and taxes. She supplemented her grant with income from doing laundry and watching her older daughter's children, but did not leave the relief roll until her son secured a full-time job in 1942.[50] Thus women who had supported families with WPA income were removed from their jobs to receive ADC. The grants, which barely covered their children's needs, required supplementation through odd jobs, including doing laundry, taking in boarders, or providing child care. ADC recipients were not eligible for WPA jobs until 1942.[51]

The WPA union provided support when a group of Detroit mothers employed on WPA projects successfully protested such efforts, staging a sit-in strike to protest announced layoffs of all workers eligible for ADC. They did not want to exchange their monthly wages of eighty-six dollars (or more) for ADC grants that would provide just eighteen dollars per month for the first child and twelve dollars for each additional child: "For this group of women the Social Security Act became a threat to their minimum standard of living."[52] Two days of occupation, with the support and aid of the Wayne County Federation of Labor, the United Auto Workers, and the WPA union, yielded an exemption for the projects from Harry Hopkins in Washington DC, allowing the mothers to keep their jobs.[53]

Not all women, however, were unhappy to leave WPA jobs to remain home full-time to care for their children. Rachel Raney, an African-American mother of three children whose father had deserted the family in 1932, supported her family with day work and later a WPA sewing job, in 1938. She was laid off WPA in early 1939, but welcomed the chance to stay home. She believed her fifteen-year-old daughter needed her. She supplemented her grant with day work, and was admired by her caseworker, who believed she had done a good job keeping her family together despite the absence of her husband.[54]

Another criticism of the women's work projects was their emphasis on unskilled work, particularly in the case of sewing and domestic work, the

50. Case C7300239, reel 4535, Saginaw ADC records.

51. Case C7300215, reel 4534, Saginaw ADC records.

52. Arthur L. Stone and Martin Kahn, "Detroit Sits Down to Work," *Social Work Today* 4.8 (May 1937): 14.

53. Ibid., 15.

54. Case C7300279, reel 4536, Saginaw ADC records; Jones, *Labor of Love, Labor of Sorrow*, 224–25. Jones argues that for some black women, particularly in the urban North, "New Deal welfare programs afforded an opportunity to place family considerations over the demands of white employers."

"dumping ground" for women relief workers.[55] Few work-relief projects, in fact, except those targeting white-collar workers, translated into skills that would be marketable in private employment at reasonable wages. White-collar workers had the skills before the Depression, and such projects offered no training. Unskilled work for women did not command the wages for unskilled work for men, of course, and thus few women who needed long-term work advanced their position in the labor market. An undated press release, "The Negro and the WPA," boasted that those black women who participated in the household training programs not only secured jobs after completing the programs, but also received higher wages than they would have earned otherwise.[56] Such training programs hoped to raise the status of domestic work by "professionalizing" it through training and standards, but they proved ineffective.[57] In many cases, such programs trained women to take low-wage, low-skill jobs in their local communities, particularly in areas with a high demand for domestic or agricultural labor. Women of color were aided the least by the work-relief projects, and were even referred to as the "problem children" in the program. Speaking in part of their disadvantaged opportunities and training, the term also connotes paternalism, and is suggestive of blame on the part of black women. The women—in this formulation—were the problem, not the labor market or the work projects.[58]

Noncitizens suffered from the drive to provide employment only to citizens, whether in the private sector or in work-relief programs.[59] The WPA and private employers often refused jobs to noncitizens, fueling the belief that if they would leave, there would be enough jobs for Americans. Twenty-year-old Maria Gortez supported her entire family—her widowed mother and four siblings—with a WPA job in Saginaw, although her mother also received a small ADC grant to supplement Maria's earnings. Caseworkers noted that supporting the entire family "was too much to be expected of her." But she later lost her WPA job because she was not a citizen, and also could not obtain factory employment without having her first papers, which could take up to a year to

55. Argersinger, *Toward a New Deal in Baltimore*, 72; Blanche Weisen Cook, *Eleanor Roosevelt, 1933–1938, Volume II* (New York: Viking, 1999), 87–88.

56. "The Negro and the WPA," WPA (Record Group 69), NDBA, reel 21, 6.

57. Alfred Edgar Smith, "Negro Project Workers: 1937 Annual Report," WPA, NDBA, reel 21, 2; Jones, *Labor of Love, Labor of Sorrow*, 205–6, 218; and Cook, *Eleanor Roosevelt, 1933–1938*, 261–62.

58. "Narrative Report," Division of Women's and Professional Projects, January 1937, Press release, NDBA, reel 21.

59. Cases appear in Saginaw and Wayne regarding noncitizens denied employment either by private businesses or WPA. See also Argersinger, *Toward a New Deal in Baltimore*, 75–76; and Julia Kirk Blackwelder, *Women of the Depression: Caste and Culture in San Antonio, 1929–1939* (College Station: Texas A&M University, 1984), 128–29.

obtain.[60] Caseworkers had no choice but to increase the ADC grant to make up for Maria's lost wages.

Social workers also criticized the overall limited effects of WPA, in particular with respect to its gender and age discrimination, but paid little attention to the discrimination against people of color and the foreign-born. County WRC administrator Louise Armstrong lamented the lack of employment for women in general in Manistee County, and recognized that the work-relief programs did little to add to those opportunities.[61] Gertrude Springer, author of the Miss Bailey series in the *Survey*, agreed, noting that projects rarely taught actual skills, nor, for those women who had never worked outside the home, did the projects instruct workers in how to function in a wage environment. Springer used Miss Bailey in the articles to illustrate issues prevalent in the administration of relief. In one article, Miss Bailey believes that the programs can do much more: "It seems to me we are missing a chance in not using projects to give these women something that industry or business is likely to want and that might rescue them from being last hired and first fired."[62] The tendency toward public works projects excluded not only women but also older men. Many could no longer do the heavy work such projects required, but were able to work in a different capacity.[63] WPA was simply not enough; it was only for the best of the unemployed. And the WPA could not even serve all those eligible for work. The numbers of WPA jobs in no way kept pace with the number of employable people on the relief rolls. In July 1938, employable cases accounted for 40 percent of the direct relief caseload, but only if the WPA employment slots had been increased from 40,000 to 175,000 could that number have been reduced to 25 percent. The WPA was simply not large enough to address the employment needs of all those able to work.[64]

Both direct and work relief provided significant aid to Michigan's unemployed. Millions of dollars came to the state and helped to alleviate the considerable hardship of the Depression. Families were the target, usually through the men in the household. But such aid was not without conflict, even within families. Caseworkers—those who sought to "professionalize" public welfare—were at the center of the administration of relief. The development of social work in public welfare, and the conflicts that occurred during that process, add another layer in the relief negotiations of the 1930s.

---

60. Case C7300120, Saginaw ADC Records, reel 4533, case history from August 4, 1937, and September 20, 1937.

61. Armstrong, *We Too Are the People*, 304. See chapter 10, "Women and Creeds and Christmas Toys."

62. Gertrude Springer, "Border Lines and Gaps," *Survey* 71 (November 1935): 333.

63. Ibid., 332.

64. Granger and Klein, *Emergency Relief in Michigan*, 88–89.

CHAPTER FIVE

"These So-Called Case Workers"

RELIEF WORKERS AND PROFESSIONALIZATION

IN NOVEMBER 1933, just weeks after county emergency-relief offices opened, E. M. Zuver, chairperson of the Van Buren County Welfare Relief Commission, issued a statement refuting information that WRC employees earned nine hundred dollars for two weeks of work. A neighboring county's newspaper had just published salary figures inflated by as much as three or four times.[1] The incident was not uncommon. A major criticism of the emergency-relief system centered on administrative costs, particularly the salaries of clerical workers, caseworkers, and supervisors employed in the relief agencies. Local officials believed they could do the work more economically than "these so-called case workers," and SERA issued more than one report defending its administrative expenses.[2] Critics included local officials, community members, and some recipients who compared their meager grants to the salaries paid caseworkers. Low salaries angered relief workers and social workers, supposed professionals who, in their eyes, were not paid as such. The events of the 1930s prompted significant debates about professional social welfare, both within and outside the profession. Contrasting ideas of what expertise was needed to administer relief, rooted in the gendered nature of professionalization, were one of the focal points of debate about welfare reorganization

---

1. "Denies Report of Expense of County Welfare Commission," *Hartford Day Spring,* November 15, 1933, 1.

2. Quote from Van Buren County Board of Supervisors' resolution, "Proceedings of the Board of Supervisors, Van Buren County," February 16, 1934, 92.

in Michigan. Two visions of professionalism—one from the social work camp and the other from local officials—clashed in these debates.

The Great Depression and the New Deal changed social work permanently, despite the continuities in policy before and after the Great Depression. A relatively new profession, social work was still engaged in defining its professional identity when its services were in demand as never before. Social workers and social work organizations participated in public policy development during the Depression and eventually the New Deal.[3] The profession faced a huge influx of new relief workers, few with formal training, hired to staff the emergency-relief agencies around the country. The 1930s saw the rise of the "new social worker": usually a young person, often female, with some college education but little or no formal social work training. The profession greatly expanded, both in numbers and in influence, as social workers entered the public welfare arena to a much greater degree. The United States was estimated to have about 30,500 social workers in 1930, largely employed by private agencies; their ranks doubled by the time Franklin Roosevelt was inaugurated in 1933.[4]

By the 1920s, social work developed the tenets of a profession. No social work schools existed in the United States in 1898, but the United States and Canada together had forty by 1928.[5] The Charity Organization movement organized in the National Board of Corrections and Charities in 1874—and would reorganize as the National Association of Social Work in 1917. The American Association of Social Workers, established in 1921, published its own professional journal, the *Compass,* later *Social Work.*[6] Another major professional social work journal was the *Survey,* published by the Russell Sage Foundation and considered to be the voice for all social workers, rather than for a specific professional organization.[7] By the 1920s, the AASW represented

3. The Family Welfare Association began as the National Association of Societies for Organizing Charities in 1911. It changed its name to the FWA just before the Great Depression and became the Family Service Association in 1946. See Peter Romanofsky and Clarke Chambers, eds., *Social Service Organizations, Vol. I* (Westport, CT: Greenwood Press, 1978), 22–23, 302–3.

4. Walter I. Trattner, *From Poor Law to Welfare State: A History of Social Welfare in America,* 4th ed. (New York: Free Press, 1989), 269–70; Winifred Bell, *Aid to Dependent Children* (New York: Columbia University Press, 1965), 37–38.

5. Linda Gordon, *Heroes of Their Own Lives: The Politics and History of Family Violence* (London: Virago Press, 1988), 63; Trattner, *From Poor Law to Welfare State,* 217–22.

6. John H. Ehrenreich, *The Altruistic Imagination: A History of Social Work and Social Policy in the United States* (Ithaca: Cornell University Press, 1985), 78; Gordon, *Heroes of Their Own Lives,* 63; and Walkowitz, "The Making of a Feminine Professional Identity: Social Workers in the 1920s," *American Historical Review* 95 (October 1990): 1054.

7. James Leiby, *A History of Social Welfare and Social Work in the United States* (New

between 15 and 20 percent of professional social workers. Usually members were the "elite" among social workers, often executives of private agencies or higher-salaried caseworkers.[8] The 1936 AASW directory included primarily social workers from private agencies.[9] The majority of relief workers were not AASW members, and their inability and, in some cases, unwillingness to attain "professional" standards would fuel the union movement among social workers.

Casework formed the core curriculum for the new social work schools that emerged by the 1930s. The use of volunteers as the backbone of social welfare agencies declined further.[10] A social worker was no longer a friendly visitor or volunteer Lady Bountiful, but instead was "the 'scientific' Miss Case-Worker, an 'objective' social investigator."[11] Social workers were to help clients deal with

---

York: Columbia University Press, 1978), 120. The *Survey* was first published in 1909 and was connected to several other publications, including *Charities* and *Commons*. Between 1923 and 1948 the *Survey* had two publications, the *Midmonthly*, directed at professional social workers, and the *Graphic*, for a wider audience. See Clarke A. Chambers, *Paul U. Kellogg and the* Survey: *Voices for Social Welfare and Social Justice* (Minneapolis: University of Minnesota Press, 1971), 7; Daniel J. Walkowitz, *Working with Class: Social Workers and the Politics of Middle-Class Identity* (Chapel Hill: University of North Carolina Press, 1999), 224–25.

8. Walkowitz, "The Making of a Feminine Professional Identity," 1054. Membership in the National Association of Social Workers held similar requirements, although that organization was more flexible in terms of replacing practical experience for formal social work education. Junior members had to have at least one year of supervised experience or one year of social work experience, and full members had to have at least four years of experience unless they were graduates of an approved school of social work. See "Membership Requirements before 1930," National Association of Social Workers Records, Box 5, Folder 46, Membership Applications.

9. Jessica H. Barr, ed., *Directory of Members of the American Association of Social Workers, 1936* (New York: AASW); AASW Records, Box 6, Folder 56; Trattner, *From Poor Law to Welfare State*, 270. Michigan members included some welfare-relief commission administrators (John Ballenger of Detroit and Victor Woodward of Flint) and several people connected to the State Emergency Relief Administration (assistant administrator George Granger, field representative Philip Shafer, Director Ruth Bowen, and WPA district supervisor Anne Hutchings). The American Public Welfare Association, comprised of social workers interested in public welfare issues, organized in 1930 and had several thousand members by the end of the decade. An outgrowth of the National Conference on Social Work, its members worked to shape federal and state relief policy and to improve public social services. See Trattner's chapter 11, "The Quest for Professionalization"; Jennifer Mittelstadt, *From Welfare to Workfare: The Unintended Consequences of Liberal Reform, 1945–1965* (Chapel Hill: University of North Carolina Press, 2005), 5–6; and "American Public Welfare Association," *Social Service Organizations*, 131–34.

10. Linda Gordon, *Pitied But Not Entitled: Single Mothers and the History of Welfare* (New York: Free Press, 1994), 103–4. Mary Richmond's *Social Diagnosis*, published in 1917, was the primary manual for casework for social workers. See Walkowitz, *Working with Class*, 57–58.

11. Regina Kunzel argues that casework was the defining skill or element of the social work profession and was "a kind of litmus test to separate professionals from amateurs and to advertise their professional status to a skeptical public." Regina G. Kunzel, *Fallen Women, Problem*

issues of social adjustment that obstructed their ability to function in society as needed, but the "objective" part was important; moral judgments were not to be a part of the diagnosis.[12] Social workers diagnosed the problems only "to indicate limits and possibilities in a systematic way, to point toward a reasoned plan of action,"[13] not to judge.

One significant continuity existed in the profession: Lady Bountiful and Miss Case-Worker were women, and the image of a social worker remained female throughout this era of professionalization.[14] Social workers were employed largely by private agencies before 1930, and in 1920 about 60 percent were women. A decade later, 79 percent were female. Only the teaching profession had a higher percentage of women.[15] Detroit's social work staff was 87 percent female and also 94 percent white in 1936.[16] Whether the fact that the profession was dominated by women was the "cause" of the low status, or if the low status and low pay deterred men from entering the profession, was debated.[17]

Feminized professions not only were numerically dominated by women, but also practiced professional values different from the more traditional (often male) professions.[18] Historian Robyn Muncy argues that gender was often a key reason for differences in the professionalization process and its definition.[19] Muncy connects the values these professionals espoused and

---

Girls: Unmarried Mothers and the Professionalization of Social Work, 1890–1935 (New Haven: Yale University Press, 1993), 42; Walkowitz, *Working with Class*, 57–58, 75–76, 87.

12. Roy Lubove, *The Professional Altruist: The Emergence of Social Work as a Career, 1880–1930* (New York: Atheneum, 1983), 77–78; Sydnor H. Walker, "Privately Supported Social Work," in *Recent Social Trends in the United States: Report of the President's Research Committee on Social Trends, Vol. II* (New York: McGraw-Hill, 1933), 1170–71.

13. Leiby, *A History of Social Welfare and Social Work*, 122–23, 182–83.

14. Walkowitz, *Working with Class*, 87.

15. Ibid., 88; Ehrenreich, *The Altruistic Imagination*, 81; and Walker, "Privately Supported Social Work," 1189.

16. Cecil M. Whalen, *Tenure, Training, and Compensation of Detroit Social Workers* (Detroit: Bureau of Governmental Research, 1938), 3.

17. Ehrenreich, *The Altruistic Imagination*, 81.

18. Robyn Muncy, *Creating a Female Dominion, 1890–1935* (New York: Oxford University Press, 1991), xii–xiv, 17–22, 68–70; Gordon, *Pitied But Not Entitled*, 72–73. Margaret Rossiter analyzes the experiences of women entering both male- and female-dominated professions, as well as the strategies they employed. See Margaret W. Rossiter, *Women Scientists in America: Struggles and Strategies to 1940* (Baltimore: Johns Hopkins University Press, 1982), 55–65. Clarke Chambers argues that social work was a profession "created by an equal partnership of women and men working in coalition." His argument may hold true for those women in national leadership positions, but I am not convinced it was true at other levels. See Clarke Chambers, "Women in the Creation of the Profession of Social Work," *Social Service Review* 60 (March 1986): 6. See also Walkowitz, *Working with Class*.

19. Muncy, *Creating a Female Dominion*, xiii–xiv. The standard work on the history of professionalization is Burton J. Bledstein, *The Culture of Professionalism: The Middle Class and*

practiced to gender, rooted in beliefs about the natural abilities of women and men. Male professional values centered on efficiency, expertise, competition, education, and research. Female professions tended to emphasize popularizing expert knowledge, an extension of the notion of women as educators, and service.[20] Female professions, like social work, nursing, and teaching, capitalized on beliefs about the nurturing abilities of women. Muncy ties this to the need to justify women's professional role in the context of traditional notions of what was appropriate behavior for women. A 1982 essay also argues that feminization occurred in professions "because there was a 'fit' between economic need and cultural conceptions of gender roles."[21] As social work developed as a profession, social workers sought to distance their work from notions about natural abilities based on gender. Regina Kunzel argues that the social work profession, in its efforts to distinguish itself from the friendly visitors and volunteers of the earlier era, was distancing itself from such beliefs about natural abilities and social work. Social work was a profession, and not a "natural" occupation for women, but it was a difficult image to erase.[22]

These contrasting professional values, rooted in gender stereotypes, emerge vividly in the welfare-reorganization debates of the 1930s. The debate was a clash between professional social workers and local officials, two groups with very different ideas of precisely what expertise welfare administration required. Social workers sought to shed the notion that their field was a "natural" one for women, and abandoned such arguments by the 1930s.[23] The values embedded in the two kinds of professionalization Muncy describes surfaced

---

the Development of Higher Education in America (New York: Norton, 1976), 86–92. Bledstein's work documents the culture of *male* professionalism, with no attention to gender and minimal attention to those professions termed "female."

20. Muncy, *Creating a Female Dominion*, 21–22. Muncy notes that while male professionals, such as doctors and lawyers, also included the idea of service, it was more abstract and directed toward the "public interest" rather than helping a specific group or individual. She also argues that in the early days of social work, female professionals relied on wealthy benefactors for support and thus had to interpret or "sell" their work to laypeople. They also had to persuade clients that their services were necessary: "At precisely the time when those traditional male professions were seeking to increase their fees and status by emphasizing esoteric knowledge, women were creating professions that depended on the cooperation of lay people" (20). For a discussion of gender and professionalism in psychiatry, see Elizabeth Lunbeck, *The Psychiatric Persuasion: Knowledge, Gender, and Power in Modern America* (Princeton: Princeton University Press, 1994), 37–38.

21. Joan Jacobs Brumberg and Nancy Tomes, "Women in the Professions: A Research Agenda for American Historians," *Reviews in American History* 10 (June 1982): 283; Bledstein, *The Culture of Professionalism*, 118–20.

22. Kunzel, *Fallen Women, Problem Girls*, 47.

23. Even within social work, a hierarchy of gender emerges. Men tended to dominate administrative and supervisory positions, while women filled the ranks of entry-level social work. See Walkowitz, *Working with Class*, 94–95, 167.

in the welfare debates in Michigan. Local officials argued that business and efficiency, the male professional qualities described by Muncy, were critical to relief work; they accused professional social workers of coddling relief recipients. Such values were not connected to the sex of professionals, but rather to the ideologies they espoused. Local officials adopted, however unintended, the gendered language of professionalism in their efforts to retain control of relief administration, rejecting the belief that social work education was necessary.

Michigan's experience in the 1930s highlights the narrow definition of social worker in standard histories of the profession. One scholar argues that "it was the county agents, all males, who were the first true social workers in Michigan."[24] Michigan's public welfare system—staffed by county agents who administered child welfare and, at times, mothers' pensions; township supervisors; and superintendents of the poor, who administered relief funded by county dollars—was the dominant welfare system in Michigan prior to the 1930s. And it was a system dominated primarily by men. Michigan's State Board of Corrections and Charities directed that agents be men "who were regarded as successful, knowledgeable, and moral." Women were excluded. Most of these early relief workers were of middle-class backgrounds and began to see themselves as a "new occupational group" by 1900.[25] Poor commissioners and superintendents of the poor, also predominantly men, were part of this group of early social workers. They never referred to themselves as social workers, but they did create their own sense of professional or occupational identity. They formed their own professional organizations, such as the Association of Superintendents of the Poor and the State Association of Supervisors, and held annual meetings addressing their shared problems and concerns. They sought to contrast their ideologies and practices with that of the professional social worker, building on the nineteenth-century legacy of county agents and poor officials.

Social work's professional status was uncertain, and local officials did not see the profession as central to relief administration. One critic argued that social work required "no specialized skills; it was a mediating occupation without final authority."[26] Many of Michigan's local officials, on the other hand,

---

24. Lorna F. Hurl, "Gender and Auspice in the Development of Social Welfare in Michigan, 1869–1900," *Social Service Review* 70.4 (December 1996): 574.

25. Lorna F. Hurl and David J. Tucker, "The Michigan County Agents and the Development of Juvenile Probation," *Journal of Social History* 30.4 (Summer 1997): 909–10.

26. Walkowitz, "The Making of a Feminine Professional Identity," 1053–54. William Brock argues that social workers "were a new breed to the corridors of power" in this period. They were met with much resentment and suspicion: "Their only qualification was professional competence in a field carrying little social status." Brock, *Welfare, Democracy, and the New Deal*, 3, 30–31.

did see a place for social workers, just not in public relief work. Local officials saw relief work as a business enterprise requiring business expertise, and their viewpoint directly collided with that of professional social work in the 1930s. The debate about professionalism, and the anxiety that accompanied it, took place within and outside of social work circles, and gender was very much at the center of debates about Michigan's welfare-reorganization laws in the 1930s.[27]

Although such conflict was not universal, Michigan was certainly not alone in its battles over the role of professional social work in public relief. Susan Traverso argues that Boston's relief staff became more male-dominated in the 1920s, and more men sought relief. The rise of mothers' pensions, and investigations by women, fostered resentment among those male workers. "In short, new standards, new practices, and new female social workers challenged the tradition of poor relief in Boston, a system long administered by a staff of man with the sole prerogative to determine the needs of poor families."[28] Several groups in Illinois, including unemployment organizations, the press, and legislative groups, found social workers to be "snoopy" and arrogant. One senator called the emergency-relief workers "an oligarchy whose methods they assume to be above impeachment."[29] Some local officials in West Virginia saw social workers as "outsiders," unfamiliar with local residents or needs. Gender was a fundamental point of disagreement in West Virginia, and in one case police were called in to protect a female relief administrator.[30]

Like many other professions, social work was one segregated by race both in education and employment. Nonwhite social work professionals generally worked in agencies that served their own communities, particularly the National Association for the Advancement of Colored People and the National Urban League. Aspiring black social workers could attend most schools of social work in the North, but education in the South remained segregated. This trend prompted the creation of separate schools of social work for blacks.[31] Beulah Whitby, educated at Oberlin College, was the first African-

27. Walkowitz, *Working with Class,* 48–51, 60–62; Walkowitz, "The Making of a Feminine Professional Identity," 1053–57.

28. Susan Traverso, *Welfare Politics in Boston, 1910–1940* (Amherst and Boston: University of Massachusetts Press, 2003), 48.

29. Dwayne Charles Cole, "The Relief Crisis in Illinois during the Depression, 1930–1940," (PhD dissertation, St. Louis University, 1973), 293. Cole also argues that such accusations were not true and that social workers often allied with the Workers' Alliance to demand higher relief funds (295–96).

30. Jerry Bruce Thomas, *An Appalachian New Deal: West Virginia and the Great Depression* (Lexington: University Press of Kentucky, 1998), 122–23. Thomas found political patronage to be at the center of conflicts with local officials, an issue to be addressed in chapter 7.

31. Robenia Baker Gary and Lawrence E. Gary, "The History of Social Work Education

American supervisor in the Detroit Department of Public Welfare, in 1941, ten years after the department initially hired her. She was first a caseworker and then a supervisor in the Alfred District, which was almost entirely black. But she did not visit white clients, even if they were down the street from other families she visited: "There would be two workers on the same district which was very wasteful . . . And it definitely was segregated."[32] Whitby also served the city's Muslim community, "because they didn't know what to do with them."[33] Before working for the DPW, Whitby worked for the YWCA, but in a segregated branch. She was among the few black caseworkers in Detroit's DPW. Only a small number of African-Americans, Hispanics, or other people of color entered the mainstream profession on a large scale until the 1960s, particularly in the South.[34]

Professional organizations were a key part of controlling the profession.[35] To control the education standards and institutions of the profession is, according to sociologist Magali Sarfatti Larson, to control the knowledge base of the field, and the training also serves as "a most powerful generator of deeply shared cultural assumptions."[36] Professionals, by definition in their ideal form, have autonomy in their place of work and field: "In part, professionals live within ideologies of their own creation, which they present to the outside as the most valid definitions of specific spheres of social reality."[37] A part of the process of professionalization is exclusion, often through requirements for membership. In 1921 AASW required just four years of experience in the field of social work, reflecting in part the varied educational backgrounds of practicing social workers. By 1929, however, full membership required some college education in social work, with specified numbers of courses from accredited schools of social work.[38] The profession's goal was to require a master's degree in social work. Formal education was to be the means to entrance into the profession by 1932, as for law and medicine. In effect, the stringent requirements

for Black People 1900–1930," *Journal of Sociology and Social Welfare* 24.1 (March 1994): 68–69, 71–73.

32. Oral Interview, Beulah Whitby, transcript, 6, 11–12, Archives of Labor and Union Affairs; Stephanie J. Shaw, *What a Woman Ought to Be and Do: Black Professional Women Workers during the Jim Crow Era* (Chicago: University of Chicago Press, 1996), 189–90.

33. Whitby Interview, 18.

34. Walkowitz, *Working with Class,* 17, 65–66, 213.

35. Lubove, *The Professional Altruist,* 124–25; Ehrenreich, *The Altruistic Imagination,* 78. Psychiatric social workers organized in 1926. These specialized groups, among others, formed the National Association of Social Workers in 1955.

36. Magali Sarfatti Larson, *The Rise of Professionalism: A Sociological Analysis* (Berkeley: University of California Press, 1977), 46.

37. Ibid., xiii.

38. Lubove, *The Professional Altruist,* 131, 136–37.

excluded many social work practitioners from joining the professional organization.[39] Older social workers who had social work experience but no formal social work education were eligible for membership only if they had belonged to the AASW before the requirements changed. New relief workers, hired only because they had some formal education, were often not eligible. These standards also excluded virtually all local relief officials, including county agents, township supervisors, superintendents of the poor, and poor commissioners.

Professional organizations like the Family Welfare Association (later the Family Service Association) determined what agencies could be recognized as "accredited" in the social work profession. Member agencies engaged in family social work, largely through private social work agencies. The FWA provided field-service visits to assist agencies in social work practice and to ensure that social work methods met their standards. Annual regional, state, and national conferences provided members with opportunities to learn new developments. The FWA also helped agencies develop training programs and published the journal *The Family*.[40] Individuals could become FWA members if they were AASW members and had one year of field experience in family social work. To accommodate agency board or committee members, the FWA offered associate memberships.[41]

Assessing the membership of the FWA points to changes in public welfare prompted by FERA. Both public and private agencies were eligible for membership in the FWA, although the majority of member agencies were private. Membership opened to public agencies in 1921, but a lack of trained social work personnel usually excluded them.[42] By 1931, just eight public agencies nationwide belonged to the FWA.[43] Interest in developing professional social work in public agencies grew during the Depression years, when public agency membership increased in the FWA and similar organizations. FERA's goal to separate politics from relief administration included staffing emergency-relief

39. Walkowitz, *Working with Class,* 90.

40. "New Frontiers in Family Social Work, FWA, Its Purpose, Services, and Membership," 1933, FSA, Box 17, Membership before 1946, 2–4.

41. "New Frontiers in Family Social Work," 1933, FSA, Box 17, Membership before 1946, 6–7.

42. Brown, *Public Relief,* 54; Memo by Joanna Colcord dated November 11, 1940, FSA, Box 17, Folder Membership Public Departments. Josephine Brown argues that professional social work organizations, like the FWA, established their membership requirements for agencies in a way that excluded public welfare departments. Colcord is critical of Brown's assessment of the FWA's involvement with public agencies. Brown argues that the FWA did not admit public agencies until 1926, while Colcord notes it was five years earlier.

43. Memo to membership committee, dated March 22, 1931, FSA Records, Box 17, Folder Membership—Public Departments. Agencies were in Denver, CO; Jacksonville and Orlando, FL; Chicago, IL; Clarkston, SC; Nashville, TN; Fort Worth, TX; and Madison, WI.

agencies with trained social workers. Gauging the interest and success of public agencies seeking FWA membership in the 1930s is one way to assess the degree to which professional social work operated in public social welfare.

Before the 1930s, Michigan's public relief agencies employed almost no professional social workers, and most relief workers were men. A 1917 study found county agents to be older men with almost no social work experience. Their occupations ranged from physician to mechanic, and in rural areas farmers often served in that position.[44] A 1936 study commission on welfare issues found that most of the local poor-relief administrators—township supervisors, county agents, investigators of mothers' pensions, superintendents of the poor, or welfare directors—had no training in social work and were simply the elected official or employee assigned to the task.[45] The study also noted that most superintendents of the poor were more than forty. Investigators found superintendents beyond the age of sixty in the seventeen counties surveyed. Probate judges tended to be younger, but some were past the age of fifty. The report acknowledged that while these members thus had experience, they also were not at the peak of their abilities.[46] Education was a concern as well, since few officials had even a high school diploma. Probate judges, elected to their positions, were not required to have any specific training, and some serving on the bench had less than an eighth-grade education.[47] Saginaw County's probate judge, John Murphy, was a candidate for his second term on the Democratic ticket in 1936. He had served as court register for eighteen years, but had no formal legal training and was "sensitive about it."[48] County agents, often responsible for mothers' and old-age pensions, also were found wanting: "County agents present a discouraging picture of grade school education, short service and lack of training and experience."[49]

FERA welcomed professional social workers into its relief agencies, but finding trained workers to staff its agencies was difficult. Administrators often

44. Ellis, "Juvenile Courts and Mothers' Pensions in Michigan," 8–9. The report was conducted for the state's Child Welfare Commission and included analysis of thirty-three counties. Brown is extremely critical of the county agents and the fee schedule under which they operate. See Matson, *Local Relief to Dependents,* 19–22, 38.

45. "Local Public Welfare," WRSC Records, Box 5, Folder 10, chapter V, "Present Public Welfare Organization," 81. A study of Flint's social services (Genesee County) found that Flint's Division of the Poor—later dissolved under FERA—had eighteen employees, none of whom had training or education in social work. "The Development of Community Resources in Flint, Michigan, during Depression Years," Prepared by A. C. Findlay (Flint Institute of Research and Planning: October 1938), 6–7.

46. "Local Public Welfare," 81.

47. Ibid.

48. "Sampling Survey of Local Relief Agencies, 1936," WRSC Records, Box 6, Folder 7, Saginaw, Probate Judge.

49. "Local Public Welfare," 82.

simply hired the more educated applicants. Rural areas, in particular, had few trained social workers on staff in emergency-relief agencies.[50] In 1936, ERA staff were more educated than poor-relief officials, but not necessarily in social work. Eleven of the sixteen county administrators surveyed had some college education, and five had college degrees. Among casework supervisors, the numbers were eleven and eight, respectively. Seven had social work experience, three were teachers, and the rest had business experience.[51] Manistee and Van Buren counties both hired staff with college educations of some sort, but only Manistee's Louise Armstrong had formal social work experience. Detroit's case was similar; a 1936 survey found that about 80 percent of the staff had some college education, but only 2.4 percent had undergraduate certification in social work, and only 1.6 percent had a graduate degree.[52] Marquette and Saginaw counties also hired relief workers with college educations.

To address this problem, FERA and social work organizations offered training in social work methods to new relief workers. Time precluded graduate degrees in social work, so FERA officials sent workers to summer institutes for short courses and provided semester leaves for staff to attend college. Agencies trained staff using in-house programs, office libraries, and subscriptions to professional journals. Summer institutes provided intense training for relief workers.[53] The University of Michigan also offered some courses, both on and off campus. Institutes at what was then Michigan State College dated to the mid-1920s, but served many emergency-relief workers once the Depression hit and FERA began. The emphasis was on social casework and investigations. More than five hundred workers attended the 1934 institute.[54]

FERA provided grants to states to send social workers to schools of social work for a semester of study.[55] One thousand students attended more than twenty different professional schools in 1934–1935.[56] Officials targeted states with particularly low numbers of trained social workers, and eleven states

50. Ehrenreich, *The Altruistic Imagination,* 107–8; Brown, *Public Relief,* 277–79; Koch, "The Development of Public Relief Programs in Minnesota, 1929–1941," 71–72; and Walkowitz, *Working with Class,* 126–28.

51. "Local Public Welfare," WRSC Records, 82.

52. Sullivan, "'On the Dole,'" 180; Whalen, *Tenure, Training, and Compensation of Detroit,* 14.

53. Whalen, *Tenure, Training, and Compensation,* 12–13; "Seventh Annual Institute for Social Workers," Michigan State College, July 15–19, 1935; and Josephine Brown, "Brief Summary of the Experience of the FERA with Summer Institutes, 'In-Service' Training and Training in Schools of Social Work," FERA Records, Social Service Training (hereafter cited as FERA SST), Box 1, Folder 2.

54. SERA Letter #374, June 5, 1935, SEWRC Papers, Box 1, Folder April to June 1935; SERA Letter # 590, June 4, 1936, SEWRC Papers, Box 1, Folder April to June 1936.

55. Letter dated September 18, 1934, from Josephine Brown to the Rev. Joseph Husslein, Dean, St. Louis School of Social Work; FERA SST, Social Work, Box 71, Folder J–Z.

56. Brown, *Public Relief,* 282.

never participated. Only schools that were members of the Association of Schools of Social Work were acceptable sites of study, because of the lack of time to ensure that other programs were of the appropriate quality.[57] Maintaining professional social work standards was a key reason behind the limited number of schools eligible to participate. Many state schools had social work courses in their departments of sociology, or began new programs, with the rising demand for social workers, but were not able to participate in the FERA training program. Attendance at all programs of social work increased during the 1930s.[58]

Professional social work education, fueled by the demand for social workers, made significant strides in Michigan during the 1930s. The growing programs also had ties to the emergency-relief personnel at the state level; SERA administrators later took teaching positions at the major social work programs in Michigan, and schools worked with state officials in developing a social work curriculum. A 1938 Michigan State College report noted that "this department is becoming a potent force in the Welfare activities of the State of Michigan."[59] The University of Michigan offered courses in the 1920s, and began issuing certificates in social work in 1927. The school created its Institute for Health and Social Sciences in Detroit in 1935, offering a two-year master's program.[60] Wayne University began offering courses in social work in Detroit in 1930; this evolved into a school of public affairs and social work in 1935, when it granted its first degrees.[61] Michigan State College offered summer institutes and courses through its sociology department in the 1930s. Demand for social work education led to a one-year social work certification program in 1940.[62] Michigan's universities responded to the demand for social workers by working quickly to offer programs to educate workers.

Despite the obvious benefits of these programs, they served only a fraction of relief workers. Surveys of students reported that the education focused on urban social work; rural workers received little help in adapting urban

---

57. Ibid., 282–83. The states that did not participate included Massachusetts, Connecticut, Rhode Island, New York, Pennsylvania, Delaware, New Jersey, Maryland, and Ohio.

58. Ibid., 283.

59. Report of the Dean of Liberal Arts, *Seventy-seventh Annual Report of the Secretary of the Board of Agriculture* (Lansing: 1938), 77; Wilfred B. Shaw, ed., *The University of Michigan: An Encyclopedic Survey* (Ann Arbor: University of Michigan Press, 1941), 259–60. http://www.hti.umich.edu/u/umsurvey/.

60. Shaw, *The University of Michigan,* 259–60.

61. Whalen, *Tenure, Training, and Compensation,* 13; Leslie L. Hanawalt, *A Place of Light: The History of Wayne State University* (Detroit: Wayne State University Press, 1968), 238.

62. Report of the Dean of Liberal Arts, *Seventy-ninth Annual Report of the Secretary of the Board of Agriculture* (Lansing: 1940), 85. All three schools were accredited with the American Association of Schools of Social Work: University of Michigan in 1927, Wayne State in 1941, and MSC in 1952.

casework practices to their rural agencies. Some graduate social work programs emphasized private social work. Relief workers, however, needed further training in public, emergency-relief work, and in the specific policies and regulations that work entailed.[63] For workers in the northern part of the state and the Upper Peninsula, travel to programs such as those at MSC was not necessarily practical. (A social worker in Marquette faced a four-hundred-mile drive to East Lansing to attend an institute.)[64]

Relief workers gained most of their training in their own offices, from their supervisors. Programs ranged in formality from a deliberate set of training steps, including supervised fieldwork and competency examinations, to informal staff meetings that addressed policies, case practices, and social work. Wayne County provided a series of thirty orientation classes to new workers in 1934. Staff met weekly in small groups for further discussion and training.[65] By mid-1935, Kent County had a training schedule for all new workers. In addition to an office library and training manual, the staff developed a series of lectures by supervisors, covering a range of topics in social work. Some focused specifically on emergency-relief practices while others centered on general social work methods, including interviews, psychiatry in social work, rural problems, and ethics. The course's final stage was a written examination. Kent County's WRC also conducted a rural institute, bringing in outside speakers to cover rural social work.[66] A published staff bulletin, weekly staff meetings, and district conferences provided an ongoing training system for all relief workers. Kent County's WRC also sought to familiarize its workers with the community's resources and businesses through tours of local industries, businesses, and community agencies.[67] Weekly meetings included practical casework discussions with active case files. Staff members also took a

63. Brown, *Public Relief*, 289–290. State officials also warned staff about unaccredited correspondence courses for social work. One was advertised through a Washington DC office, but SERA warned relief workers that it was not connected to FERA and was not an appropriate way to secure additional training. SERA Letter #350, April 30, 1935, SEWRC Records, Box 1, Folder April to June 1935.

64. Social workers in the Upper Peninsula also did not have the Mackinac Bridge (completed in 1957) connecting the upper and lower peninsulas of Michigan; instead, travelers had to rely on car ferries to cross the five-mile span of water.

65. Suzanne Copland, "Detroit's In-Service Training Program," *Social Work Today* 7.5 (February 1940): 19.

66. "Training Program of the Social Services Division," Kent County Welfare Relief Commission, May 1935; FERA SST, Box 1, Folder Michigan; "Outline for Agency Self-Evaluation," August 1934, FSA Correspondence, FSA Records, Box 58, Grand Rapids Folder.

67. "Training Program," Kent County, FERA SST, Box 1, Folder Michigan. The city of Detroit and Wayne County also had formal training programs for their relief workers, covering many of the same topics. Wayne County also dealt with the rural or out-county aspects of relief work. "Intake Outline," City of Detroit ERA, and "Wayne County—Rural and Suburban Division," FERA SST, Box 1, Folder Michigan.

seventeen-week course in family casework at the University of Michigan through an extension program.[68]

Although county agencies sought to provide education for new relief workers, inadequate training was a continued problem for Detroit's DPW in the 1930s. A lack of training facilities was cited as a key concern in 1933 by the FWA, although staff were able to attend periodic seminars as well as state conferences and institutes to further their social work education. The DPW established a training center by 1937 to provide in-service instruction for DPW employees, and also to make fieldwork available for college students of social work, who were largely from the University of Michigan and Wayne University. DPW employees pursuing college degrees in social work could do their fieldwork in the Detroit agency or a private agency. Major obstacles to the continued training of social workers were funding, facilities, and a lack of support from DPW superintendents and the city government.[69]

Some Michigan counties embraced, albeit briefly, the professional practices and values of social work. Professional social workers, either on the Welfare Relief Commission or in the relief agency, were central to these efforts. Two Michigan counties earned membership in the FWA. Kent County was the first WRC in 1934; Detroit's DPW (operating as the Wayne County WRC) became a member in 1935.[70] Oakland County, in southeastern Michigan, sought membership in late 1935, but little action is recorded in the surviving files. Bay and Midland counties both began inquiries in 1939, but a car accident that seriously injured the women pushing for it stalled those efforts.[71] Genesee County sought membership in 1933, through the WRC chairperson and city manager, John Barringer. Barringer was active in the local community chest and anxious to have the newly created public department adopt social work practices. He disagreed with the director of public welfare, Milton Van Geison, a former clerk with the Buick personnel department and ardent home rule proponent. Van Geison argued that investigators were to be detectives and that relief "should be made hard for the families . . . in order to encourage them to be self-supporting." He held great disdain for professional social work

68. "Training Program," Kent County, FERA SST, Box 1, Folder Michigan.

69. Rose Porter, Memo dated July 1933, FSA Correspondence, FSA Records, Box 57, Detroit Folder 1929–1934; Questionnaire, April 21, 1937, 4, Detroit Folder, 1936–37; Rosemary Reynolds, Field Visit, Oct. 16–20, 1939, 4, FSA Records, Detroit Folder, 1938–39.

70. Memo dated January 19, 1937, FSA Records, Membership Folder. Seventeen public agencies held full membership in the FSA by 1936.

71. Rosemary Reynolds, Memo dated June 21, 1939, FSA Correspondence, FSA Records, Box 57, Bay City Folder; Rosemary Reynolds, Extra Mural Conference, June 21, 1939, FSA Correspondence, FSA Records, Box 58, Midland Folder.

in relief administration.[72] The two men's views again illustrate the divide over the question of who should administer relief. Three years later the agency still had not gained membership, although it was recognized by the FWA as one of Michigan's highest-quality public agencies.[73]

Social workers in Detroit's Department of Public Welfare first inquired about membership in 1924, although the DPW was divided on its commitment to professional social work and casework.[74] In 1929 the FWA sponsored a two-week educational institute on casework principles for DPW staff; DPW Superintendent Thomas Dolan supported professionalizing the department, although he had no formal training in social work. The revised city charter in 1918 granted the department the power to do so, but it remained largely a relief-giving agency.[75] The reality of the budget crises of 1930 and 1931 placed professionalization of the department, and membership in the FWA, on hold. Caseloads were running as high as 300 to 400 per worker, and morale was low. "[DPW social workers] said quite regretfully that each winter saw them plunged into a similar emergency situation and that the period between the emergency situations was spent chiefly in recuperating from the emergency before."[76] Professional social work practices were a luxury the DPW could not afford in the early Depression crisis. But by 1935 caseloads had dropped to between 80 and 125, and the department had established a training program for its staff. The FWA granted the DPW membership in June 1935.[77]

Federal officials recognized Kent County as having one of the best Michigan county agencies.[78] The agency first inquired about membership in February 1934, and seven months later the agency became an FWA member. Quick

72. Consultation Visit, Rose Porter, April 28 to May 11, 1933, 3, FSA Correspondence, FSA Records, Box 58, Flint Folder. Van Geison was a formidable opponent and would lead the fight to preserve local control of welfare—and its punitive nature—in the battle over welfare reorganization later in the decade.

73. FWA field investigators were doubtful about the motives for membership. They reported that the county WRC wanted the benefits of membership but was not eager to assume its responsibilities. Consultation Visit, F. R. Day, December 10, 1936, FSA Correspondence, FSA Records, Box 58, Flint Folder.

74. Consultations, David Holbrook, December 15, 1924, FSA Correspondence, FSA Records, Box 57, Michigan Prior to 1928 Folder.

75. Consultations, Ella M. Weinfurther, May 2, 1930, FSA Correspondence, FSA Records, Box 57, Detroit 1928–1935 Folder.

76. Ibid., 7–9.

77. Consultation Visit, FSA Correspondence, FSA Records, Box 57, Detroit 1931–35 Folder.

78. Memo from field representative Howard Hunter to Harry Hopkins, June 1, 1934; Harry Hopkins Papers, Box 58, FERA-WPA Narrative Field Reports, Michigan, 7. Hunter reported to Hopkins that Kent County's relief organization was "one of the best in the state" and credits social welfare activism with leading "an uprising of citizens," resulting in a new city council.

granting of membership likely arose in part from the casework supervisor, Alice Yonkman, who had both public and private social work experience. Yonkman had worked with the public agency in the early 1920s before moving to the Red Cross. The Family Service Association, a private agency and member of the FWA, hired her in 1929.[79] FWA field visitors commended Yonkman's direct manner and the quality of her case records, which showed "increasing case work treatment and more thoughtful work, and real participation on the part of the client."[80] By 1933 she had the support of Howard Hunter, head of the community chest, to lead the local WRC. Yonkman later left the FSA to work in the WRC.[81] New staff members had formal social work training, and Yonkman was committed to professional social work standards in the agency.[82] The proliferation of caseloads, which ranged from 187 to 230 per caseworker, was a concern of the FWA. But membership was recommended and the Kent County WRC joined the FWA.[83]

A county WRC board sympathetic to social work was critical in the professionalization of local agencies. All three men—a business executive, an attorney, and a township trustee—on Kent County's commission supported professional social work ideals and took an active and positive interest in its development in the public agency. When the commission changed under the revised administrative rules in early 1936, support for a social work organization continued under Probate Judge Clark Higbee, a member of the Welfare and Relief Study Commission.[84] Detroit's Public Welfare Commission (PWC) and the Wayne County WRC included some members who had backgrounds in social work and social work education, and who were active in either public or private welfare work in the city. James Fitzgerald, who was PWC chairperson for several years, was executive secretary of the city's St. Vincent de Paul Society. Other members had affiliations with the Jewish Social Service Bureau, the Council of Social Agencies, and the city's medical community.

---

79. *Polk's Grand Rapids City Directory* (Grand Rapids: Grand Rapids Directory Company, 1922), 907. From 1922 to 1925 Yonkman was listed as a social service worker, but with no place of employment specified. By 1926 she was a supervisor with the city social service department and in 1929 began working for the FSA. She disappeared from the city directory in 1935.

80. E. M. Weinfurther, "Summary of Contacts," March 19, 1931, FSA Records, Box 58, Grand Rapids folder.

81. Consultation Visit, Rose Porter, July 17–18, 1933, 4–6; Consultation Visit, Rose Porter, June 13–14, 1934, 4, FSA Records, Box 58, Grand Rapids Folder.

82. Rose Porter, Consultation Visit, June 16, 1934, 4, FSA Correspondence, FSA Records, Box 58, Grand Rapids Folder.

83. Consultation Visit, Margaret Wead, October 1934, FSA Correspondence, FSA Records, Box 58, Grand Rapids Folder.

84. Consultation Visit, Rosemary Reynolds, November 9 and 12, 1937, FSA Correspondence, FSA Records, Box 58, Grand Rapids Folder.

Fitzgerald also served as chair of the county's WRC. Other members included Frederic Siedenburg, a Catholic priest active in the Council of Social Agencies, and Ruth Whipple. Whipple served on the Plymouth City Commission and also was active in the Women's Christian Temperance Union, the League of Women Voters, and the Business and Professional Women's Club.[85] City officials were often hostile to social work in the administration of public welfare, but the social work background of commission members helped to counter their opposition.

The FWA was willing to work with those public agencies that chose to instill professional social work into their programs. But such efforts were not very successful during the 1930s. Just two of Michigan's eighty-three counties actually gained membership, and only a handful more sought FWA support. Thus the active drive for professionalization was small and brief, as events would further reinforce by the decade's end. Most county agencies professionalized only to secure federal and state funds, and resisted even that.

THE REALITY OF RELIEF WORK

The rhetoric of professionalization rang hollow for some relief workers, and speaks further to the competing visions of professionalization in this period, even within the profession. College-educated but untrained in professional social work, these workers were at the heart of debates about the definition of social work and the expertise needed for welfare administration. Low salaries continued to be one of several issues relief workers—experienced and not—faced in the emergency-relief period, and yet their salaries were the focus of criticism regarding SERA's administrative costs. Relief workers, however, saw their wages and working conditions as grievances to be addressed. The contest over professional standards and labor issues prompted some new relief workers to pursue union organization as a means to gain higher wages and job security. These relief workers did not entirely reject professionalization but, rather, used it to further their cause. The union movement met opposition within the profession, and social work union activists faced reprisals for their outspoken advocacy on behalf of themselves and their clients.

Despite the rhetoric of professionalization, relief workers did not earn a professional wage, even before the 1930s. Salaries among the "elite psychiatric and medical case workers" in urban areas were about $150 per month

85. Consultation Visit, Florence Day, FSA Correspondence, FSA Records, Box 57, Folder Detroit 1936–37; Herbert S. Case, ed., *Who's Who in Michigan* (Munsing: 1936), 357, 423.

($1800 per year), while most social workers, concentrated largely in family- and child-welfare agencies, earned between $90 and $125. Wages for social workers increased just 3 percent from 1913 to 1926, and most social workers earned slightly less than skilled industrial workers. Daniel Walkowitz argues that a wage of $1,800 in the 1920s earned social workers a "bare existence." Few social workers earned a middle-class standard of living.[86] This continued to be true in the 1930s, when wages rose little and SERA constantly faced criticism about administrative costs and high salaries. The average caseworker salary in 1936 was $1,573, a monthly salary of about $131. But 20 percent of the welfare department in Detroit earned more than $2,500 per year, "nearly twice as much as the average auto worker."[87] This group likely included administrators and supervisors. The average relief worker earned much less.

According to SERA, Michigan's casework supervisors earned an average monthly salary of $127.93, while caseworkers and investigators earned an average monthly salary of $89.31 in the first year of SERA's operations. The average salary for other workers, largely clerical and office staff, was $85.97.[88] Investigators, home visitors, and aides were paid between $70 and $90; the positions required a high school education and a "desire to learn to do social work." Caseworkers earned between $90 and $105 and were required either to be a college graduate with a year of social work experience, or to have two or more years of experience in a related field along with a year of formal social work training. Senior caseworkers earned between $105 and $130 and had to be eligible for junior membership in the AASW; their responsibilities included supervision of other caseworkers. Supervisors earned from $120 to $175. Administrators' salaries depended on the county's population, with larger counties having higher-paid administrators. Monthly salaries ranged from $90 to $300. Clerical workers were paid from $60 to $100, depending on the level of responsibility.[89] Van Buren County's administrator received $140 per month ($1,680 per year) in October 1934, while the deputy administrator and supervisor each received $130 per month. Caseworkers received $80 per month and the stenographer's monthly salary was $70.[90]

86. Walkowitz, *Working with Class*, 100; Walker, "Privately Supported Social Work," 1191.

87. Sullivan, "'On the Dole,'" 180, footnote 68; see Whalen, *Tenure, Training, and Compensation*, 35, 51. Sullivan mistakenly quotes that annual median income is $1,673.

88. Haber and Stanchfield, *Unemployment and Relief in Michigan*, 61.

89. SERA Letter #188, October 16, 1934, FERA SST, Box 4, Michigan—Personnel Folder. Van Buren and Marquette fell in the second-tier salary schedule, while Saginaw was in the third tier and Wayne County in the fifth tier. Placement was based on population.

90. State Personnel Dept., Salary Schedule, Van Buren County, October 25, 1934; Records of Van Buren County Emergency Welfare Relief Commission (hereafter cited as VB EWRC Records), Archives and Regional History Collections, Western Michigan University, Box 1, Folder 23.

To refute the charges of waste and excessive spending, SERA published the report *Cost of Administration in the Emergency Relief Program* in 1935, and also addressed the issue in its first two annual reports. The reports state that SERA's administrative costs were just 8.5 percent of first-year expenditures, and 9.4 percent the second year.[91] SERA also reported that 6.7 cents of each dollar spent went to pay salaries of employees in the first year (the rest paid for travel, office supplies, and rent), or about 8 percent of the total cost of relief programs.[92]

To limit relief spending and to refute charges of wasteful spending, SERA regularly ordered reinvestigations to ensure that people receiving relief remained in need.[93] Such reinvestigations were another issue of contention for relief workers. Public criticism regarding the number of "chiselers" on the relief rolls prompted SERA to undertake a major reevaluation of its caseload in December 1934. Every head of household on relief received a letter stating that their case would be closed; if the family was still in need they had to reapply. Each letter included a two-week grocery order, which would allow the family "that length of time to make other plans." When possible, a different caseworker was assigned to those people who did reapply, to avoid any preconceptions about the family.[94] Van Buren County's acting administrator, M. D. Cook, announced the program in a front-page article in the *Hartford Day Spring* in February of 1935, and new caseworkers were hired to help. The WRC dropped between forty and fifty cases each week.[95] Cook advised that the WRC was not seeking to deny relief to anyone in need, but wrote that "the burden of proof for such need will rest entirely with the applicant . . . Applicants who have not proven the need for relief will be rejected and so informed."[96]

Some welfare-relief commissions sought the assistance of local citizens to uncover anyone cheating the system, a practice not endorsed by SERA but

---

91. Haber and Stanchfield, *Unemployment and Relief in Michigan*, 60; Haber and Stanchfield, *Unemployment, Relief, and Economic Security* (Lansing: 1936), 27; and Michigan State Emergency Welfare Relief Commission, *Cost of Administration in the Emergency Relief Program* (Lansing, 1935), 7. The latter publication found that administrative costs were just 8.14 percent in the first three months of FERA.

92. Haber and Stanchfield, *Unemployment and Relief in Michigan*, 61. Comparable figures are not available for the second year.

93. SERA Letter #156, September 20, 1934, SEWRC Papers, Box 1, Folder July to September 1934; SERA Letter #352, May 1, 1935, SEWRC Papers, Box 1, Folder April to June 1935.

94. Haber and Stanchfield, *Unemployment, Relief, and Economic Security*, 219.

95. M. D. Cook, "Welfare Rolls in Van Buren to Be Revised," *Hartford Day Spring*, February 6, 1935, 8.

96. Cook, "Welfare Rolls," 1.

nevertheless implemented by some agencies.[97] The use of "gossip" in welfare investigation was not new, and is a significant continuity in relief work. In some cases, agencies invited "spying" by residents, and fostered the assumption that relief recipients were likely dishonest.[98] Manistee County, which undertook its own reinvestigation independent of the WRC in November of 1934, also sought information provided by residents. The *Manistee News-Advocate* ran front-page forms for residents to use to report so-called "chiselers" (see figure 5.1). The cases were then reinvestigated by a special committee appointed by the mayor.[99] Clients had to prove their need and agencies encouraged citizens to inform on their neighbors and fellow residents. Although administrators rejected the notion that they asked their workers to be detectives, some did pressure caseworkers to do so.[100]

Reinvestigations did reduce the relief rolls. SERA reported that about 15 percent of cases in some counties remained closed, although reports noted that increased employment opportunities in industry and agriculture explained some of the decline in need. SERA found that between 5 and 7 percent of relief recipients were not entitled to aid.[101] Van Buren closed 213 cases (more than 30 percent of the caseload) in the first three months of its reinvestigation. Two-thirds of those dropped never reapplied for relief, and apparently either had the resources to manage or simply did not want to endure the extensive reinvestigation. Most of the remaining cases simply had "adequate resources," according to the WRC report.[102]

97. Cook, "Welfare Rolls," 8; Haber and Stanchfield, *Unemployment, Relief, and Economic Security,* 219–20. Haber and Stanchfield do not discuss using residents to report on relief recipients in their coverage of this program. See "Anti-Chiseling Group Carries on with Work," *Manistee News-Advocate,* November 22, 1934, 1, 8; copy in Armstrong Papers, Box 1, Reviews Folder.

98. Margaret Hillyard Little, "'He Said, She Said': The Role of Gossip in Determining Single Mothers' Eligibility for Welfare," *Journal of Policy History* 11.4 (1999): 434, 442–43, 446; Little documents the use of welfare hotlines in more-contemporary welfare administration in Canada. Melanie Tebbutt, *Women's Talk? A Social History of "Gossip" in Working-Class Neighborhoods, 1880–1960* (Brookfield: Ashgate Publishing Company, 1995), 1–2. Tebbut's work is on working-class women in Great Britain. Few scholars have directly considered gossip in the administrative operation of American social welfare.

99. "Welfare Group Issues Complaint Call," *Manistee News-Advocate,* November 15, 1934; Edward W. Pfeiffer, "Your Cooperation Is Needed! Please Help," *Manistee News-Advocate,* November 22, 1934. Pfeiffer was the editor of the *Manistee News-Advocate.*

100. Frances Fox Piven and Richard A. Cloward, *Regulating the Poor: The Functions of Public Welfare,* Rev. Ed. (New York: Vintage, 1993), 177. The authors argue that professionalism in social work did little to improve the dispensing of relief, and they assert that although social work was to make the process more humane, the results were not that different from those of poor-relief methods.

101. Haber and Stanchfield, *Unemployment, Relief, and Economic Security,* 220.

102. "Van Buren Cuts 213 Families off Its Relief Rolls," *Hartford Day Spring,* May 8, 1935, 1.

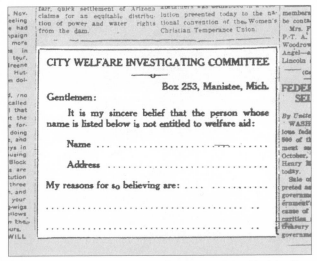

Figure 5.1 Form published on the front page of the *Manistee News-Advocate,* November 15, 1934, seeking information on welfare fraud.

Detroit also underwent several investigations to purge the relief rolls, particularly under the leadership of conservative mayors intent on removing chiselers. Richard Reading, elected mayor in 1937, specifically targeted the city DPW's practice of allowing the United Auto Workers to investigate members seeking relief. Reading used police officers to investigate current welfare recipients' cases. He also sought to have all relief applicants sign a "notarized affidavit attesting to their financial status and need." Having such a document would make it easier to prosecute relief recipients who defrauded the DPW. He "urged that a program be worked out whereby the so-called chiselers and drones would be entirely eliminated from relief rolls."[103] Professional social workers harshly criticized Reading's plans, but to little avail. His crusade did result in closed cases, but found fraud in just one in three hundred cases, and restitution agreements brought in just under twenty-four thousand dollars—far less than the cost of the investigation to the department.[104]

Despite efforts to reduce the number of relief recipients, caseloads for relief workers remained high. Social work guidelines warned against more than 150 cases for each public relief investigator. However, only twenty-six of Michigan's eighty-three counties had caseloads below 150 in January 1935; the

103. Fine, *Frank Murphy: The New Deal Years,* 472–73; Detroit Public Welfare Commission minutes, February 15, 1938, 143.
104. Sullivan, "'On the Dole,'" 205, 207–11; Detroit Public Welfare Commission minutes, January 11, 13, 18, 28, 1938, 118–19, 122–24, 130.

state average, excluding Wayne County, was actually 175. Forty-two counties had caseloads between 150 and 250 and thirteen counties averaged more than 250 cases per investigator.[105] In December of 1936, Van Buren County's WRC reported that its caseload was 285, not including service-only cases, which were about fourteen per investigator.[106] The problem persisted throughout the emergency-relief years. When SERA told the Van Buren County WRC that staff numbers had to be cut in 1939, administrator Louise Wilkinson argued that any reductions in investigators and caseworkers were impossible. Caseloads were already as high as seven hundred, and a resolution by the county's WRC reiterated her position.[107] Such high caseloads placed incredible pressure on relief workers who sought to investigate that many families properly.

Autonomy and control over daily tasks are key to the definition of a profession.[108] Relief workers did have some measure of control over their workday, although high caseloads and limited budgets placed great strain on maintaining a forty-hour workweek. Clerks prepared work schedules for social workers to enable caseworkers to leave the office shortly after reporting for work. In a two-week cycle, relief workers spent eight days in the field, visiting families and conducting home visits. Caseworkers returned to the office in the early afternoon to dictate case histories and submit relief requisitions for that day. They had one day each week in the office for appointments (for families they had difficulty finding at home or for complaints), and used their remaining time after field visits for emergency requests and work on new cases.[109]

The day of a caseworker was thus controlled in some measure by the office, but caseworkers determined what families to visit and set appointments and office visits. They were not confined to the office and determined their day within the larger time frame of field and office work. Clerical staff provided

105. SEWRC, *Cost of Administration,* 10. The SERA study included data for only eighty-one of the state's eighty-three counties. A study by *Social Work Today* found that the average caseload in twenty-three agencies was 129. Caseloads ranged from 80 in New York City to 250 in Milwaukee. Ten of the public agencies surveyed were in the Midwest, although the study does not list which cities were included; Detroit likely was one. George Hedin, "Salaries and Working Conditions in Public Relief Agencies," *Social Work Today,* 2.6 (May 1935): 12.

106. Letter from Van Buren WRC to Helen Daley, Field Case Representative, December 30, 1936; VB EWRC Records, Box 1, Folder 10. Service-only cases were those that received no material relief but were eligible for surplus commodities and clothing; clients under the WPA and Rural Resettlement programs were among those classed as "service only."

107. Letter from Helen Daley to George Granger, December 30, 1936; VB EWRC Records, Box 1, Folder 10.

108. Larson, *The Rise of Professionalism,* xii, 182–87. Larson defines social work as an organizational profession, dependent on the state's expansion of social services. "True" professions (she cites the example of the medical profession) have complete control over their workday, with no outside interference.

109. Report by Irene Murphy, supervisor of casework for Detroit Department of Public Welfare, 1935; FSA Correspondence, Wayne County folder; FSA Records.

support by typing case histories and correspondence, and preparing checks and relief requisitions, but a typical relief worker faced long and hectic days trying to successfully serve the high caseload assigned. Each case, when first investigated, required significant document collection and verification, including financial information, birth and marriage documents, medical statements (if applicable), residence verification, and employment checks. In Detroit, a caseworker might visit fifteen families on a given day.[110] Home visits were the primary contact with clients, although how often caseworkers visited families depended on their caseload, since on a given day they also may have had to contact other individuals or agencies, including schools, private welfare agencies, and businesses, to investigate a child's school attendance, other aid received, or the employment status of a member of the household. Cases that involved questions about eligibility or suspicion of the validity of a client's claims demanded much more time and attention. Caseworkers faced hostility and distrust on many visits, and often were the targets of verbal abuse from recipients, at times for issues beyond their control. It is easy to envision the harried nature of such work and the frustrations of high caseloads with too little time to complete the work.

UNIONIZING RELIEF WORKERS

Low salaries and high caseloads were among the issues that fueled the rise of the union movement, known as the rank and file movement, in the 1920s and 1930s. Social workers employed in private agencies in New York City were the original organizers of the movement,[111] which spread outside of New York by 1932; the following year it had thirteen organizations in private agencies in eight cities, including Detroit. In 1934 unions began to enter public agencies, but remained concentrated in the largest American cities, including Chicago, Detroit, Los Angeles, Minneapolis, and New York City.[112] The movement's leadership began publishing *Social Work Today,* the journal dedicated to trade unionism and the rank and file movement, in 1934, and held its first national conference in 1936.[113]

110. Report by Irene Murphy, 1935.
111. Rick Spano, *The Rank and File Movement* (Washington, D.C.: University Press of America, 1982), 45–47; Walkowitz, *Working with Class*, 122–25.
112. Rick Spano, *The Rank and File Movement*, 68–69; Koch, "The Development of Public Relief Programs in Minnesota," 264–65; and "Rank and File: Detroit and Cleveland," *Social Work Today* 1.2 (May–June 1934): 23.
113. Leslie Alexander, "Organizing the Professional Social Worker: Union Development in Voluntary Social Work, 1930–1950," (PhD dissertation, Bryn Mawr College, Graduate School of Social Work, 1976), 84, 86–87.

The influx of new relief workers was one factor in the growth of social work unionism in the 1930s.[114] Rank and file members challenged the AASW's standards, and offered an alternate vision of professionalization.[115] Many of these workers could not meet AASW professional guidelines; the shift in emphasis to formal education placed professional recognition farther out of reach for most relief workers. Low salaries, long hours, poor working conditions, a lack of grievance procedures, and little job security were the chief concerns of relief workers. Public agency workers faced the worst conditions. Many of them had the highest caseloads and the poorest working conditions of any social workers. Because professional organizations were not at their disposal, some turned to unions to address their problems.[116] But union members did not entirely reject professionalization; many employed professional language and credentials in their negotiations on behalf of themselves and their clients.[117]

Michigan's social work union movement originated in Detroit, and expanded to include four other counties and cities as well as a statewide organization by the decade's end (see map 5.1). The Wayne County Social Workers' Association formed in 1934 and, like many public agency groups, affiliated with the Congress of Industrial Organization, in 1937, as Local 79, under the State, County and Municipal Workers of America.[118] Some unions, including the Detroit group, represented not only caseworkers but also clerks and Detroit Receiving Hospital support staff.[119]

114. Jacob Fisher, "Trade Unionism in Social Work," *Social Work Year Book, 1937* (New York: Russell Sage Foundation, 1937), 502.

115. Leslie Leighninger, *Social Work: Search for Identity* (New York: Greenwood Press, 1987), 39–42.

116. Alexander, "Organizing the Professional Social Worker," 64–67; Walkowitz, *Working with Class*, 83–85, 136–40. Walkowitz assesses the involvement of the AASW in grievance procedures for caseworkers, illustrating that some relief workers did not share the AASW's vision of social work.

117. For a discussion of language and professionalization, see JoAnne Brown, "Professional Language: Words That Succeed," *Radical History Review* 34 (1986): 33–51.

118. The Wayne County group originally organized as the Detroit Association of Social Workers but changed its name a year later. See "Directory of Rank and File Organizations," *Social Work Today* 2.3 (January 1935): 31. "A Budget for Human Needs: Analysis of the Department of Public Welfare Budget, 1940–1941," Research and Standards Committee, Local 79, State, County, and Municipal Workers of America, Pre-1970s Vertical Files, ALUA, Box 59, Folder: Public Welfare—1940s, 34. Local 79 represented only city workers; county workers organized in Local 116 of the SCMWA. Most public social workers who unionized organized within the SCMWA, the American Federation of Labor's AFSCME. Social workers in private agencies often joined the United Office and Professional Workers of America, also affiliated with the CIO. Alexander, "Organizing the Professional Social Worker," 136; Walkowitz, *Working with Class*, 121.

119. Sharon Hartman Strom argues that social service employee unions—often comprised largely of women—tended to include clerks and other support staff in their groups. She also

Map 5.1 Rank and file unions, 1934–40

No details of Local 79's membership are available, but a 1938 study of Detroit social workers found that the DPW's social workers were 87 percent female and 94 percent white.[120] Clerical workers were also largely female by the Depression years, and thus women likely made up a major portion of the union's potential membership.[121] Although concentrated in a minority of

---

argues that the Congress of Industrial Organizations gave little support or encouragement to its government employee unions (United Federal Workers; State, County, and Municipal Workers of America; and the United Office and Professional Workers of America). In addition, their options were more limited because they could not strike, which also would have gone against the rank and file movement's dual purpose of aiding both workers and clients. Sharon Hartman Strom, "'We're no Kitty Foyles': Organizing Office Workers for the Congress of Industrial Organizations, 1937–1950," in *Women, Work, and Protest: A Century of US Women's Labor History,* ed. Ruth Milkman (Boston: Routledge & Kegan Paul, 1985), 212–15; Strom, "Challenging 'Woman's Place': Feminism, the Left, and Industrial Unionism in the 1930s," *Feminist Studies* 9 (Summer 1983): 371–72.

120. They were also relatively well educated, with just 14 percent with no college credits. Whalen, *Tenure, Training, and Compensation,* 3, 55, 57.

121. Mark McColloch, *White Collar Workers in Transition: The Boom Years, 1940–1970* (Westport: Greenwood Press, 1983), 21; Strom, "'We're No Kitty Foyles,'" 212–15; and Strom,

public agencies, the union movement nonetheless is significant for the issues it raised and for its involvement in cases that attracted the attention of labor and civil rights groups. The movement first appeared at the Michigan State Conferences of Social Work in December 1935. Reports in *Social Work Today* noted that the rank and file sessions attracted "real if somewhat skeptical interest" and that the final session was attended by more than fifty social workers.[122]

One result of the state conference was the formation of a Michigan State Coordinating Committee of Rank and File Groups to serve as a centralized state network of rank and file groups, and to assist other local groups in organizing. The state committee participated in national rank and file conferences, giving Michigan social workers a voice in the national movement.[123] It evolved into the Michigan Federation of Social Agency Employees, organized at a state rank and file conference in January 1936, becoming one of just three state organizations in the rank and file movement.[124] Twenty-three county public agencies and twelve private groups sent delegations, and membership in the state organization was open to all employees in social agencies in Michigan.[125] Formal unions organized in Washtenaw County (centered in Ann Arbor) in 1935, and caseworkers in Kalamazoo and St. Clair counties organized rank and file groups in 1936. Agency workers in Dearborn, also in southeastern Michigan, organized in 1939.[126] (See map 5.1.)

Union representatives' negotiations with their respective agencies reflected the dual purpose of the organized social work movement: to ensure that social services provided adequately for clients' needs while also addressing the labor and professional issues important to the caseworkers. Union members believed their two goals were connected: only a trained, professional staff, in conjunction with adequate relief budgets, could make certain that clients received the

"Challenging 'Women's Place,'" 371–72. Historians have documented the feminization of clerical work in several works, including Margery W. Davies, *Woman's Place Is at the Typewriter* (Philadelphia: Temple University Press, 1982), and Lisa M. Fine, *The Souls of the Skyscrapers: Female Clerical Workers in Chicago, 1870–1930* (Philadelphia: Temple University Press, 1990).

122. See telegram regarding rank and file movement and the Michigan Conference of Social work, October 24, 1935, FERA State Series, Michigan, Box 140, Complaints, Folder T–Z; and "Detroit Salutes the Conference," *Social Work Today*, 5.2 (November 1937): 27. The Wayne County Social Workers Association sponsored a lecture at the conference by Dr. Tucker Smith, President of Brookwood Labor College, in 1937.

123. "Rank and File: At State Conferences," *Social Work Today* 3.3 (December 1935): 26; "Relief; Work; Staff: Where Workers in Public Agencies Stand," *Social Work Today* 3.4 (January 1936): 11–12.

124. Others formed in Ohio and Pennsylvania. See "Directory of Rank and File Organizations," *Social Work Today* 3.1 (October 1935): 31.

125. "From the Field," *Social Work Today* 3.6 (March 1936): 26.

126. "From the Field," *Social Work Today* 4.1 (October 1936): 26; "Trade Unions in Social Work," *Social Work Today* 6.9 (June 1939): 40.

services and assistance they needed.[127] The constitution for the Kalamazoo County Federation of Social Workers "provide[d] for the protection of the interest of both employees and clients," and St. Clair County workers called for "collective action for client and worker security."[128] Detroit social workers aimed to "further cooperative action and mutual understanding between the various divisions within the Department of Public Welfare . . . and to improve the professional standards of its members."[129] Unions sought to work for improvement of larger social services, such as the expansion of the provisions of the Social Security Act. They protested cuts in travel allowances and pushed for grievance procedures; they also fought for more-adequate food budgets for clients when food costs rose steeply.[130]

Perhaps the most visible role for the unions was defending the right of social workers both to organize themselves and to participate in the organization of their clients. Union activity could have severe consequences for relief workers, regardless of their experience or ability. Caseworkers in both Wayne and Washtenaw counties were fired or demoted because of organizational activities. Wayne County's Local 79 did not appear before Detroit's Public Welfare Commission or Common Council until 1937, when it mobilized to protest the suspension of several employees, including Rachel Norber, a founding member of Local 79, for alleged inefficiency. The case galvanized the union around the right of employees to a fair hearing before discharge and the right to unionize. Unionization was recognized as a means not only to protect professional workers' rights as employees, but also to safeguard professional standards for those workers.[131] Norber eventually regained her job five months after her discharge, when the Civil Service Commission ordered the PWC to reinstate her and to pay her for the time off, and she lost no seniority

127. Walkowitz, *Working with Class*, 124–25; Alexander, "Organizing the Professional Social Worker," 10, 50, 64–67.

128. "From the Field," *Social Work Today* 4.1 (October 1936): 26.

129. "Directory of Rank and File Organizations," *Social Work Today* 2.3 (January 1935): 31.

130. Florence Gardner, "Not Without Protest," *Social Work Today* 5.1 (October 1937): 22; "A Budget for Human Needs." Martin Sullivan makes no mention of the union movement among social workers in his study of relief in Detroit and argues, "At no time during the Thirties did Welfare Department employees in Detroit participate in, or lend overt support to, demonstrations by clients or by radical pressure groups." While this may be true for many of the DPW's employees, it is too broad a statement and ignores the efforts of the Wayne County social worker union. Sullivan, "'On the Dole,'" 180.

131. Ibid. Union members also voted to affiliate with the SCMWA of the CIO during this period, and their issues overlapped with those advocated in the eight-point program of the state SCMWA. See Alexander Taylor, "State, County Union Lists Important Gains," *Michigan CIO News,* September 25, 1939.

or vacation credit.[132] In addition, the union gained the PWC pledge to allow all employees a hearing before the commission considered their discharge.[133] Several months after the Norber case was decided, the commission revisited the issue of discharging and suspending employees, adopting a formal four-step process. The revised policy again guaranteed employees a hearing before either a discharge or a suspension.[134] The union would use the strength it gained from this battle to defend the rights of both union members and relief recipients.

In this case, Local 79 defended professional status as it fought for Norber's job and union rights. Norber had received no advance notice of her suspension or her discharge. Following critical reports by the director of personnel at a special public welfare commission meeting, with the support of Superintendent Gerald Harris, the commission voted to discharge Norber in June of 1937.[135] In response to the charges, one month later Norber argued that she had lost her job because of her union activism, and not because of inefficiency, a stance supported by the national rank and file journal *Social Work Today*.[136] She based her defense on her abilities as a trained social worker. Hired in 1930 as a family investigator, Norber had passed the civil service examination in 1935 and had then been promoted to student caseworker.[137] She was working on her bachelor's degree in social work from Wayne University, and had received at least one educational leave in 1936 to pursue that goal.[138] Norber questioned the validity of the report on her inefficiency because it was drafted by the Field Work Observation Bureau, an agency, she charged, that knew little about social work or casework practices or DPW policy. She was a professional social worker, even though she did not yet have her degree, and was judged, she argued, by those who did not have the appropriate credentials. Their information, subjectively and inaccurately presented, was then used by

132. Numerous other organizations joined to support Norber and the union's cause, including the Wayne County and Michigan Conference for the Protection of Civil Rights, the Professional League for Civil Rights, the Women's Auxiliary of the UAW, the WPA Union, and other local unions. Samuel Kellman, "Detroit and Los Angeles Victories," *Social Work Today* 5.4 (January 1938): 13; "Regains Her Job in Welfare," *Detroit Times*. November 23, 1937; Gardner, "Not Without Protest," 22; and "Civil Rights Body Protests Firing of Social Worker," *Detroit Labor News,* June 25, 1937.

133. "Proceedings of the Public Welfare Commission," vol. 11, June 11, 1937, 7.

134. "Proceedings of the Public Welfare Commission," vol. 12, October 25, 1938, 30.

135. "Proceedings of the Public Welfare Commission," vol. 11, June 11, 1937, 6–7.

136. Gardner, "Not Without Protest," 21–22.

137. "Proceedings of the Public Welfare Commission," vol. 11, June 11, 1937, 6.

138. "Proceedings of the Public Welfare Commission," vol. 10, June 23, 1936, 135; Whalen, *Tenure, Training, and Compensation,* 21–24.

her supervisors to obtain her discharge.[139] Her professional status, even though she had not completed her formal study, was the cornerstone of her defense.

In contrast, the union apparently remained silent about the removal of the family investigators, or those untrained relief workers hired in 1930 and 1931—like Norber—to help with rising caseloads. The 1937–38 reclassification plan eliminated that job category; most family investigators who had not been promoted as Norber had faced either dismissal or demotion. The group argued that their six to seven years of service qualified them as professionals. They had attended conferences and professional training programs, and often worked overtime with no additional compensation because they had been told they were professionals.[140] Significantly, the group did not use the union, either Local 79 or any other employee organization, to pursue its case. The union's silence on this issue, just a few months before Norber's situation, illuminates its commitment to a trained, professional staff that employed professionalization as a means to further unionization.

Washtenaw County's social workers engaged in a similar battle with their supervisors. Milton Kemnitz, a supervisor, was demoted to caseworker, because, co-workers alleged, of Kemnitz's efforts to organize the unemployed and relief clients.[141] Henry Meyer, an agency caseworker, was fired for protesting Kemnitz's demotion. The WRC issued a statement shortly after the incidents, outlining policies prohibiting employees, both on and off work, from engaging in organizational activities that "might lead to controversial discussions regarding relief policies of the organization, or which might lead to criticism from the general public." The commission also stated, however, that it was "not opposed to the organization of case workers or other employees."[142]

---

139. "Proceedings of the Public Welfare Commission," vol. 11, July 13, 1937, 19–20.

140. Letter to Mayor Frank Couzens from Family Investigator Group, March 9, 1937; Detroit Mayor's Papers, 1937, Box 7, Burton Historical Collections.

141. Letter from Washtenew County Rank and File Social Workers to Aubrey Williams, Assistant FERA and WPA Administrator, dated October 8, 1935; FERA State Series, Michigan, Box 140, Complaints, Folder T–Z; "Michigan Cracks Down," *Social Work Today* 3.2 (November 1935): 3; "Review of Case of Washtenaw County Welfare Workers Discriminated against for Organizational Activity," Conference for the Protection of Civil Rights, Detroit, and letter to Frank Martel, President, Detroit and Wayne County Federation of Labor, from J. H. Bollens, Chairman, Conference, dated November 15, 1935, Wayne County AFL-CIO Collection, ALUA, Box 23, Welfare Department Folder; and Letter from Edith Foster, Regional Social Worker to Elizabeth Wickenden, Asst. Director, WPA, dated January 3, 1935; FERA State Series, Michigan, Box 140, Complaints, Folder T–Z. I believe the date on this letter is an error; it should be January of 1936, given the sequence of prior events.

142. Memo to "All Employees of the Washtenaw County Welfare Commission," from C. H. Elliot, administrator, n.d., FERA State Series, Michigan, Box 140, Complaints, Folder T–Z.

The case attracted the attention of labor and civil liberties groups, including the Detroit and Wayne County Federation of Labor, as well as several other rank and file groups. An investigation by state and federal officials, working with the Conference for the Protection of Civil Rights in Detroit and an Ann Arbor civil liberties group (both of which were active in defense of the caseworkers), found that the WRC had "acted in anger" and without the knowledge or approval of the casework supervisor.[143] At a review of Kemnitz's case, clients and caseworkers supported his work, while public officials, including local mayors, spoke against his performance.[144] Meyer was reinstated as a caseworker, but was transferred to Battle Creek.[145] The resolution of Kemnitz's case is unclear regarding his demotion, but he apparently did not leave the agency.[146]

The position of the State Emergency Relief Administration on unionization is not clear. SERA administrator William Haber believed in the right of social workers "to organize into a union for the purpose of improving their own condition." Haber did not take a public stand on the issue, but did tell union members that they "may rest assured that the entire matter will be presented very sympathetically to the State Relief Commission."[147] He did not support "active participation in the organization of clients by the case worker," but left the final decision to the state commission.[148] But while Haber opposed the alliance of caseworkers with their clients, he did back the right of social workers to organize, particularly to address issues such as low salaries.[149]

143. Letter from Foster to Wickenden, January 3, 1935 [sic]; "Civil Liberties in Michigan," *Social Work Today* 2.4 (January 1936): 19.

144. Public officials also criticized Manistee County administrator Louise Armstrong, who refused to follow the tenets of local officials and instead followed state rules. When pressed to resign, she refused, and SERA supported her. The critical difference, apparently, is that she was not attempting to organize relief clients. See Armstrong, *We Too Are the People*, 188–89; SEWRC Minutes, April 10, 1934, Box 1, Folder 1; "Rengo, Peterson Desire to Quit Welfare Body," *Manistee News-Advocate*, April 12, 1934; "Will Act upon Resignations Late Next Week," *Manistee News-Advocate*, April 13, 1934; and "Local Welfare Problems Increase," *Manistee News-Advocate*, November 9, 1934.

145. "Civil Liberties in Michigan," 19.

146. Rank and file members also mobilized against the dismissal of another Washtenaw County social worker, Louise Stellwagen, who was secretary of the rank and file group. The outcome of that case is also unclear, although the circumstances were similar to the case of Kemnitz, who regularly contributed articles to *Social Work Today* about rank and file activities in Michigan. See "Difficult to Supervise," *Social Work Today* 3.4 (January 1936): 25.

147. Letter from Haber to Frank Martel, Detroit and Wayne Federation of Labor, dated November 22, 1935, Wayne County AFL-CIO Collection, ALUA, Box 23, Welfare Department Folder.

148. "Civil Liberties in Michigan," 19. The minutes of the SEWRC include no references to the unionization of social workers.

149. "Civil Liberties in Michigan," 20.

The rank and file movement remained concentrated in large cities but had organizations in fifteen states, including Michigan, Ohio, and Illinois, by 1938. Public agency organizations tended to affiliate with the State, County and Municipal Workers of America while private agency groups were affiliated with the United Office and Professional Workers of America, both a part of the Congress of Industrial Organizations.[150] Active in four counties and one city in Michigan, the rank and file movement did strike a chord with social workers, particularly those in public agencies. An important question is why social workers organized in those counties but not in others, including Marquette, Saginaw, and Van Buren. The lack of organization in Saginaw County is the most puzzling, as the area already had a union presence in the auto-related factories and was also the site of organized protests by work-relief recipients. But no evidence of an organization of relief workers is evident. Regional representatives were able to minimize the influence and appeal of the rank and file movement, but it is likely that many relief workers shared the frustrations and concerns articulated by the rank and file movement.[151]

Roadblocks to social work unions in general were significant, including ideological conflicts between labor organizing and professions, the high turnover in relief-agency staff, and regional hostility to unions. As a profession, social work seemed to some to be in direct conflict with labor organizing. Unions were for workers, not professionals. The rank and file movement sought to reconcile those apparent contradictions, creating a new social worker identity, which Daniel Walkowitz calls "The Professional Worker."[152] Many AASW members viewed unions with hostility, and while some AASW chapters made efforts to build relationships with the unions, the issue of membership standards continued to preclude unity.[153]

Unions organizing relief workers often dealt with people who did not have a long-term commitment to the field. Many relief workers, often white and middle-class, were teachers or nurses, and thus returned to their own fields when those job prospects improved. The elimination of federal funds for relief in 1936 also resulted in cuts in staff. Civil service merit requirements, instituted in 1936, gave rise to qualifying examinations for all relief employees.

150. "Directory of Trade Unions in Social Work," *Social Work Today* 5.9 (June 1938): 24; Jacob Fisher, "One Year of the CIO in Social Work," *Social Work Today* 5.9 (June 1938): 21. Two agencies joined unions of the American Federation of Labor. See "Addenda to 'Directory,'" 36, same volume.

151. Edith Foster reported that the rank and file group, although active in state conferences, was generating "little interest . . . even in Detroit." See Foster to Wickenden, October 21, 1935, n137.

152. Walkowitz, *Working with Class*, 119–20.

153. Leighninger, *Social Work*, 40–42.

About 12 percent of those examined failed to qualify for their positions, and thus lost their jobs, adding to the turnover in relief workers.[154] A majority of relief workers were women, and thus arguments related to the difficulty in organizing women workers and the problems women faced in unions are significant.[155] The demographics of relief workers, then, played a role in limiting union development.

Regional hostility to unions and to social workers further complicated social work organizing. Some regions of Michigan, such as the mining district of the Upper Peninsula, which included Marquette County, and also southwest Michigan, including Kent County, were hostile to labor organizations in general. While Detroit had an active labor movement on several fronts, Grand Rapids and Marquette did not.[156] A final factor with respect to restricted union development was the hostility toward professional social work, which the rank and file movement was allied to some degree. At the same time that relief workers argued for higher salaries as professionals, opponents advocated the removal of social work from relief administration entirely, because of what they viewed as the high salaries. New Deal measures protecting labor unions and workers, and the successful sit-down strikes in Flint against General Motors, only heightened animosity and exacerbated fears about Communists in unions.[157] While no direct accusations about Communism appear in the surviving records, it is not difficult to imagine the link made by critics. Accusations of Communism in the WPA unions likely touched relief workers seeking better aid for their clients. Given the barriers to social work organization in Michigan and elsewhere, individuals willing to risk their jobs in uncertain economic times were probably the exception rather than the rule.

Some recipients of relief had little sympathy for caseworkers, deeming them to be overpaid, nosey investigators and, like other critics of the program,

154. "State Organization for Public Welfare in Michigan," March 1937, Welfare and Relief Study Commission Records, Box 5, Folder 4, 211–12, 221. Another 5 percent of those examined failed to qualify for their current position but passed tests for a position with a lower classification.

155. For a review of this debate, see Alice Kessler-Harris, "Where Are the Organized Women Workers?" in *U.S. Women in Struggle: A Feminist Studies Anthology,* ed. Claire Goldberg Moses and Heidi Hartman (Urbana and Chicago: University of Illinois Press, 1995), 110–33, and Dorothy Sue Cobble, "Rethinking Troubled Relations between Women and Unions," same volume, 166–88. It is unclear how gender played into the social worker unions, particularly in relation to the role of women and their access, or lack of access, to positions of leadership in the union movement.

156. Lankton, *Cradle to Grave,* 211–12; Lorence, *Organizing the Unemployed,* 58–63.

157. Labor issues were a major debate in the 1938 elections, and some historians believe that Governor Frank Murphy's support of labor rights and the General Motors strikers cost him the election that year. See Fine, *Frank Murphy: The New Deal Years,* 510–11; Dunbar, *Michigan: A History of the Wolverine State,* 530–31.

not seeing the need for "professional" workers. Historian James Lorence argues that protests by Houghton County's relief recipients "revealed deep worker resentment against welfare bureaucrats whom they perceived to be hostile towards the clients they served."[158] Some recipients also resented the income caseworkers earned in comparison to relief grants. Jobs with the county emergency-relief agencies were not categorized as work relief, and thus were not open to those most in need unless the applicant was qualified for the position. Some Houghton County residents saw the money paid in salaries to caseworkers and clerical employees as money diverted from direct or work relief, arguing that the $65 monthly salary earned by ten welfare investigators could be better spent on clothing for relief recipients.[159] Another common complaint was that while a work-relief recipient's earnings might be cut from $44 to $22, the office workers continued to draw their full pay. Salaries for relief workers averaged $1,573 in 1936, more than four times the relief grant awarded a family of four.[160] In the case of women's work, little enough money was spent on projects for women, compounding the problem. The minimal requirements for a caseworker—a high school education and preferably college and some social work experience—excluded many relief applicants. While the requirements for clerical workers were less tied to formal education, few women outside the white middle class held the skills necessary to obtain a job as a stenographer or bookkeeper, let alone an investigator or caseworker.

Amanda Lorenson held a particularly hostile view of the emergency-relief agency. Lorenson, a divorced mother of six children, two of whom lived at home, was a constant critic of the Saginaw County social welfare programs. She wrote numerous letters complaining about the size of her grants, her ex-husband's failure to pay court-ordered alimony, and the personnel in the social welfare agency. Several of the caseworkers assigned to her reported that their visits consisted of "continuous complaints."[161] They argued that she often withheld information about income or alimony when it was received, and few of the caseworkers trusted her. She received relief beginning in 1933, supplementing the earnings of her older children. Most had left home, and she was dependent upon public aid. A college graduate who had taught elementary education for three years, she was later a file clerk in the county's WRC, but was discharged in 1936. Lorenson maintained it was because she was eligible for Aid to Dependent Children; agency officials, however, stated that she was

158. Lorence, *Organizing the Unemployed,* 86.

159. Letter from Emil Kangas to Harry Hopkins, dated December 20, 1934, FERA State Series, Box 140, Folder G–H.

160. Whalen, *Tenure, Training, and Compensation,* 35, 51.

161. Saginaw County ADC Case C7300045, quoted from case history dated March 19, 1940.

unable to do the job.[162] She complained to several officials, including the governor. She wrote that she had been given high praise for her earlier work, and couldn't understand "why [county administrator] Mr. Howlett should lay me off and keep on his negroes, it is more than I can account for."[163] As a white woman, she believed she deserved first consideration for employment. As an educated woman, she would have been an attractive candidate as a relief worker, let alone a file clerk, but clearly the WRC staff did not agree.

Lorenson also criticized the young women who worked in the office, and had nothing good to say about any of the caseworkers she encountered in the five years she received aid. Her experience, age, and education placed her above these young women, in her view, and she deeply resented that they had such control over her life through the relief program, first under the WRC and later through ADC: "It would be impossible to state on paper the suffering I have undergone at the hands of young girls who have no interest in older people. A girl who is single and spends most of their time smoking cigarettes in a rest room has no right to dictate to older people who have a college education."[164] It was her belief that the relief workers did not need these jobs, and were indeed working for amusement, with no children to support: "I was given a pension of $32.97 to care for two children and myself for one month, while [they] draw no less than $80 for pin money."[165] Lorenson wanted a job, preferably with the WRC, or a larger grant, and wrote that she would not take anything less simply "because of some young girl's whims."[166] She did not see caseworkers as women with families to support, but as single young women benefiting from employment in a "poor man's institution" at the expense of those in need.[167]

Gender factored into other recipients' outlooks as well. Martin Sheets, a Van Buren County applicant, wrote several letters to Michigan Governor Frank Fitzgerald because he had no patience or use for the women in the WRC office. Caseworkers approved a grocery order of $1 per week, the amount allowed for single men. He had received $650 in compensation for an ampu-

162. Employment application dated July 27, 1938; Letter from Ella Lee Council, field representative, to SERA, August 15, 1938, Case C7300045, Saginaw County ADC Records, State Archives of Michigan.

163. Employment application dated July 27, 1938; Case C7300045, Saginaw ADC.

164. Letter from Lorenson to SERA, Lansing, dated July 28, 1938; Case C7300045, Saginaw ADC.

165. Letter from Lorenson to SERA, Lansing, dated July 28, 1938; Case C7300045, Saginaw ADC.

166. Letter from Lorenson to Dora Heilman, supervisor, December 30, 1940, Case C7300045, Saginaw County ADC. She did not receive the increased grant, as she was already receiving the maximum grant of twenty-four dollars under state law.

167. Letter, July 27, 1938, Case C7300045, Saginaw ADC.

tated arm, and also had a son in Chicago with whom he could live. Sheets told the caseworker, a woman, that the WRC needed to pay his room and board and food until he was eligible for an old-age pension. He was refused and the case rejected because he would not accept the aid offered.[168]

Sheets first contacted SERA and Fitzgerald about his need before he applied for relief, according to the WRC. He told Fitzgerald that he was not able to work and that he was entitled to relief: "Now I can't live on snow balls or grass."[169] He claimed that he had no money left from his arm-injury award: "I am not begging, never did, never stole a cent."[170] He was an honest laborer, he insisted, who had earned help. He refused to take no for an answer, and the office workers also would not budge, even when his son wrote that he could not support his father.[171] Caseworkers believed he was trying to get something for nothing, and that he should still have insurance money to live on or that he could go and live with his son; the people he listed as references reported that he should have money left. Sheets wrote Fitzgerald: "Beg I never will. It would [please] this lipstick and powder puff office here to [*sic*] well."[172] A former salesman who had divorced twice, Sheets believed the women in the office were the problem. Thus he turned to male "higher authorities," although it did him little good.

The profession of social work faced contention on many fronts in the 1930s. They sought to differentiate their status from that of the earlier social workers, many of whom were the most vocal critics of professional social work, while also protecting their status from untrained relief workers within their own ranks. Relief workers were not full members of the profession in which they worked. For many, true membership in the profession was a college degree out of reach. Engaged in a debate over the definition of social worker, and what qualifications were needed for that job, many relief workers were likely looking for meaningful work at a decent pay. Some probably shared the concerns of one anonymous critic of the relief worker's position, who signed an article of complaint "by a white collar worker who is getting a trifle hot under the collar."[173] The 1930s witnessed a debate over not only welfare policy in Michigan, but also who should administer that policy. There was also a dispute over the very notion of social worker identity, both within and outside the profession.

168. Case history, March 24, 1936, Case #8351, VB ERA, Box 3, Folder 3.

169. Letter to Fitzgerald dated December 27, 1935; Case #8351, VB ERA, Box 3, Folder 3.

170. Letter from Sheets to Fitzgerald, dated March 13, 1936, Case 8315, VB ERA Records, Box 3, Folder 3.

171. Letter from son to agency dated February 1, 1936, Case #8351, VB ERA, Box 3, Folder 3.

172. Letter to Fitzgerald dated March 13, 1936, Case #8351, VB ERA, Box 3, Folder 3.

173. "Vademecum fur Herrn Haber," William Haber Papers, Bentley Historical Library, Box 33, Folder MSERA-4, 7.

CHAPTER SIX

"I Can't Make a Go of It"

NEGOTIATING RELIEF WITH THE FAMILY AT THE CENTER

RECIPIENTS OF RELIEF in Michigan in the 1930s faced a welfare land-scape different from the old system, but with some familiar landmarks. The expansion of federal and state involvement in welfare opened new avenues for appeal and protest. Emergency-relief programs provided many families and individuals with much-needed assistance at a time when their own resources were exhausted.[1] Michigan recipients welcomed the programs initiated by the federal government, but not all agreed with the programs' policies. The process of applying for relief entailed a maze of interactions on the part of both recipients and caseworkers. Casework was an interactive process, driven by negotiations between recipients and their caseworkers. But these negotiations also included other community agencies and professionals, such as police, the courts, the schools, physicians, private welfare agency personnel, public officials, and family members outside the immediate household. Neighbors and those in contact with the recipients also injected their views at times through informal communication networks. At the center of these negotiations was the family and expectations of how families should behave, which were rooted in legal expectations of relatives' obligations to support one another. Behavior that was rendered a private concern for those not in need became a public

1. Gordon, *Pitied But Not Entitled,* 138–39, 294; Cohen, *Making a New Deal,* 252–53; and Edsforth, *Class Conflict and Cultural Consensus,* 142–43, 149–51.

issue for those receiving public assistance. These negotiations operated in the realm of a welfare discourse different from the dominant narrative, and spotlighted questions about why welfare recipients acted as they did.

Under Michigan law, families were legally required to support one another. This responsible-relative clause represents an important continuity in Michigan social welfare policy and was also used to contest the meaning of responsibility with respect to race, gender, family, and finances. Its very existence highlights the integral role that notions of family played in welfare administration in America. This rule mandated that parents, spouses, adult children, and grandparents were legally responsible for family support. In practice, the responsible-relative clause prompted significant conflict between social workers and welfare recipients, and also between recipients and other family members. Social workers were not looking for a specific family type or organization, such as two-parent families with a male breadwinner and a mother as caretaker. Rather, it was the dynamics in those families—whatever their makeup—that interested them. Much like child and spousal support, the responsible-relative rule was a means to minimize the financial burden the needy placed on the state.[2] The responsible-relative clause was a key way in which welfare administration regulated families receiving relief.

While some historians argue that the stigma against "the dole" declined during the New Deal years, applying for relief was not easy for many people in the Great Depression.[3] Instead of seeking aid from a township supervisor or superintendent of the poor, applicants went to the office of the county welfare-relief commission. The process of applying for relief required providing information about property ownership, bank-account listings, and debts, as well as verifying birth and citizenship records; the latter were critical for the Aid to Dependent Children and Old Age Assistance programs. Caseworkers computed a monthly budget (including shelter, clothing, food, and utilities) to determine the amount of relief needed, which was then offset by any income sources the family had. Caseworkers also verified wages of any employed household members.[4] Noninstitutional medical care could be included, but hospitalization was a local welfare obligation.[5] Thus applicants sometimes

2. Willrich, "Home Slackers," 463; Igra, *Wives without Husbands,* 86–87.

3. Robert S. McElvaine, *The Great Depression: America, 1929–1941,* Rev. Ed. (New York: Random House, 1993), 176–79.

4. Age and citizenship were defining factors in the old-age pension program. Recipients of old age pensions had to be citizens for fifteen years and seventy years of age.

5. Armstrong, *We Too Are the People,* 62–63; Carothers, *Chronology of the Federal Emergency Relief Administration,* 7–9; Haber and Stanchfield, *Unemployment and Relief in Michigan,* 70–71; and *Michigan Emergency Relief Administration Budget Manual* (Lansing: 1937).

dealt with both the WRC offices and local poor-relief officials, and perhaps private agencies as well, to gain the help they needed.

Case files generally contained at least one application form on which case-workers recorded the home condition, family background and education, statements about household members and relatives, employment history, and health status, as well as whether the family attended church. Some workers encouraged applicants to develop the best plan for themselves, particularly in the ADC and OAA cases later in the decades. Emergency-relief caseworkers recorded a report on collateral information: what did the applicant's references, often a township supervisor or poor official, say about his or her need for relief? The goal of casework was to analyze the family's information in order to attempt to address any larger problems, beyond unemployment, that had prompted the family or individual to seek relief in the first place.[6] The caseworker was to present a composite picture of the family, and then to deter-mine the best course of action, ideally with the recipients' input.

Case-file records from the early years of Michigan's categorical-aid pro-grams offer an opportunity to assess an alternate welfare discourse: why relief recipients circumvented the system. Cases generally originated in the New Deal years, and were among those eventually transferred to either the Old Age Assistance or the Aid to Dependent Children programs in the late 1930s. Case records are inherently subjective, as virtually all information, except for correspondence directly from the recipient, is filtered through a caseworker's perspective and bias.[7] Despite these limitations, case-file records also are rich sources of information about the daily administration of welfare, and offer a window into the power relations between recipient and caseworker, or "the ways in which state power infiltrated civil society."[8] Case records provide an opportunity to analyze the discourses and practices of welfare administra-tion, including those employed by caseworkers and policy makers, as well as by recipients.[9] The exchange of information rendered casework a negotiation

6. Kunzel, *Fallen Women, Problem Girls,* 126–27; Gordon, *Heroes of Their Own Lives,* 62–63.

7. Both the caseworker and the applicant are engaged in "performing" in this process. Caseworkers know that their records will be read by supervisors, and recipients often framed their answers to ensure they would get aid. Little, "He Said, She Said," 439; Franca Iacovetta, "Gossip, Contest, and Power in the Making Suburban Bad Girls: Toronto, 1945–60," *The Canadian Historical Review* 80.4 (December 1999): 606–12.

8. Franca Iacovetta and Wendy Mitchinson, "Introduction: Social History and Case Files Research," in *On the Case: Explorations in Case History,* eds. Franca Iacovetta and Wendy Mitchinson (Toronto: University of Toronto Press, 1998), 9–10.

9. For a discussion of the use of poststructuralism in case file analysis, see Iacovetta, "Gossip, Contest and Power," 591–92, 621, and Gordon, *Heroes of Their Own Lives*; Kathleen Canning, "Feminist History after the Linguistic Turn: Historicizing Discourse and Experience,"

throughout the process. Recipients told caseworkers only the information that they wanted to share, and framed their narratives in ways they thought might best result in aid. Caseworkers also sifted the information with their own perspective, and their case histories—supposedly containing objective facts important in the diagnosis of the family's problem or need—included many personal assessments. Many social workers, for instance, commented on the lack of education or desire to work on the part of clients and on the intellectual or psychological abilities of recipients or members of their families, even after one brief visit. Racial, ethnic, and class biases were also evident. Social workers often found it impossible to remove their own judgments from their work.[10]

Investigations involved gathering information through informal communications, including gossip, and this method was key in enforcing family support. Gossip reinforced family support by providing information that could lead to obtaining additional family financial assistance. The provenance of the gossip might be a letter or telephone call, or the result of a conversation with a neighbor. Caseworkers might seek information from the local grocer, school personnel, a police officer, a landlord, or another family member. Caseworkers might hear about an ex-husband who was employed and could afford child support, or about a son or a daughter who had a job and thus could contribute to the family income. The content of these informal communications rested almost exclusively on the two issues of morals and money. Accusations of immoral behavior, including sexual relationships or consumption of alcohol, or the misuse of agency funds, including hiding income, employment, or assets, were the most common. Regardless of the content of the accusation, one nearly universal outcome was increased scrutiny on the case and efforts to secure information about other sources. Caseworkers and policy makers focused primarily on rooting out those who broke the rules rather than on interrogating why recipients did so, in large part because of the dominant discourse about welfare. This discourse, evident in casework practice, stereotyped the welfare recipient as one who lacked moral character instead of questioning the structural problems in the program's administration and the economy in which recipients lived.[11] Many recipients who operated outside the boundaries of agency regulation generally felt compelled to because they

---

Signs 19.2 (Winter 1994): 368–404.

10. Kunzel, *Fallen Women, Problem Girls,* 137–39; Gordon, *Heroes of their Own Lives,* 14–18.

11. Sharon Hays makes a similar argument about recipients and the 1996 welfare-reform law. Welfare law ignores the larger structural and institutional barriers to independence and focuses on the individual. Hays seeks to explain not only the choices recipients make but also the context in which they make them. Hays, *Flat Broke with Children: Women in the Age of Welfare Reform* (New York: Oxford University Press, 2003), 60–61, 123.

needed to support their children, but this experience was a much less recognized welfare discourse in this period.[12]

Most scholars define gossip as information that is shared informally between people who often know each other. Margaret Little, who argues that welfare administration is an arena in which gossip is used in the public sphere, rather than in private communications, broadens the definition of gossip to "a form of communication exchanged about other people's activities and behaviors that may or may not be substantiated."[13] Gossip is often used to control or change the behavior of individuals in the community, or to ensure that community mores are followed. In the case of welfare administration, its persistence as an investigative tool rests in part on its effectiveness. Unsubstantiated gossip and informal communications that would not be admitted as evidence in a court of law enabled caseworkers to discover information about recipients they might otherwise not obtain. Informal communication was an effective investigative tool that prompted caseworkers to focus on individual behaviors rather than larger contextual issues, including limited employment opportunities, budget shortfalls, and family conflict.

The position of the recipient in American society played a significant role in justifying the use of informal communications in these investigations. As a condition of receiving aid, recipients signed away their right to privacy regarding virtually all aspects of their lives. They were no longer full, independent citizens within the welfare system. Actions by those with financial means that might have been accepted, or at least not investigated, by public officials were subject to criticism and censure when a person asked for public assistance. Moral issues intersected with fiscal concerns, as agencies sought to enforce behavior deemed acceptable by larger community customs, a part of the bigger goal of limiting welfare costs. The New Deal was the period in which the link between welfare and dependency solidified, but Nancy Fraser and Linda Gordon also argue that "this use of the term [*dependency*] was fundamentally ambiguous, slipping easily, and repeatedly, from an economic meaning to a moral/psychological meaning."[14] Economic need was still equated largely with individual failing, despite the widespread unemployment during the Great Depression, and the nineteenth-century goal of determining those who were "deserving" of aid continued. This effort required "constant vigilance . . . to ensure that [the undeserving] did not slip in, disguising themselves as

---

12. Canning, "Feminist History after the Linguistic Turn," 381–82.
13. Little, "He Said, She Said," 434; Tebbutt, *Women's Talk?*, 1–2.
14. Nancy Fraser and Linda Gordon, "A Genealogy of *Dependency*: Tracing a Keyword of the U.S. Welfare State," *Signs* 19.2 (Winter 1994): 319.

deserving."[15] By the 1930s the ADC program, like other public assistance programs of the period, "continued the private charity tradition of searching out the deserving few among the many chiselers."[16] Gossip and anonymous tips were effective methods to do that, and their continued use reinforced the status of welfare recipients in American society.

REGULATING THE AMERICAN FAMILY

Social welfare programs were designed to provide aid only when all other avenues, including family support, were exhausted. Caseworkers designed the aid a family received, whether it was ADC, OAA, or work relief, around the needs of the family, and not around the individuals within that family or household. Those who followed the "family ideal" of support received the compliments of caseworkers. In contrast, families who did not support one another were often seen as "problem cases," usually because individuals within the family failed to fulfill their roles. In some cases, relatives would leave the household or community rather than conform to social welfare regulations, oftentimes allowing their family members to regain their relief benefits. In other cases, recipients of relief also used this provision to secure the aid of social workers in enforcing their own authority in their families.[17] The efforts to enforce support often yielded unintended results, including exacerbating family conflicts or prompting the departure of family members from the household. The responsible-relative clause resulted in negotiations, and sometimes heated conflicts, between caseworkers, recipients, and their families.

Child support or alimony, usually from the fathers, was the major source of support checked for ADC recipients. Before caseworkers would even begin to investigate ADC applications, mothers who received no alimony or child support at the time of application had to file a complaint of nonsupport with their local prosecuting attorney. Enforcement by the prosecutor varied from county to county and case to case, but recipients had to initiate the process of securing alimony to receive ADC. If the court did not order alimony, or if an estranged or ex-husband did not pay it, the woman could receive ADC, but

15. Ibid., 320.
16. Ibid., 321.
17. Mary Odem describes the latter trend in her study of laws governing age of consent in California. Odem argues that parents used age of consent laws to control their daughters' behavior when traditional family controls failed. See *Delinquent Daughters: Protecting and Policing Adolescent Female Sexuality in the United States, 1885–1920* (Chapel Hill: University of North Carolina Press, 1995).

she had to file the complaint. Sarah Forbes hoped to avoid the courts in getting her husband to support her, but when that failed, she filed a complaint so she could receive ADC. When her husband stopped paying alimony, caseworkers increased her grant to make up the difference.[18] This case was typical of ADC cases of nonsupport.

The enforcement of family support went far beyond spousal and child support to include other family members. Conflicts usually centered on the amount of a child's wages that had to be budgeted as family income. When determining a recipient's eligibility for aid, social workers computed a family budget based on the needs of all the household members. They then offset that amount with any other support the recipient had, such as income from a part-time job, boarders, alimony, or family earnings. For children and parents living in the same household, caseworkers considered 60 percent of each person's income from private employment as family resources, after deducting for employment and personal expenses.[19] If a family member was employed on a public works job (such as the Works Progress Administration, the Civilian Conservation Corps, or the National Youth Administration), caseworkers considered 100 percent of the income as family resources, since a public works assignment was granted to provide for the support of the entire family.[20]

Adult employable children were often the targets of support-enforcement efforts. Marion Rose, of Saginaw, was widowed in 1929. She received a mothers' pension and emergency relief before qualifying for the ADC program in 1936. Her son, Frank, helped his mother with work from the Civilian Conservation Corps, the National Youth Administration, and later the WPA, before joining the army in 1941. At that point, a married daughter and her husband moved into the home, and their income fell under the responsible-relative clause. They asserted that they were not permanent members of the household, and the son-in-law told the caseworker "not to monkey around with his wages." The caseworker allowed two weeks for them to move, but sent a wage-verification form to the son-in-law's employer. Three weeks later, the couple was still there; the caseworker calculated their contribution to be sixty-

18. Case C7300142, Saginaw ADC Records, reel 4533.

19. This policy remained until 1945, when the State Social Welfare Commission allowed adult children to pay a "going rate" for room and board, rather than 60 percent of their wages. Investigation by staff found that cost of the change was not that high (fifty thousand dollars statewide over a year, even if the caseload doubled), and commission members felt it would be more practical. State Social Welfare Commission Minutes, August 28, 1945, 16–17, Box 2, Folder 1.

20. Donald S. Howard, *The WPA and Federal Relief Policy* (New York: Russell Sage Foundation, 1943), 341–50, 381–82.

two dollars per month, which covered the family budget. She did not close the case, although she told them she would. Instead, she held their checks at the welfare office. She hoped the threat to cancel the grant would prompt them to leave or accept their responsibility to help support the mother.[21] The daughter protested in a letter to the State Department of Welfare, two months after the checks were held. She rejected the notion that she and her husband were financially responsible for her mother. "I think it is your place to wright [sic] and tell them to send checks immediately to my mother for when my husband married me he didn't marry the whole fambley [sic]."[22] They refused to support the mother, but did eventually move.

When social workers enforced the responsible-relative clause, the recipient often paid the price, either through family unrest or financial hardship. Marion Rose was caught in the middle. According to the caseworker's notes, she wanted her daughter to move out, but they would not leave. She lost her ADC grant but could not depend on her son-in-law to contribute. She pleaded with state officials to send a check, or "I will be out on the road bcuse [sic] I don't got no muney [sic] to live on."[23] Rose sought the aid of the caseworker, who agreed to interview the son-in-law and other children. She did not have the power in her household to force her daughter and son-in-law to contribute or leave. Because she lacked that authority, the agency stepped in, at her request. The caseworker, by simply holding the checks rather than closing the case, saved Rose the time of reapplying, but she remained without support for months.

Caseworkers determined aid based on the needs of the family, and at times agency workers used work relief to force children to support their parents. Donna Barker, a Van Buren County resident, was a divorced mother of two. She earned three dollars per week caring for her grandchildren while her daughter worked, and earned extra during the fruit season. These wages were not enough to support her, and her son, Frank, who was twenty-two, was unemployed. She applied for emergency relief in December of 1937. Caseworkers reported that Barker "tried to impress worker with how badly she felt about applying for relief, and how she has always tried to keep off relief." According to the township supervisor, "That boy is too lazy to do a thing."[24] Caseworkers noted that Barker had no control over her son, and recommended work relief for the son. So while Barker had little authority over her son, the agency could attempt to control him by providing him with a public job to support his

21. Saginaw County ADC Case C7300218, quote from case history June 30, 1941.
22. Saginaw County ADC Case C7300218, letter in file dated September 16, 1941.
23. Saginaw County ADC Case C7300218, August 4, 1941.
24. VB ERA Records, Case 5229.

mother. Five months later, Barker was living with her daughter, and the case record ends there.

Recipients at times encouraged caseworkers to enforce their children's support, either through letters or visits from the agency. Barker's voice is relatively silent in the case record, and it is not clear whether she supported the agency's efforts to enforce her son's responsibility to support her. But other recipients hoped that agency workers might influence relatives in ways that family members could not.[25] Soliciting the aid of the caseworker to enforce support, however, did not necessarily imply positive feelings toward the agency. Amanda Lorenson, first introduced in chapter 5, complained about the size of her grant and about the budgets relief workers calculated for her family. She also was upset that she herself was not hired as a caseworker, a job she sought on more than one occasion. The hostility evident in her interactions with the relief agency, however, did not prevent her from seeking the help of social workers to enforce the support law. She turned to them to collect alimony, and also sought their aid in garnering support from her single son, Olsen. He was twenty-four years old and employed at Saginaw Auto Sales, earning twenty-four dollars per week in May 1941. Lorenson told caseworkers that he spent his wages on his girlfriend, but she thought his money should be going to her, his mother. At her request, the social worker visited her son, who refused to help either parent. He agreed to provide support for his sister, Evelyn, but preferred to help her directly rather than through his mother. The social worker was able to negotiate with Olsen some support for the family, but not in the way that Lorenson had hoped.[26]

The presence of employable adult children in a household receiving categorical aid (such as ADC) under the Social Security Act, as in Sandy Eckett's case in St. Charles Township in Saginaw County, endangered the household's grant. Eckett was a widow with six children, and her three eldest—all beyond the age of seventeen—were reluctant to take employment to help support the family. Walter had two WPA assignments, which helped cover the family's budget, but the other two sons, and later an older daughter, were less cooperative. Another son refused a CCC assignment in October 1940, and none made any effort to register at the local employment office. The caseworker pressured them to search for employment, and when they failed to make the effort, he canceled the ADC grant. He believed the sons "want[ed] to sit around and

25. Historians analyzing case-file records have found that the recipients of aid or regulation often employed those services in ways never intended by policy makers. See Odem, *Delinquent Daughters*, 49–52; Gordon, *Heroes of Their Own Lives*, 164–65, 234–35, 293–95. See also Ruth M. Alexander, *The "Girl" Problem: Female Sexual Delinquency in New York, 1900–1930* (Ithaca: Cornell University Press, 1995).

26. Saginaw County ADC Case C700045.

live on [their] mother's ADC grant." The caseworker attempted to prevent the sons from living off money intended for the minor children.[27] The family wrote a letter to the bureau supervisor, arguing that only one person was working (Walter on WPA), and that there was no work. Bureau supervisor Dora Heilman replied that the family had the WPA income, and that there was no evidence any of the children had seriously sought employment: "Your problem is really that they need work and we believe they can find it if they try."[28] The bureau believed that three employable sons and one employable daughter could support the family of seven, particularly with a base income from WPA, and the case remained closed.

Budgeting practices frustrated many recipients, who resorted to deception simply to make ends meet.[29] Budgets computed for the program allowed for only a minimum standard of living. ADC was not a generous program. Grants were intended for children's expenses, and federal guidelines did not include support for the parent.[30] In 1938 a parent with one child was eligible for a maximum grant of eighteen dollars per month; additional children garnered twelve dollars.[31] Some counties, including Wayne County, supplemented federal grants with local and state funds, but not all counties did so. Barely enough to cover rent, let alone anything else, an ADC grant was indeed "partial support."[32] All women faced limited employment opportunities, but none more so than black women, who were largely confined to domestic work and who paid higher rents for poorer housing.[33] Most ADC recipients

27. Saginaw County ADC Case C7300478, case history dated October 14, 1940.

28. Saginaw County ADC Case C7300478, letter to recipient, October 18, 1940.

29. Kathryn Edin and Laura Lein discuss this trend in contemporary welfare programs in *Making Ends Meet: How Single Mothers Survive Welfare and Low-Wage Work* (New York: Russell Sage Foundation, 1997). See also Hays, *Flat Broke with Children*.

30. Linda Gordon, "Putting Children First: Women, Maternalism, and Welfare in the Early Twentieth Century," in *U.S. History as Women's History: New Feminist Essays*, eds. Linda K. Kerber, Alice Kessler-Harris, and Kathryn Kish Sklar (Chapel Hill: University of North Carolina Press, 1995), 81–82; Suzanne Mettler, *Dividing Citizens: Gender and Federalism in New Deal Public Policy* (Ithaca: Cornell University Press, 1998), 138–39.

31. Gordon, "Putting Children First," 83; *A Manual for Aid to Dependent Children* (Lansing: Michigan State Emergency Relief Commission, 1938), 1. By 1940 minimum grants had increased to twenty-four dollars and sixteen dollars. Michigan's average grants tended to be higher than in some other states, especially in the South. Robert C. Lieberman, *Shifting the Color Line: Race and the American Welfare State* (Cambridge: Harvard University Press, 1998), 126–28.

32. Joanne Goodwin, "'Employable Mothers' and 'Suitable' Work: A Re-Evaluation of Welfare and Wage-Earning for Women in the Twentieth-Century United States," *Journal of Social History* 29.2 (Winter 1995): 253–74; Goodwin, *Gender and the Politics of Welfare Reform*, 172–74.

33. See Wolcott, *Remaking Respectability*, 52, 60; Kevin Boyle, *Arc of Justice: A Saga of Race, Civil Rights, and Murder in the Jazz Age* (New York: Henry Holt, 2004), 108–10.

were single mothers who had to work any paid employment around their children. Critics argued that ADC rules discouraged employment. Caseworkers deducted all employment income from the grant unless a budget deficit existed; thus for every dollar recipients earned, they lost a dollar from their respective grants.

The agency's budgeting system was not always the problem; rather, it was sometimes a caseworker's overzealous interpretation of the budgeting practices.[34] One Wayne County caseworker, for instance, received a report that Georgia Evans was employed at a local beer garden, and a check with the employer found that she had indeed worked there, briefly, and was paid one dollar. Despite the small amount of income (Evans paid rent of thirteen dollars per month for herself and her son), the caseworker admonished her that she had to report all income.[35] Elizabeth Kurzawski denied any outside employment, and said she worked at the local farmer's market on Saturdays for chicken and eggs. Her caseworker was unconvinced, even after a letter from the market stated that Kurzawski had received a dozen eggs. The caseworker deducted two dollars—the estimated value of the produce—from the woman's budget.[36] When Mary Stevens was confronted by her caseworker about the furniture she had purchased, she said that "she was tired of having her budget decreased . . . Each time she instructed her worker that she was working she would cut her budget." She no longer told the agency when she earned extra income, because, she told the caseworker, "they don't give you enough anyway and then they deduct what you make and you have to work very hard to earn this money."[37] When Norah Robbins's case was closed in 1944, after her children obtained employment, she admitted she had not always told caseworkers of her children's earnings, or of her alimony, asserting that the "agency had always been so rigid in budgeting policies that this was the only way that she could manage."[38]

34. For a discussion of budget practices under the SEWRC, see *A Manual for Suggested Policies and Procedures for Use by County Relief Administrators* (Lansing: Michigan Welfare Emergency Relief Commission, 1938), 3–8.

35. Wayne County ADC Case C8204988, case history from February 16, 1939. Neighbors also alleged that Mrs. Evans' roomer was her common-law husband, but the charge was never proved. The case was closed two years later when her son, Melvin, entered the CCC and was no longer in the home.

36. Wayne County ADC Case C8206148, case history from October 30, 1939; November 3, 1939; November 9, 1939. The case was closed in early 1943 when Mrs. Kurzawski obtained employment at a local defense factory.

37. Wayne County ADC Case C8202382, case history from May 22, 1942.

38. Wayne County ADC Case C8203039, reel 4647, case history from May 9, 1944.

DECIDING TO LEAVE

In some cases, state regulation of family responsibility prompted children to leave home. Some children accepted public employment but rejected the program's rule that they relinquish all of their wages to the family, opting to move out or even leave the area. Frank Perelli, for example, moved in with his grandparents to escape the harassment of caseworkers and their insistence that he find work.[39] Cynthia Wright's son, Burton, refused to accept a WPA assignment if it meant supporting the entire family. He saw that income as his, regardless of the source, and refused to "work under those conditions." He had had a previous WPA assignment, and resented his monthly wage of thirty-eight dollars going to the family. The caseworker informed him that if he refused the WPA job, he would be removed from the family's food budget and receive no aid. He relented and agreed to be recertified. But one month later, Burton left the city before his recertification went through, and the caseworker had to increase Wright's ADC grant to compensate for the lost wages.[40]

Family members who secured private employment and lived in the household applying for aid did not face the same rules governing public employment. Their contribution was set at 60 percent of their income (after deductions and employment expenses). But some refused to do even that. Sarah Harding, a mother of two living in Detroit, began receiving an ADC grant in 1938. Having been deserted by her husband the year before, Harding relied on ADC and on the earnings of her older daughter, Lilly, for support. But Lilly moved out in mid-1942 rather than support the family. Her mother sympathized with her, and refused to tell the caseworker where her daughter lived. The caseworker spent two months trying to locate Lilly, advising Harding that her case would be closed if Lilly did not come to the office. Eventually, Lilly did return home, and called in September to notify the caseworker that she would support the family.[41]

Not all children, however, returned after leaving home. Rachel Raney, a black woman whose husband deserted the family in 1932, supported her three children with a WPA sewing job in Saginaw. She was cooperative, and caseworkers admired her efforts to keep her family together. When her WPA project ended in 1939, she applied for ADC because she wanted to stay home to supervise her teenage daughter. Her grant was reduced, however, when her

39. Marquette County ADC Case C5200174, case history from April 25, 1938.
40. Saginaw County ADC Case C7300200, case history from August 16, 1939; September 18, 1939.
41. Wayne County ADC Case C8205153, case history from July 12, 1942; August 27, 1942; September 26, 1942.

son, Garland, entered the CCC. Later, a wage check found her son earning enough at a local factory to support the family. But Garland Raney refused those terms, and was gone a month later. When Rachel Raney finally received her grant in mid-October, she was trying to support her family with occasional housework, for which she earned $1.50 per day.[42] Employment opportunities in Saginaw and other Michigan cities were scarce for black women such as Raney. Day work was among the few options.[43] Limited in employment opportunities because of race and caught in the middle of the social agency's bid to enforce family obligations, Raney and her two younger children struggled to make it in a labor market segregated by race and gender.

Caseworkers, in their efforts to enforce family support, often expected the person with perhaps the least power—often the stay-at-home mother—to enforce that responsibility with her adult children, as in the case of Raney. But parents dependent on public aid likely carried little authority with their adult children, particularly their sons, who saw themselves as independent adults with a right to the money they earned. Parental efforts to enforce family support, and later efforts to do so by the welfare agency, did worsen or rupture relationships. When Edith Walton of Detroit applied for ADC for her two young daughters in 1938, her son Clyde was working, and his brother Arthur was on WPA. Consequently, the application was denied. Two years later she reapplied, after Arthur had married. The caseworker again denied the application because Clyde was employed by Dodge and earning thirty-two dollars each week, 60 percent of which easily covered the family expenses. Clyde threatened to leave both the household and his mother with no support. But he also realized his mother was physically unable to work and thus Clyde stayed in the home.[44]

Walton reapplied again five months later. Her son Clyde had become verbally and physically abusive in the meantime. She preferred dependency on the state to her son's behavior. The agency approved a small grant, but not enough to relieve Clyde of his obligations. A few months later, he married and moved out. He would not contribute anything to his family's support, and the mother reported that they were barely speaking. She eventually found defense work in Detroit, and her case was closed in early 1943. The damage to her family's relationship, however, had already been done.[45] Although it is impos-

---

42. Saginaw County ADC Case C7300279.

43. Wolcott, *Remaking Respectability,* 80–85, 231–39; Thomas Sugrue, *The Origins of the Urban Crisis* (Princeton: Princeton University Press, 1996), 25.

44. Wayne County ADC Case C8207798, case history from June 27, 1940; November 4, 1940.

45. Wayne County ADC Case C8207798, case history from April 23, 1941; February 11, 1942; March 19, 1943.

sible to know if the agency caused the problem, their zeal likely exacerbated the conflict. It placed the mother in an abusive situation, however unintended. This case also highlights the centrality of the family unit's well-being over that of individual family members. The family dynamics, with a son providing support for his mother and siblings, overrode what might have been in the best interest of the mother, who was placed in a vulnerable position economically and forced to depend on a son reluctant to support her.

Efforts to enforce a child's responsibility prompted some parents to side with their children, opposing their children's obligation to provide for the family. Betty Johnson, an African-American mother of two daughters, offers one such example. Widowed in 1938 after her husband died from tuberculosis, Johnson also had to cope with living with an arrested case of the disease herself, and her children were monitored because of their exposure.[46] Early entries in the case record describe a family who lived in a nice residential district. The caseworker wrote that the "relationships within the family are excellent and it seems apparent that Mrs. [Johnson] is giving the children excellent care."[47] Problems arose when the two daughters began working. Betty was employed at Ex-Cell-O Products, but her mother told the caseworker that "Betty was giving her too much now and it was none of the worker's business how much she gave the family." A wage check found that Betty was earning forty dollars per week, but planned to move, with the full support of her mother.[48] She would rather have the case closed, she said, than allow caseworkers to intrude even further in her family's life. The case was closed the next month.[49]

The probate court was another avenue to enforce support. At times caseworkers encouraged family members to seek aid through the court system, if their efforts proved unsuccessful. The probate court had long been the agency to enforce support through court orders, as caseworkers could only threaten to end or refuse aid. When sixty-seven-year-old Diane Strand of Saginaw was referred to the Welfare Relief Commission for an OAA grant in late 1937, her son, David, lived with her and worked part-time at the local Chevrolet parts factory. His mother told the caseworker outright that he was irresponsible. Strand, a widow since 1926, was in poor health and suffered from asthma; she could no longer work as a domestic and laundress and relied on her son and

---

46. For the treatment of TB, see Barbara Bates, *Bargaining for Life: A Social History of Tuberculosis, 1876–1938* (Philadelphia: University of Pennsylvania Press, 1992), and Georgina D. Feldberg, *Disease and Class: Tuberculosis and the Shaping of Modern North American Society* (New Brunswick: Rutgers University Press, 1995).

47. Wayne County ADC Case C8201132, case history from December 6, 1941.

48. Wayne County ADC Case C8201132, case history from July 21, 1943.

49. Wayne County ADC Case C8201132, case history from August 17, 1943.

OAA for support.[50] Her son's arrest for lewdness a few months later involved the police, who asked the caseworker to stop Strand's OAA grant, arguing that she used it for her son. Investigation found that David Strand earned more (fourteen dollars per week) than a WPA wage, although he was employed only part-time. He also had a car, and refused to get rid of it. The Strands were told the grant would be canceled, and returned later with an attorney, to no avail.[51] The caseworker consulted probate court officials, and all agreed it was better to enforce the son's responsibility to support his mother. Diane Strand did not agree, and protested the closure in a letter to supervisor Dora Heilman. She had no money and questioned the power the caseworker and the agency held over her grant: were they "the judge and jury?" The caseworker apparently had told her that she had spoiled David, but Strand refuted this, writing that she had to leave him alone often after she was widowed to clean houses to earn a living. He had been forced to take care of himself, she wrote, at a very young age.[52] Caseworkers did not reinstate her grant, but did secure a WPA assignment for David, and Strand later obtained full-time employment with Chevrolet in Saginaw.[53]

Some recipients reluctantly sought help through the probate court. Joan Yates, a widow with four children, did file a support complaint. Yates, a seventy-one-year-old native of Mississippi living in Saginaw County, was initially denied OAA in late 1936 because she had two employed men (a son and a son-in-law) living with her, and also because she lacked the proof of age and residency required for a grant. She applied again in 1937 and was approved. A 1939 investigation found a daughter, Leslie, and her husband and four children living with Yates, but these family members asserted they had enough resources only for themselves. Another son, Warren, also lived there, but told the agency he could not help his mother. He had debts to pay and was separated from his own wife. Agency supervisor Dora Heilman wrote that he would "never be responsible for his mother's support."[54] Two years later another caseworker found Warren earning $190 per month; his contribution, using the agency's formula, covered the budget deficit. The caseworker, after consulting with Heilman, closed the case and referred Yates to the probate court. Yates came to the office and told the caseworker that she could not

---

50. Saginaw County OAA Case A7302543, reel 3015, case history from November 18, 1937.

51. Saginaw County OAA Case A7302543, case history from March 21, 1938.

52. Case A7302543, case history from April 26, 1938; letter from Strand to Heilman, dated June 1, 1938.

53. Case A7302543, case history from June 23, 1938; December 9, 1938.

54. Saginaw County OAA Case A7301193, reel 3003, case history, April 12, 1939; April 18, 1939.

take her son, whom she called "a whiskey head," to court, and that it was not fair for "this agency to expect me to rely on him for support." Warren again refused to help her, but her case remained closed. With no other options and no other children to help, Yates reluctantly filed a petition for support with the probate court. The court found that because of the shutdown of local factories employing the woman's children, support could not be ordered.[55] The woman reapplied, but died one month later before her case had been investigated. Because she had not been an approved OAA recipient, no burial allowance was permitted.[56] In this case, the pursuit of court-ordered support caused much grief for the recipient with no resulting support.

Combining court-ordered support with pressure from caseworkers also prompted children to leave home rather than support their parents. Pauline Ristav, a forty-five-year-old widow with six children, faced conflict with several of her children over their support for her and their younger siblings. Ristav, who was a recipient of an ADC grant before her husband's death from tuberculosis, in late 1938, had her case closed at one point because of sufficient income, likely from her older children. She invested her insurance money in a home. Her son Avery left home because of the amount he was expected to contribute. Ristav went through the probate court, which ordered Avery to pay three dollars' support per week. She told the caseworker that the court-ordered support had soured her relationship with her son. Her eighteen-year-old daughter, Laurie, who worked part-time and contributed four dollars per week in room and board, later balked at paying sixty dollars per month, which had been computed on the basis of her higher factory wages; Laurie was expected to contribute 60 percent. She would pay only eight dollars per week in room and board, however, and argued further that since her brothers did not pay, she would not.[57] Laurie moved out rather than pay the ordered support, and her mother refused to go through the probate court again. Without a court order, Laurie was not obligated to pay the support. Caseworkers did not decrease Ristav's grant for her younger children, ages six and ten, as she had endeavored to enforce support and other children were helping, most likely. But when the caseworker received word that Avery had claimed his mother as a dependent on his draft form, in the hopes of getting an exemption, Ristav's ADC check was held, pending investigation. If the report were true that Avery claimed he was supporting Ristav for draft purposes, the agency would

55. Case A7301193, case history from August 11, 1941; August 24, 1941; November 24, 1941; December 15, 1941.

56. Case A7301193, case history from January 19, 1942 and February 20, 1942.

57. Saginaw County ADC Case C7300548, reel 4540, case history from December 28, 1939, to February 4, 1942.

eliminate the ADC. However, he had apparently not claimed her as a dependent, and the state office, when asked, allowed the ADC to continue despite the ability of relatives to help, because they had been unsuccessful in enforcing support.[58] Again, efforts to enforce support only increased family friction and resulted in Ristav losing what little help her children had provided.

Some recipients simply refused to allow family members to be interviewed for support. This occurred in Sarah Harding's case, described earlier, when she refused to tell caseworkers where her daughter, Lilly, lived. Another case involved James and Ellie Stern, who lived with their son, employed at the Saginaw Foundry. They had deeded their home to him in exchange for support. The Sterns did receive a small Old Age Assistance grant, as their daughter-in-law was an invalid and their son had large medical bills to pay.[59] When the caseworker suggested contacting their daughter to see if she could help, the son refused. He would assume full support, despite the burden, rather than see her investigated. The case was closed, although the father wrote to Governor Murray Van Wagoner, pleading for his grant; his son could not do it all. State officials joined the negotiations when they requested a report from the Welfare Relief Commission, and also suggested a small grant. State officials backed off immediately when the local officials explained the case, and encouraged the family to allow the daughter to be contacted. They continued to refuse, and the case remained closed. State officials deferred to local caseworkers in this instance, as they had direct knowledge of the case and clearly were following agency regulations.

Property ownership was a problem unique to OAA cases. Property transfers to children were relatively common, and did not always remove eligibility, as in the Sterns' case, depending on the income of the children who received the property. The property transfer usually was in exchange for continued housing and financial support. Carl Janetzka, for instance, a native of Czechoslovakia and a U.S. citizen, received a rather small OAA grant—just $2.50 per month—for clothing and incidentals. He had lived with his son and daughter-in-law for more than a year, since his wife had died, and they got along well. But when the caseworker found that his grant was for "pocket" money, rather than essentials, and also found a deed transfer, she closed the case. Under the terms of the property transfer, it was up to the son to provide for his father, and he had sufficient means to do so.[60] Janetzka was in the OAA office a few

58. Case C7300548, case history from March 16, 1942, to January 25, 1944.

59. Saginaw County OAA Case A7301106, case history from July 30, 1936; April 14, 1937.

60. Saginaw County OAA, Case A7301375, reel 3005, case history from September 2, 1938; December 4, 1939; and May 1940.

months later, seeking a WPA job, as he needed clothes and did not want to ask his son. The caseworker told him he had already paid for the clothes with his land, and that his son was legally obligated to provide for him.[61]

Not all cases involving property transfers and parental support were so amiable. In the Janetzka case, the son did not protest his responsibility to his father, but others did, often exerting extreme stress and hardship on their parents. John Arnold, who had farmed just west of Saginaw, began receiving aid in late 1935 because of ill health, and later was transferred to the OAA program. He lived with his son, George, a farmer. Arnold's small grant covered clothing and medical care, as his son's wife was rather ill and their income was limited. At that time his son did see his father's care as his duty, and continued to provide for him, although the other children did not contribute.[62] A year later, however, George asked his father to leave. Arnold planned to move in with his daughter, but later moved to Bay City to live with a brother. Prompted by a comment by the brother, the caseworker found that Arnold had deeded his property to his son, and that the terms of the agreement included a life lease, space for a garden, medical care, and burial. After consulting with the state office, the caseworker closed the case, since Arnold had never been entitled to the original grant.[63] The son immediately protested, arguing that his father did not know what he was talking about, but was chagrined when the caseworker told him that his father had said nothing about the deed. The tragedy was that the son refused to take Arnold in again, and asked him to leave for good. The caseworker intended to visit the son, but nothing was recorded. Apparently Arnold stayed with his brother until his death, three years later, at the age of ninety.[64]

Property requirements served as a deterrent to the OAA program. A significant number of Wayne County's recipients (nearly 7 percent) withdrew their applications before they were investigated, and the most common reason was a refusal to sign over their property to the state. Many opted to forego aid rather than sign that form. More than half were later approved for aid anyway, but the property requirement likely dissuaded some from applying. The 1947 Recovery Act enabled the state and county to make a claim against a deceased recipient's estate for OAA grants during his or her life.[65] State officials saw an

---

61. Case A7301375, case history from August 9, 1940. The man died two years later.

62. Saginaw County OAA, Case A7300761, reel 2998, case history from September 13, 1938.

63. Case A7300761, case history from July 19, 1939; July 25, 1939; September 5, 1939.

64. Case A7300761, case history from September 11, 1939.

65. Public Act 262 of 1947, *Public and Local Acts of the Legislature of the State of Michigan* (Lansing: Franklin, DeKleine Company, 1947), 393–94.

immediate 3 percent increase in closings, which they attributed to the new law.[66]

Caseworkers and policy makers were aware of the difficulties the enforcement of relatives' support had on families. They discussed how best to pursue such support, and some acknowledged that their efforts were "very apt to be harmful to the family relationship."[67] In 1946 the Michigan Social Welfare Commission recommended rethinking the budgeting of relatives' contributions. Budgets should include only support that was actually received, rather than expected, because "many aged persons are barred from receiving assistance, or are compelled to subsist on reduced payments" due to relatives refusing to fulfill their responsibilities.[68] But the commission's overall support for the law remained and continued to be used to limit the state's welfare costs.

THE MODEL CASE

Families who conformed to welfare administration's expectations of support earned the respect and compliments of caseworkers, and were often described as model cases for the program. What is most compelling about these trends is that the family structure or marital status of the ADC grant recipient was less significant than the dynamics operating within the family. In fact, the case-file sample shows that married or widowed recipients accounted for about half of all cases in both Saginaw and Wayne counties, even among ADC recipients (see table 6.1). Single women in Wayne County are the smallest group, but 22 percent of Saginaw County's cases were unmarried. The numbers reveal that although married and widowed women, long defined as the most "deserving" recipients of mothers' pensions, comprise more than half of the Saginaw and Wayne ADC pool, nearly half were divorced, deserted, separated, or even never married.[69] Men also accounted for some recipients in all counties: 36 percent in Marquette County, just 2.3 percent in Saginaw County, and 7 percent in Wayne County. Male recipients were found almost exclusively in the married or widower category in all three counties.

66. *Fifth Biennial Report of the Michigan Social Welfare Commission, July 1946–June 1948* (Lansing: December 1948), 17–20.

67. Field Report by Ella Lee Cowgill, Kent County, June 4, 1943, 1–2, Narrative Field Reports, Archives of Michigan, Box 6, Folder 10.

68. *Fourth Biennial Report*, 2–3.

69. Linda Gordon analyzes the long-term stigma of single mothers of all types in welfare history and also documents the early bias against separated, divorced, deserted, and never-married mothers. ADC's early advocates remained silent about the latter groups of women, but in Michigan they did receive aid. Gordon, *Pitied But Not Entitled*, 26–29, 105, 280–81.

TABLE 6.1
MARITAL STATUS OF ADC RECIPIENTS (%)

County and Program	Married	Divorced or Deserted	Separated	Single	Widow	Widower
Marquette ADC	67	6	9	2	4	0
Saginaw ADC	18	21	21	22	37	1
Wayne ADC	13	31	10	1	42	3

The ADC program was far more inclusive racially in the sample than other studies have shown, particularly for Wayne County. One-third of Wayne County's ADC recipients in the sample were nonwhite, far higher than their share of the population. Saginaw County's sample included 10 percent that involved nonwhite recipients. But the sample also shows that while married and widowed recipients are a significant share, they are not a majority. Forty-four percent of Saginaw's nonwhite ADC recipients were either married or widowed. The rest were divorced, deserted, or separated. Just under 4 percent were unmarried, again the smallest group in the sample. For Wayne County's nonwhite recipient population, 49 percent were widowed, and just a little more than 5 percent were married. Deserted, divorced, and separated recipients accounted for 43 percent of the cases, but unmarried women accounted for just 1 percent.

Family dynamics were central to a caseworker's perception of a case. Regina Schultz, a forty-one-year-old mother of four, began receiving a mothers' pension from Saginaw County in 1931, after her husband died of a heart attack. Schultz's youngest child was two, and she also cared for her elderly mother. She supplemented her mothers' pension with domestic work and sewing, and fortunately had a place to stay in her mother's home. Schultz's case was transferred to ADC in 1936.[70] She continued to receive ADC until 1947, but despite her lengthy partial dependence on public aid, caseworkers saw this case as a model that justified public social welfare programs.

Caseworkers found Schultz to be an excellent housekeeper and mother. As her children grew older, they began to supplement her ADC grant with part-time jobs. Her siblings also assisted with the care of her mother. Her children never balked at helping support their mother, and she eventually lived with one of her married children. The caseworker who closed the case in July of 1947 wrote, "The situation in this home is one that is really beautiful. The

70. Saginaw County ADC Case C7300182, reel 4534.

children are obviously fond of their mother and she of them. The grandmother is a welcome and loved member of the household."[71] Schultz's case clearly followed the "family ideal" of support: she raised her children to be independent but also accept their familial responsibility, and thus reduced her long-term dependence on the state.

Case-file analysis also shows that race was not the determining factor in model cases. Families who worked together and accepted responsibility for other members were not only white, middle-class widows, as Schultz was. White widows often were portrayed as the most "deserving" of America's poor, but women in other categories could also be a part of this model group. This is not to say that marital status, race, and class were irrelevant, but positive family relations could, in some sense, overcome other factors that might have contributed to a negative view of a case or family. Positive family relations—which followed the white, middle-class model—could result in what caseworkers termed a "high type" case. Divorce, desertion, or illegitimacy did not carry the stigma in 1930s Michigan social work that is found in earlier periods.[72] Minorities and noncitizens did receive aid from the state social welfare programs in the Depression, although not in proportion to their rates of unemployment. Caseworkers entered homes of Mexicans, African-Americans, and the foreign-born with different expectations than in those of white homes. In a sense, minorities and lower-class whites had to "prove" their worth in ways that other families did not. But some were successful, and exhibiting family relations of harmony or unity was one such way.

Marcella Hernandez of Saginaw was one case in point. A Mexican citizen with one daughter, Hernandez suffered from tuberculosis, the same disease that had killed her husband in 1930. She spent six years in the local sanitarium while her sister cared for her daughter, Beatrice. She was released in May 1938, although not fully cured, and applied for an ADC grant. From the start, she impressed the caseworker "as being exceptionally honest and trustworthy and was most anxious to cooperate." She lived with her sister and brother, who had supported the family with a job at the Saginaw Foundry. He had been laid off, however, prompting her to seek ADC for her daughter.[73] The application was approved, and Hernandez received aid for the next six years. The daughter earned excellent citizenship marks, and a caseworker in 1942 referred to her as "a high type Mexican girl."[74] The mother returned to the hospital briefly in 1944, and again the sister cared for her child. When Hernandez was released,

71. Case C7300182, quote from case history from July 18, 1947.
72. For a discussion of marital status, race, and welfare, see Mink, *The Wages of Motherhood*, 36–41.
73. Saginaw County ADC Case C7300010, case history from May 5, 1938.
74. Saginaw County ADC Case C7300010, case history from January 16, 1942.

her daughter secured a part-time job to help her mother, who could also work only part-time. When Beatrice finished high school in 1947, she planned to secure full-time work and support her mother, whose health still precluded any job more than part-time. The social worker saw the Hernandez case as an exemplar, one that served as "a good advertisement for the ADC program."[75] The lengthy partial reliance on public support was not a problem, and neither was the woman's race or citizenship status. Rather, it was the family network and feeling of responsibility—illustrated through the sister and brother's willingness to help their sister with child care and financial support, and later her daughter's assumption of part of that responsibility—that made this an ideal case. The ADC program enabled the mother to care for her daughter, who grew up to be a responsible and self-sufficient adult. Beatrice's willingness to support her ill parent precluded other long-term support for her mother at that time.

Rose Moore, a Detroit African-American mother of four, earned the praise of caseworkers for similar reasons. Her husband died in 1930, when her oldest child was eleven. She received a mothers' pension before her case was moved to ADC, whereupon she supplemented that grant with day work. Her home was always neat and clean, and she lived in a "good negro district."[76] Her children helped with part-time jobs as they grew older. By 1942 her son Fred, who was eighteen, was able to support the family on his income, and the case was closed.[77]

Caseworkers also sometimes helped noncitizens who faced restricted employment opportunities. Hilda Weber was a divorced mother of a two-year-old son when she applied for aid. A native of Germany, she had never obtained citizenship. Her ex-husband did not have a job, and thus she had no support. When she needed a tonsillectomy two years later, the county denied her, telling her to get a job. She would have to pay for child care, and only factory work paid enough. As a noncitizen, however, no one would hire her. Thus she was caught; she needed employment that paid enough to enable her to obtain care for her child, but had limited options because of her lack of citizenship, circumstances that county officials failed to see. At the encouragement of her caseworker, she started the citizenship process, unsure whether she could afford the fees, but she eventually did and obtained factory work, leaving the ADC program.[78]

75. Saginaw County ADC Case C7300010, case history from May 8, 1947.

76. Wayne County ADC Case C8200720, reel 4630.

77. Wayne County ADC Case C8200720, case history from January 10, 1941; September 23, 1942.

78. Saginaw County ADC Case C7300184, reel 4534, case history from July 13, 1939; October 1, 1941; August 20, 1942.

When Juan Gortez, a Mexican citizen and sugar beet worker, was diagnosed with tuberculosis, in 1938, his family began receiving ADC while he recovered in the Saginaw County TB Hospital. His wife, a Mexican-American woman born in Texas, cared for their children on the ADC program and with domestic work until he recovered. But upon his release, he found himself unable to secure employment, as he had no citizenship papers. His caseworker, along with bureau supervisor Dora Heilman, contacted local churches and community members to help with the process. As a result, he became a citizen and found a good factory job that enabled him to support his family.[79] The family was well liked by the entire community, as evidenced when their home burned down in 1943. All four children died in the fire, and a collection produced one thousand dollars for a new home for the couple. The caseworker recorded: "In spite of all the hardships they endured they held to their purpose to rise above the level of itinerant beet worker and to make a place for themselves as respected citizens." The caseworker classified the family as "high type," again a model Mexican family who "disproved" the stereotypes so common among the agency staff.[80]

In the case of Beulah Beloiz, a son faced marital troubles over the issue of helping his mother and siblings financially. Beulah Beloiz was widowed in 1934. A naturalized citizen, she received a mothers' pension and then ADC for her four children. Josef was the oldest, and, in 1940, had left his wife, in part over disputes about his financial support of his mother, who spoke little English and required Josef's help in order to navigate the language barriers. One caseworker commended the "strong feeling of family responsibility on the part of each to the group as a whole." By October 1940, two daughters were employed, one on WPA and another at Dodge. Josef was divorcing his wife and planned to help as well, and the case was closed.[81]

The case of Anthony Benilli is a unique one, in that a father was the recipient of ADC for his children. Left a widower in 1936, Benilli received ADC for his six children, the eldest of whom was born in Italy. His citizenship status made employment difficult for him and his eldest son; he was laid off WPA when rules precluded the hiring of noncitizens.[82] Benilli also was a man of pride, and therefore did not always tell caseworkers when his children lost jobs; he made do rather than seek a higher grant. Caseworkers reported that

79. Saginaw County ADC Case C7300444, reel 4538, case history from April 3, 1939; January 10, 1940; December 10, 1940.

80. Case C730044, case history summary from August 29, 1947.

81. Wayne County ADC Case C8201050, reel 4633, case history from January 23, 1940; April 2, 1940; October 24, 1940.

82. Wayne County ADC Case C8203480, reel 4650, case history from October 21, 1940.

the children were always willing to help their father and siblings, and commended the cooperative feeling they shared. By 1942, two of the children had
steady employment. Benilli told the caseworker they no longer needed aid,
although he gave no details, and the case was closed.[83]

Efforts to enforce support were moderately successful, although many
family members quietly did their part with no vocal objection to caseworkers.
Fifteen percent left the Marquette County OAA program because they had the
means to support themselves, either through family members or through the
sale of assets, often a home or farm. Nine percent of Saginaw's OAA recipients left the program when relatives were able to support them, and another
4 percent found other means, often through the sale of assets, to regain their
independence from government programs. Just 3 percent of Wayne County
recipients, however, were able to leave the program through family support or
other reasons. More than a third of the ADC cases in both Saginaw and Wayne
counties were closed when a family member—either a parent or child—found
employment sufficient to support the family.[84] Thirteen percent in Saginaw
found other sources of income, usually from more than one area, including
alimony, part-time work, or a military allotment from a son or other relative.
The war years saw an increase in cancellations due to family resources, since
the war's employment opportunities enabled more families to support their
elderly parents.[85] In 1940 and 1942, increased family resources accounted for
about half of all ADC closures in the state.[86]

Work-relief programs also proved to be an important means for people to
leave the direct relief programs. Half of the Van Buren emergency-relief recipients found employment, either in the private sector or on a works program.
Twenty-seven percent of the Van Buren cases listed private employment as
the reason for closing the case; in one case a son secured a job to support the
family. Another 3 percent found "unsteady" employment, but since their case
was not reopened, someone in the family likely was able to find full-time work.
Sixteen percent received WPA assignments, and in two of those cases it was
for a son in the household. Three percent received assignments on a National

83. Wayne County ADC Case C8203480, case history from June 24, 1942.

84. In Saginaw, 35 percent of the cases listed private employment as the reason for closing
the case. Employment of children accounted for 15 percent, employment of the mother comprised another 15 percent, and in 5 percent of the cases a husband was again able to work. For
Wayne County, mothers were employed in 8 percent of the cases while fathers accounted for 4.4
percent. Children's employment resulted in closure in 22 percent of the cases.

85. *Second Biennial Report, Michigan Social Welfare Commission, July 1940–June 1942*
(Lansing: December 1942), 35.

86. *First Biennial Report, Michigan Social Welfare Commission, July 1938–June 1940* (Lansing: December 1940), 40; *Second Biennial Report*, 39.

Youth Administration project (two were students), and one case included a CCC assignment for a son. The works programs proved critical for Van Buren residents, where 23 percent were able to leave the direct-relief rolls to secure some type of public work. For those recipients, work relief provided interim employment until a job could be found in the private sector.

The categorical-aid programs of the Social Security Act also were important to a significant portion of Van Buren's relief population. Twenty-seven percent of the cases analyzed qualified for either OAA or ADC. The other 3 percent received ADC (one moved as well), and two others likely received ADC, although it is not clear from the record. Thus about a quarter of the cases continued to receive aid under the Social Security Act, indicative of the entrenched welfare needs that became so evident during the Depression years.

Studies of ADC often overshadow the OAA program, when the latter served far more Americans than ADC until the mid-1950s and was a critical force in reducing extreme poverty among the elderly. Nationally, more than 2 million elderly received OAA in 1940, while just 131,000 received social security benefits. OAA caseloads were twice that of ADC in 1940, and "even as late as 1949, Old Age Assistance beneficiaries outnumbered those of Social Security by a third—2.49 to 1.67 million."[87] Long waiting periods for applicants was the norm in the first years of the program. Michigan had a backlog of 32,000 cases in 1940 with a nineteen-month waiting period; by 1942 the backlog was just 3,151.[88] By 1946, OAA served more than a quarter of all Michigan residents above the age of sixty-five, and 22 percent two years later.[89] The OAA caseload peaked in Michigan at 100,000 cases in September 1950; that same year the ADC caseload was just over 27,000.[90]

The records of the other three counties show stark differences in the two categorical-aid programs. Most OAA recipients received governmental help for the remainder of their lives. The chief reason for closing an OAA case was the death of a recipient: this was true in two-thirds of the Marquette County cases, 80 percent of the Saginaw cases, and 82 percent of Wayne County cases. Another 18 percent of Marquette County's clients were institutionalized in

87. Katz, *The Price of Citizenship*, 4–5.

88. *Second Biennial Report, Michigan Social Welfare Commission, July 1940–1942* (Lansing: December 1942), 33; *Third Biennial Report, Michigan Social Welfare Commission, July 1942–1944* (Lansing: December 1944), 7–8.

89. *Fourth Biennial Report, Michigan Social Welfare Commission, July 1944–1946* (Lansing: December 1946), 20; *Sixth Biennial Report, Michigan Social Welfare Commission, July 1948–1950* (Lansing: December 1950), 11.

90. *Seventh Biennial Report, Michigan Social Welfare Commission, July 1948–June 1950* (Lansing: December 1950), 34–35, 47.

a hospital until their deaths, while 7 percent in Saginaw and 5. 3 percent in Wayne County shared that fate. Statewide, death prompted the closure of at least half of the OAA caseload, and those numbers climbed to about 65 percent by the 1950s.[91]

UNSUITABILITY

Part of enforcing family responsibility was ensuring an appropriate environment for children, a key goal of the ADC program, which called for a "suitable home with reasonable standards of care and health," but it was up to local agencies to establish and enforce those standards. The 1938 program manual advised measuring the existing standards against available options: "This does not mean contentment with low living standards, but measurement in terms of alternatives."[92] Michigan's suitable-home clause was approved by the Social Welfare Commission on April 22, 1940. An unsuitable home was defined as one in which children suffered from "indifference, ill health," or a lack of material care (food, clothing, medical care, etc.). Parents were to see that their children attended school and were to provide a positive "example of socially desirable behavior." They were also to make sure children were loved and wanted, and that they enjoyed both security and respect.[93]

Unsuitability was not an issue in a lot of cases; less than 3 percent of the Saginaw cases and 3.4 percent of Wayne's cases resulted in an unsuitable-home finding or the removal of children, either because of neglect or delinquency. The low numbers of cases closed for unsuitability is somewhat surprising, as the application of such regulations to police recipients is found in studies of later periods.[94] This evidence points to a period in the program when the suitable-home provision was simply used less in the closure of cases. This observation does not mean, however, that caseworkers were not concerned with issues of morality. Moral issues—including promiscuity, prostitution, unmar-

91. *First Biennial Report,* 35; *Second Biennial Report,* 35; *Third Biennial Report,* 11; *Tenth Biennial Report, Michigan Social Welfare Commission, July 1956–1958* (Lansing: December 1958), 30.

92. *A Manual for Aid to Dependent Children* (Lansing: Michigan State Emergency Welfare Relief Commission, 1938), 5.

93. Minutes of State Social Welfare Commission, Box 1, Folder 1, April 22, 1940, Archives of Michigan.

94. Scholars link the increased use of suitable-home provisions to the growing number of nonwhite and nonwidowed recipients in the program in the 1950s and 1960s. Winifred Bell, *Aid to Dependent Children* (New York and London: Columbia University Press, 1965), 111–23; Mittelstadt, *From Welfare to Workfare,* 46, 86–87.

ried cohabitation, and alcohol use—appeared in 4.4 percent of Saginaw's cases, 18 percent of Marquette's cases, and 9 percent of Wayne County's sample. Recipients both resented and denied many charges about morals issues, and experienced heightened inspection and attention, but few had their respective ADC cases closed in this period.

The majority of morals concerns were related to sexuality. Recipients were often accused of cohabitation; a man was living in the house, and thus was suspected of providing economic support. Some recipients were accused of promiscuous behavior, particularly if they had illegitimate children while on ADC, and a few cases involved prostitution. Alcohol was also an issue, although often it was connected to another problem, as was neglect. Several of the recipients also were labeled "feeble-minded" or of "low intelligence." Both black and white recipients endured such scrutiny, although black women did so in greater proportion than their share of the caseload. African-Americans assumed 35 percent of all morals cases in Wayne County, and more than 20 percent in Saginaw County.

Gossip was inextricably linked to the investigation of morals in these cases. Caseworkers often relied on reports from neighbors, landlords, and other family members, in addition to their own surveillance. While few recipients lost aid because of such accusations, they did face increased scrutiny. Recipients tired of investigators' intrusions and investigations, and many did not believe that their relief status warranted such intrusion. Jane Mansfield, an African-American widow in Detroit, was a model recipient in her first years with the agency, but later came under intense investigation. She told the caseworker in 1939 that she preferred not to work—although she had done day work in the past to supplement her mothers' pension—because her children needed her at home (the youngest was ten). The caseworker reported that the home was suitable and that "no complaint has been received by our office."[95] Complaints began after Mansfield's stepson left for the military. Neighbors reported alcohol use and loud parties and said a man, employed at Ford Motor Company, was living with her. The caseworker became concerned about the home's suitability and the woman's honesty, despite the nine years of no complaints with the mothers' pension program and no corroboration of the accusations. Mansfield denied the allegations, and told the caseworker she had already gone through this with the mothers' pension department as well. She "talked at length concerning the fact that her case had been thoroughly investigated, why she did not know, and she was definitely tired of it." She decided to seek private employment, and told the caseworker that if the agency wanted to close

95. Wayne County ADC Case C8200569, case history from July 16, 1940.

the case, that was fine with her. Less than two weeks later, in September 1943, Mansfield called the office to report that she was employed at Ford Motor Company in defense work, earning eighty-five cents per hour, and wanted her case closed.[96]

But rigorous inquiry like this was uneven. The accusation of a male living in a home did not guarantee such invasion. A Saginaw caseworker received a report of a man living with Sally Reynolds in 1938, but accepted that it was likely a rumor started by her estranged husband. Three years later she had a male roomer and his son living with her. The roomer paid rent, they shared child-care responsibilities, and he helped with home repairs. But again, caseworkers raised no questions about his status. The case was closed at Reynolds's request when she secured employment at a local factory. She worked days, and the roomer worked nights.[97] Other than the early report, which Reynolds attributed to her estranged husband, the case record has no hint of suspicion regarding the relationship. The case of Beulah Shoren, who was separated from her husband, was similar. Caseworkers found her relationship with her roomer questionable at one point, but did not pursue it.[98] Both women were white, as opposed to Jane Mansfield, but it is hard to know if race was a decisive factor, given the limited sample.

At times caseworkers sought to avoid labeling some closures an unsuitable home, particularly if another reason existed. Local officials actually did not favor those laws in many instances, as recipients denied or cut off from ADC had to turn to local relief, which did not receive federal funds. Fiscal localism, and a desire to minimize the obligations to use local funds, again appears. Local officials also tended to see other alternatives, including removal of children from homes, as expensive and not always warranted.[99] Caseworkers, therefore, may have sought to appease these officials by avoiding such classifications. In one Wayne County case, caseworkers did not tell the mother the closure was for unsuitability, "given her [mental] instability."[100] At times,

96. Wayne County ADC Case C8200569, case history April 16, 1943; April 28, 1943; April 30, 1943; September 17, 1943; September 30, 1943.

97. Saginaw County ADC Case C7300054, case history March 21, 1939; February 29, 1940; October 8, 1941; March 4, 1943.

98. Saginaw County ADC Case C7300135, case history from January 16, 1940.

99. See *Proceedings of the Annual Convention of State Association of County Social Welfare Boards and State Association of Supervisors,* 1946, 15–26. A 1962 law required counties to provide direct relief when ADC was denied or ended because of an unsuitable home, but the law had little effect on the direct-relief caseloads. *Thirteenth Biennial Report, Michigan Social Welfare Commission, July 1962–June 1964* (Lansing: December 1964), 17; Public Act 195 of 1962, *Public and Local Acts of the Legislature of the State of Michigan* (Lansing: Speaker-Hines and Thomas, Inc, 1963), 432.

100. Wayne County ADC Case C8204271, case history from February 23, 1942.

they simply avoided the label for reasons specific to the case. Gossip alleged that Susan Morrow, an African-American recipient in Saginaw, was living with a man employed at a local factory, a situation confirmed by the man. Caseworkers found that the man had listed Morrow as a dependent on his draft application, and closed Morrow's case because of sufficient income.[101] Another Saginaw case involved Erin Hartz, a white mother of two children who was unmarried. The probate court record criticized the lack of training and guidance Hartz had given her children, but Hartz was approved for an ADC grant in part because of a lack of alternatives. Caseworkers had reports of men in the house and neglect of the children, and Hartz became pregnant again. A psychiatric evaluation said she had "no moral sense," and she also contracted gonorrhea. The case team—including the casework supervisor, Associated Charities staff, and probate court officials—agreed that the home was in no way suitable. Hartz eventually agreed to be sterilized after the child's birth, and to have her children placed, and the case closed. The reason listed, however, was not an unsuitable home, but "receipt of other public or private aid."[102]

To caseworkers, ADC was one of several options for a child's care, and, in some cases, the preferred one, because the family's status as ADC recipients allowed caseworkers to supervise the household beyond its financial needs. Such was the case for James Bellwood, one of the few fathers in the ADC records. A resident of Saginaw and father of six, he had one son living with him in 1939. He worked irregularly due to arthritis and a nervous disorder, which doctors attributed to his service in World War I. Neighbors complained of his drinking and violent behavior. He had a housekeeper, who also received ADC for her daughter, to help with his son's care, and they planned to marry once her divorce was finalized. Caseworkers were concerned with the safety of both children in the home, but did not want to close the case because of unsuitability without an alternate plan for the children. A married daughter, who was caring for two of her older sisters, agreed to take the son into her home, but before that could occur, Bellwood received a veteran's pension and asked that his case be closed.[103] Caseworkers clearly did not think the home was suitable, but with the removal of Bellwood's financial need, they lost the ability to monitor the case. They did not officially close the case, in the hope

101. Saginaw County Case C7300379, case history from January 8, 1941; March 5, 1942; March 9, 1942; March 12, 1942.

102. Saginaw County ADC Case C7300630, case history from February 26, 1940; October 4, 1940; October 15, 1940; November 14, 1940; November 12, 1940; November 19, 1940.

103. Saginaw County ADC Case C7300017, case history from April 14, 1939; May 13, 1939; February 16, 1940; March 29, 1940.

that they could still have some influence, but Bellwood then retrieved his daughter from the older daughter's home. While caseworkers could not prevent this, they referred the matter to the probate court. What makes this case interesting is that caseworkers clearly ignored the "woman in the house," the housekeeper. Their relationship was not simply employer and housekeeper, given their intention to marry, but the caseworkers did not even allude to it. This could point to the gender double standard, in what they expected of their female recipients in contrast to the men, whose numbers were much smaller. The safety of the children in the house likely overrode the moral concerns, in part because the housekeeper provided Daniel's care, serving as a buffer between him and his father. Again, no better alternative existed, in the eyes of caseworkers, who thus adjusted their expectations.

Trying to provide what was best for the child within ADC guidelines emerges in another Saginaw County case. Rose Garner was a long-term recipient about whom caseworkers had very little positive to say. They criticized the family's intelligence, labeling most "feeble-minded," and had numerous conflicts with the older son, Warner, about his financial contributions to the family. Anonymous letters told caseworkers of men living in the home and unexplained luxuries not possible on the family's reported income. Several of the children had conflicts with the law, and more than one spent time in juvenile detention homes. Budget cuts, however, prevented the court from removing the children entirely as long as ADC was allowed. The case was the subject of a staff conference, but caseworkers agreed that ending ADC with no other plan was not in the children's interest, since the receipt of ADC allowed caseworkers to supervise the family. Although caseworkers clearly believed the home was unsuitable, the ADC grant continued.[104]

Recipients could protest decisions by the agency via requesting a fair hearing, which involved a state field representative, as well as the county administrator, case supervisor, and caseworkers.[105] A transcript of the hearing was then sent to the state office, which either upheld or reversed the agency's action. Generally a copy of the case history was also enclosed—a vivid example of when caseworkers were under scrutiny for their handling of a case. Very few recipients in the sample requested fair hearings: less than 1 percent in both Saginaw and Wayne counties, and none in the Marquette County sample. Recipients requesting one of the three hearings in the Wayne sample, and one of the five in Saginaw County, withdrew their respective requests before a hearing was held. What made the fair hearings unique were both the chance

---

104. Case C7300003, case history dated February 8, 1940; February 23, 1940; April 9, 1940; April 11, 1940; May 1, 1940; May 2, 1940.

105. *A Manual for Aid to Dependent Children*, 16.

for the recipient's view to be recorded unfiltered through the caseworker—the transcript was to be verbatim—and the type of evidence considered. Weight was generally given to either direct observations of caseworkers or evidence presented by either the courts or the police; gossip from neighbors, landlords, or family members was not given the credence it might have been in an investigation.

The sample is small enough to render broad generalizations difficult, but the reasons for the hearings are illuminating. All three cases in Wayne County were categorized as unsuitable homes, while just one of five in Saginaw County dealt with an unsuitable home. Two of the three in Wayne involved black women, while just one of the five in Saginaw was black, but that case also involved issues of morality and unsuitability. The more common reason in Saginaw was budgetary; either recipients contested the budget allotted them or disputed the closure of cases based on sufficient income. Here the fair-hearing process intersects with the enforcement of family support. Recipients used the fair hearing, at times, to contest the responsibility of their children to support the family.[106]

Questions of morality were central to the fair hearings in Wayne County. The case involving the withdrawn request focused on the mental stability of the mother, who was deemed of "low intelligence." Caseworkers believed her mental health precluded her employment, and the case record documents caseworkers' concerns about the son's lack of attendance at school and the care his mother provided. The case was closed and referred to the DPW with a suggestion to remove the child.[107]

Court findings concerning accusations of running a house of prostitution proved key in the state's validation of the agency's closure in the case of Tammy Dunbar, an African-American. The Department of Public Welfare record contains several references to such accusations, although the ADC caseworker in this instance noted that he had seen nothing to indicate prostitution. A court case involving a paternity suit filed by a woman who said she had conceived the child in that house prompted the case closure. Again, the caseworker wrote that he had seen nothing, and that Dunbar denied the allegations, but the case was nevertheless closed. The state based its decision on the court record, finding the court testimony compelling, despite the caseworker's comments. Dunbar may have been guilty, but also may have been

---

106. A 1954 law allowed recipients to request a review, through the probate court, of the contributions expected of relatives. The contribution would not be budgeted until the court review was complete. *Eighth Biennial Report, Michigan Social Welfare Commission, July 1952–June1954* (Lansing: December 1954), 15.

107. Wayne County ADC Case C8204271, case history from May 31, 1940; February 23, 1940; April 20, 1942.

the victim of a racist court system, which provided the basis for the closure of her case.[108]

Carol Barnes, an African-American ADC grant recipient in Saginaw, endured similar charges and also had her case closed because of unsuitability. In her case, the testimony of a black police officer was central to the state's decision. The officer believed she was running a "sporting house" and testified that the red light and jukebox in her apartment were evidence enough. According to the caseworker, Barnes had also posed as the wife of her boyfriend on more than one occasion. The state supervisor criticized much of the information presented by the caseworkers, finding it largely hearsay, circumstantial in nature, but he did find the police officer's "evidence" compelling. He upheld the agency's decision.[109]

The alternate discourse of welfare emerges vividly in these cases. Labeled immoral and unsuitable by caseworkers, these women saw themselves in a different light. Dunbar and Barnes likely were engaging in what Victoria Wolcott describes as illicit leisure businesses, which included liquor trafficking, buffet flats, and houses of prostitution. (Barnes had served jail time in Georgia for alcohol violations before moving to Michigan.)[110] But Wolcott argues that such businesses were a means to fight the low wages and high rents endured by black women; Dunbar and Barnes rejected day work, the most common occupation open to black women, and sought different and more lucrative means to support their children. Such entrepreneurial efforts, however, contradicted the goals of respectability set forth by black reformers, including the Detroit Urban League, as well as by the public welfare system.[111] Thus both women ultimately lost their aid.

Another fair hearing involving Martha White, also a black recipient, resulted in the reversal of the agency's decision. Caseworkers asserted that White had hidden income and also had represented herself as the wife of her boyfriend on more than one occasion, once to an agency employee. The hearing transcript unfortunately did not survive, so we do not know the basis for the state's reversal, but clearly they found some error in the county agency's policy. White was reinstated to the ADC program, and no further morality issues appear in the record.[112] In this instance, she pushed her case and won.

108. Wayne County ADC Case C8210470. Virginia Wolcott documents the racist bias in the court and police system in Detroit in the interwar period. Wolcott, *Remaking Respectability,* 103–5.

109. Saginaw County ADC Case C7300312, case history from January 8, 1942; January 15, 1942; hearing transcript.

110. Saginaw County ADC Case C7300312, case history from March 7, 1940.

111. Wolcott, chapter 3, "The Informal Economy, Leisure Workers, and Economic Nationalism in the 1920s."

112. Wayne County ADC Case C8205611.

Financial issues were at the center of some hearings, and while not all recipients were reinstated, their suits did prompt some behind-the-scenes action. The effects of the responsible-relative clause, and the flexibility within that policy, appear in Rachel Wood's case. When Wood's son, Donald, quit the WPA, in early 1939, caseworkers removed him from the family budget and reduced the grant; this decision was the final straw for the Saginaw widow, who was already upset at the small grant she was receiving, and blamed her son's convictions for stealing on the agency's expectations that he support the family.[113] Caseworkers did allow Donald to keep twelve dollars of his monthly fifty-dollar WPA wage, which contrasted the usual practice of having the entire salary go to the family. Because of the son's history, the caseworker clearly felt this might appease him. It did not, and he came to the office to confront the caseworker. His mother backed him; it was not Donald's responsibility, she contended, to support the other children, three of whom were only his half siblings. The caseworker suggested that she request a fair hearing, and she did.[114] The state agency upheld the budget decision, and Wood continued to receive ADC. But in the hearing summary—although not in the letter to Wood—Philip Schafer, director of social services, questioned the caseworker's attitude and handling of the case. He directed the field representative to look into the situation "relative to the adequacy of this worker to deal with problem cases." Although it did Wood no good in her situation, she did succeed in raising questions about the caseworker's actions. Unfortunately, Wood died a year later from a severe heart attack, at the age of forty-five, and her children became wards of the state, as no relatives could take them.[115]

Recipients sought to maintain an active role in the planning of their cases. They spoke out when they felt wronged, and often rejected the caseworker's or the agency's assessment of their need, or lack of it. They did not see themselves as dependents spreading their disease in American society, and many believed that their own circumstances or behavior entitled them to state aid. While they exhibited a range of reactions to the relief process, and put forth a variety of justifications for aid, they were agents in that process. They took full advantage of new avenues of appeals, including petitioning officials in state and federal agencies. The recipients' narratives of relief contrast markedly with the picture painted by local officials, a situation described in the next chapter. Local officials depicted state and federal regulations, including the hiring of

113. Saginaw County ADC Case C7300354.

114. Saginaw County ADC Case C7300354, case history from February 21, 1939; March 14, 1939.

115. Saginaw County ADC Case C7300354. Hearing summary dated May 16, 1939; case history from May 27, 1940.

professional social workers, as the key problems with emergency relief; they were inefficient and fostered dependence, these officials maintained. County supervisors, superintendents of the poor, and other proponents of home rule saw themselves as the last defense against a monster centralized government intent on subverting the democratic process and local autonomy. Only in defeating the monster, in their eyes, could home rule advocates prevent the spread of dependence, and they mobilized effectively in the late 1930s to do just that.

CHAPTER SEVEN

"The Right to Rule Ourselves"

A CONTEST FOR LOCAL CONTROL

"WE HAVE NOT shirked our responsibility," E. H. Hoddenott of Lenawee County told the Welfare and Relief Study Commission in 1936. "We want that which the constitution of this nation says we could have, the right to rule ourselves, and will fight for it . . . That is the feeling of the people, and I know it is intense because we went along with the set-up for four or five years, but we feel the emergency is over."[1] Applause greeted Hoddenott's remarks at the November 10, 1936, hearing of the Welfare and Relief Study Commission.

His views represented the most vocal opinions of local officials of the welfare debates in the 1930s. These debates focused on competing narratives, at the center of which were basic philosophical differences about which level of government should administer relief (and how) and what training or experience was needed. The two visions of professionalization clashed during these final debates. Fears of the centralization of government and a loss of electoral representation fueled the conflicts. Rhetoric often focused on the invasion of local communities by the federal and state governments, and key players in that invasion were social workers. A coalition of township supervisors, county officials, and superintendents of the poor, and the organizations that represented them, successfully fought efforts to remake general relief from a local to

1. Minutes of November 10, 1936, hearing in Lansing, Welfare and Relief Study Commission Minutes, Box 1, Folder 9, 62.

a state program run by professional social workers. Reorganization of welfare proved limited in Michigan, as the ideology of home rule prevailed. By 1940 social workers primarily administered the categorical aid programs under the Social Security Act: Aid to Dependent Children, Old Age Assistance, and Aid to the Blind. General-relief programs, the third track of welfare that emerges in this period, generally returned to local control and pre–New Deal relief methods.

The end of FERA, in December 1935, signaled a shift in welfare policy in Michigan and other states. Federal funding for direct relief ceased when FERA shut down, but relief continued with local and state monies.[2] With the federal government out of the general-relief picture, the landscape changed markedly. Michigan's State Emergency Welfare Relief Commission began to give township, city, and county officials more say in the administration of relief. Federal money funded only the categorical-aid programs of the Social Security Act (ADC, OAA, and AB), and thus SEWRC had to have local contributions for general-relief programs. SEWRC no longer could use federal funds to ensure local government cooperation with its programs, and lost its major bargaining chip in negotiations for relief contributions. Change occurred on two levels: the first centered on the immediate need to adjust relief with the end of FERA, and the second—the appointment of the Welfare and Relief Study Commission—addressed long-range welfare reform in Michigan.

Governor Frank Fitzgerald, elected in 1934, worked with local officials to reshape relief after the demise of FERA. He was critical of the emergency-relief system and favored greater local control.[3] He appointed the WRSC in April of 1936, but local officials demanded immediate change. By June of that year, the State Emergency Welfare Relief Commission, working with Fitzgerald, revised the composition of county welfare-relief commissions. SEWRC appointed only one of the three members of the county's welfare-relief commission; county supervisors selected the other two. A major goal of the shift was "to secure greater public support and interest in the administration of relief."[4] Governor Fitzgerald, through an executive order, created a civil service merit system for employees and a qualifying examination for all current WRC employees. Fitzgerald and proponents of the change hoped to keep politics out

2. Brown, *Public Relief*, 301. FERA officially ended December 31, 1935.

3. Michigan Field Report from Howard Hunter to Hopkins, January 20, 1935, 1–2, FERA Michigan Field Reports, National Archives, Box 138, Folder 2; "Relief Power Return Asked," *Lansing State Journal*, April 30, 1936, 1–2; and WRSC Report, "State Organization for Public Welfare in Michigan," March 1937, 186–87, WRSC Records, Box 5, Folder 4.

4. SERA Letter #589, June 4, 1936; SEWRC Papers, Box 1, Folder April to June 1936; "State Organization for Public Welfare in Michigan," 186–87.

of relief, which was a goal of FERA, but Fitzgerald also supported a greater local role in relief administration.[5] Eventually he would be a vocal advocate of home rule, campaigning on that issue in 1938.[6] Michigan was not alone in its actions following the demise of FERA. Other states also strengthened local control, often returning control of relief to local officials to an even greater extent than Michigan.[7]

Although temporary measures to administer categorical-aid grants were approved, Michigan still faced the task of complying with the provisions of the Social Security Act on a long-term basis. Efforts in 1935 to reform welfare stalled when the legislature failed to pass either of the two major bills introduced,[8] a situation that led to Governor Fitzgerald's creation of the Welfare and Relief Study Commission in April of the following year. The WRSC's task was to recommend how to reorganize Michigan's welfare programs, "as well as to give greater service to the indigent and needy persons in the state." The Social Security Act also necessitated administrative changes if the state was to qualify for categorical-aid grants to help dependent mothers, the blind, and the aged.[9] The commission's report and the reaction to its findings framed the final welfare-reform debates of the decade.

The commission's eighteen members, two of whom were women, represented a range of occupations and perspectives on social welfare. The group included four local officials (both city and county), three business owners, three members of the state's existing welfare commissions, four current state officials, one attorney, and two physicians. Key local officials on the commission were Kent County Probate Judge Clark E. Higbee, Marquette Mayor Arthur Jacques, who also would chair the county's WRC in 1937, Oakland County supervisor Oliver Gibbs, and William Thomas, Kent County superintendent of the poor. Important state officials included SERA administrator William Haber, State Welfare Department Director Fred Woodworth, and William Norton, chair of the State Emergency Welfare Relief Commission.

5. Fine, *Frank Murphy: The New Deal Years,* 408–9; George Granger and Lawrence R. Klein, *Emergency Relief in Michigan* (Lansing: May 1939), 11–12.

6. "Fitzgerald Lashes at Centralization," *Lansing State Journal,* July 29, 1938, 14; "Fitzgerald Heads the Speakers Scoring Present Laws," *Evening News,* July 29, 1938, 1, 10; and Fine, *Frank Murphy: The New Deal Years,* 484–85.

7. Cole, "The Relief Crisis in Illinois," 267–68; Anthony Badger, *North Carolina and the New Deal* (Raleigh: North Carolina Division of Archives and History, 1981), 48; and Thomas, *An Appalachian New Deal,* 153–54.

8. Arthur Dunham, "Public Welfare and the Referendum in Michigan," *Social Service Review* 12 (September 1938): 418.

9. Minutes of the Welfare and Relief Study Commission, April 20, 1936, 4; WRSC Records, Membership list; Box 1, Folder 1, and Box 9, Folder 1; Fine, *Frank Murphy: The New Deal Years,* 411–12.

Harold Smith, executive director of the Michigan Municipal League and state budget director, was chair of the commission.[10] Arthur Dunham, a professor of social work at the University of Michigan, was secretary and eventually directed the commission's study.[11]

The 1936 commission was not the first to evaluate the state's welfare system. Two commissions—the Commission on Public Relief and Care and the Child Welfare Commission—had been established in 1917. Both recommended sweeping changes in local welfare administration, including the abolition of the superintendents of the poor. The reports' criticisms were similar to those found in later commissions, including the WRSC: local officials were often untrained political appointees who made only superficial efforts to investigate relief applications or coordinate aid with other agencies.[12] Opal Matson, in her 1933 report, *Local Relief to Dependents,* recommended a county unit because most relief activities, including mothers' pensions, county infirmaries, and juvenile programs, were organized on that basis. She also questioned the people employed to administer that relief: "There seems little reason to make the most serious and most costly service a local matter administered by untrained and often uninterested persons." She recommended the abolishment of superintendents of the poor and the removal of all welfare administration "from the hands of the supervisors and city welfare directors."[13] Commissions to study welfare in Michigan were not new, but action following them was rare. The 1936 commission would be different.

The WRSC quickly hired a staff and undertook a thorough study of all aspects of Michigan's welfare system, including SERA, the crippled-children commission, and the OAA Bureau, as well as a detailed study of local welfare services in seventeen counties in Michigan. The commission also held four public hearings in Lansing, Detroit, and Muskegon to gain input from local officials and other interested people, and met with state officials in charge of the various departments related to welfare.[14] Once the commission had an

10. Smith was a Republican but was known to have voted for Eugene Debs in 1920 and Roosevelt in 1936. He later was appointed head of the federal Bureau of the Budget by Roosevelt. See Fine, *Frank Murphy: The New Deal Years,* 269.

11. Dunham, "Public Welfare and Referendum in Michigan," 420.

12. "Preliminary Report of Commission to Investigate Public Relief," February 22, 1917, copy in WRSC Records, Box 3, Folder 8; Emma O. Lundberg, *State Commissions for the Study and Revision of Child-Welfare Laws,* U.S. Children's Bureau Publication No. 131 (Washington, D.C.: U.S. Government Printing Office, 1924), 47–49.

13. Matson, *Local Relief to Dependents,* 69.

14. Dunham, "Public Welfare and Referendum in Michigan," 420–21; WRSC Minutes, April to December 1936, WRSC Records, Boxes 1 and 2. Counties included Gogebic and Delta, in the Upper Peninsula; Hillsdale and Eaton, representing diversified agriculture; Kalamazoo and Jackson, for diversified industry; Isabella and Montcalm, oil resources; Kalkaska and

understanding of the current welfare system, members began to debate how best to improve it.

A multitude of overlapping agencies characterized Michigan's welfare system prior to its 1939 reorganization. Michigan had nine state agencies, including the State Emergency Welfare Relief Commission and SERA, established in 1933. The state welfare department, created in 1921, had a director and deputy director, and three commissions, all served by nonsalaried members: the corrections commission, the welfare commission, and the institute commission. The director of welfare also oversaw the old-age pensions (and later the OAA program) before the 1939 law. Michigan also had a crippled-children commission, State Department of Corrections, state hospital commission, and the Michigan Child Guidance Institute.[15] Local welfare systems contained another nine agencies, including the county superintendents of the poor, which oversaw the county infirmary; township supervisors, who administered outdoor relief; probate courts (responsible for mothers' pensions, dependent/neglected/delinquent children, and hospitalization); and county welfare-relief commissions. Some counties had relief commissions for soldiers and sailors, and juvenile detention homes as well. The WRSC study found a total of 1,976 state and local agencies involved in public welfare administration in Michigan's eighty-three counties.[16]

Consolidation was the key goal, and the WRSC argued largely between two possible administrative structures at the state: one department (including prisons and mental hospitals) or three separate departments (mental hygiene, corrections, and public assistance).[17] The commission eventually recommended three commissions and departments.[18] The report also recommended state supervision of local agencies, through the state department of public welfare, arguing that "sound statewide programs require statewide minimum standards and a blending of state leadership with local autonomy and initiative." Federal regulations for the Social Security Act's grants (ADC, OAA, and AB)

Montmorency, for cut-over-recreation; Saginaw and Oakland, high urbanization; Mason and Oceana, fruit; and also Allegan, Genesee, and Ingham. "Local Public Welfare," n.d., WRSC Records, Box 5, Folder 10, 18–20.

15. Arthur Dunham, *The Michigan Welfare Reorganization Act: An Analysis* (Lansing: Michigan Conference of Social Work, October 1939), 10; "State Organization," chapter 1, WRSC Records, Box 5, Folder 4, 36.

16. Dunham, *The Michigan Welfare Reorganization Act,* 12; "State Organization," 16; Dunham, "Public Welfare and Referendum in Michigan," 421–23.

17. "Michigan's Organizations for Public Welfare Services," WRSC Records, Box 3, Folder 8, 2.

18. "State Welfare Organization," 271; WRSC Minutes, July 10, 1936, Box 1, Folder 2; *Report of the Welfare and Relief Study Commission* (Lansing, December 1936), 7, 12–17.

also required state supervision if the state was to qualify for funds.[19] The hiring of qualified personnel, through a civil service merit system, was recommended for all state welfare employees.[20]

The WRSC staff, led by Secretary Arthur Dunham, undertook extensive investigation of local and state welfare programs and ultimately recommended a wholesale reorganization of the welfare system.[21] In addition to accumulating reports on state institutions and departments, staff members conducted interviews with local officials and visited the agencies in the seventeen counties; they read minutes from boards of supervisors and reviewed annual budgets. The WRSC staff report recommended consolidating all welfare programs, including ADC, OAA, direct relief, medical and hospitalization, institutional care, and relief for soldiers and sailors into a single county agency subject to state supervision. The key recommendations centered on hiring trained social workers, using professional social welfare practices, and coordinating social welfare programs. The authors rejected the argument that local officials, as residents, knew their fellow citizens better than did outsiders and could best assess their needs; that argument simply was not enough, as "too often familiarity breeds contempt."[22]

The report ultimately recommended a single, integrated county department of public welfare, governed by a three-member board: one member appointed by the state and the other two by the county board of supervisors, modeled after SERA's administrative revisions in mid-1936. The county board of supervisors could opt to appoint a member of their board, if they wished.[23] The county DPW would oversee all aspects of welfare, including the county infirmary, categorical-aid programs (ADC, OAA, and AB), medical care, hospitalization, and direct relief. A welfare director would administer the department, and also serve as secretary to the county social welfare board. The plan abolished the emergency-relief commission, soldiers' and sailors' relief commission, county old-age assistance board and investigator, and the offices of the superintendents of the poor and the county agents.[24] Personnel would be selected through a civil service merit system. The report argued that the problems with the existing system were the training and qualifications of the personnel running it, not "the indifference or insincerity on the part of the

19. *Report of the Welfare and Relief Study Commission*, 23.

20. *Report of the Welfare and Relief Study Commission*, 24; Fine, *Frank Murphy: The New Deal Years*, 412–13.

21. WRSC Records, "Local Public Welfare," Box 5, Folder 10, 22.

22. WRSC Records, "Local Public Welfare," 181–82.

23. *Report of the Welfare and Relief Study Commission*, 25–26.

24. Ibid., 8.

individuals."[25] The report's language sought to soften the blow to township supervisors and county superintendents of the poor, who had administered relief in Michigan for decades. But the report's recommendations rejected the home rule position, including the pre–New Deal model of relief administration, in favor of the position advocated by professional social workers and FERA.

WRSC member William Thomas, a superintendent of the poor, attacked the local report on more than one occasion, disputing its portrayal of the old relief and demanding to see details about the criticisms. He likely felt personally challenged by criticism of the existing system and of his colleagues. He refused to accept the possibility that perhaps not all poor-relief administrators were like he was, as suggested by other commission members. Staff did outline in their reports specifically which county official generated which criticism, but Thomas rejected the evidence presented: "You can't tell me that in those counties where the superintendents of the poor or other agencies have worked they haven't been conscientious and haven't done remarkably good work."[26]

Thomas and Fred Woodworth, state welfare department director, were the vocal proponents of home rule on the WRSC. From the first meeting they advocated allowing local governments the right to determine their welfare administration. Woodworth believed that "people of the counties should have the type of government they want," a view that Thomas shared.[27] Woodworth argued that the old system had served Michigan's welfare needs for a hundred years, and thus could certainly continue to do so.[28] Throughout the commission's six months of meetings, Thomas consistently maintained that welfare "can best be administered, in my mind, as it is now efficiently and economically."[29] He was openly critical of SERA administrator William Haber, another member of the commission, and insisted that local officials could have done the same job more effectively with one-half to one-third the cost.[30] Thomas

---

25. Ibid., 27–30, quotation from p. 34.

26. WRSC Minutes, Box 1, Folder 9, November 20, 1936, 61. In addition, records related to the county superintendent of the poor in Marquette, Saginaw, and Van Buren counties show dissension and a lack of harmony related to poor relief. See "County Poor Fund Quiz Looms before Board," *Saginaw Daily News,* October 24, 1931; "Poor Fund Inquiry Left Up to Prosecutor," *Saginaw Daily News,* October 27, 1931; "Stewart Resigns as Poor Director," *Saginaw Daily News,* July 19, 1931; and *Proceedings of the Board of Supervisors, Saginaw County, Michigan,* January 11, 1933, 52–64.

27. WRSC Minutes, August 21, 1936, 48–49.

28. WRSC Minutes, September 18, 1936, 12.

29. WRSC Minutes, August 21, 1936, 47.

30. WRSC Minutes, August 21, 1936, 50.

also criticized civil service exams, calling them a "damn fool lot of questions."[31] By the end, he was critical of the commission itself, often asserting that a few members decided issues for the whole.[32]

Thomas pushed early and hard for public hearings on reorganization, and the commission held four: two in Lansing, one in Muskegon, and another in Detroit. Hearings were conducted only in the southern part of Michigan for the most part, thus limiting the numbers of county officials who could easily attend; none were convened in the Upper Peninsula. The Muskegon hearing coincided with a meeting of the Michigan Municipal League. The November 10, 1936, hearing in Lansing coincided with the State Association of Supervisors' meeting to allow any county with representatives attending that organization's meeting an opportunity to present its viewpoint. Although Thomas characterized local officials as overwhelmingly in support of local control and the old system, the hearings' minutes reveal a different picture.[33]

The hearings reflected a more diverse opinion on relief administration than the ideas articulated by the most ardent home rule advocates or by the "sanctioned" positions of the local officials' organizations. Twenty-six people representing seventeen of Michigan's eighty-three counties spoke at the hearings held October 22, 1936 (Detroit), and the following day in Lansing. Just eight of those (31 percent) voiced complete opposition to change, in agreement with Thomas and Woodworth. Sixteen (61 percent) wanted a system that blended the emergency program and local control. Some advocated continuing the communication between caseworkers and supervisors, whose knowledge of their residents could be tapped on a case-by-case basis. While many voiced certain objections to aspects of SERA's administration, some also saw positive changes occurring. Four people (15 percent) favored consolidation of some kind, but did not necessarily reject the old system's staffing, including the superintendents of the poor. None spoke specifically against consolidation into a county unit.[34] The hearing held with members of the supervisors' association is also revealing. Although the association went on record in stark opposition to a more centralized system, just one-third of those supervisors

31. WRSC Minutes, November 20, 1936, 24, 75; Fine, *Frank Murphy: The New Deal Years,* 379–80.

32. The commission voted on various aspects of the report when a quorum was present. A majority of those members present, but not necessarily a majority of the entire commission, was needed to approve specific recommendations. Thomas often argued that a majority of the full commission should be necessary to pass any recommendations.

33. Hearing transcripts survived only for the two held in Lansing and the Detroit hearing; the Muskegon minutes are not available.

34. WRSC Minutes, Hearings held October 22, 1936, and October 23, 1936; Box 1, Folder 8.

who testified (six of eighteen) advocated a wholesale return to the old system, a percentage similar to the earlier hearings. Ten (55 percent) favored a new system that blended local and state control and supervision. Some argued that if counties were to accept state and federal funds for welfare, they needed to accept some supervision and control. Statements against SERA and for local control tended to generate applause during the hearings, but in actuality many participants did not share the extreme negative views voiced by Thomas and Woodworth. Some appreciated SERA's efforts to remove politics from relief, and believed that parts of the system had worked well.[35]

The members of the State Association of Supervisors' committee on welfare were ardent supporters of home rule and strongly opposed any loss of local control of relief. Soon after the hearings, the association presented to the WRSC, through Thomas, a resolution that put forth its own vision of welfare reorganization. The resolution called for a merging of the emergency-relief commission with the state welfare department to eliminate duplication, with a local relief commission of three to five members, appointed by the supervisors, to oversee all aspects of relief. The local relief commission would handle all hiring and fix salaries, with minimal state supervision. The association's position followed that of the home rule advocates, siding against the centralization of relief.[36]

Key targets of home rule advocates were SERA's administrative structure and the "expensive" caseworkers the organization hired. These criticisms hearkened to the early days of federal relief, reflecting feelings of anti-intellectualism and opposition to university-trained officials (and social workers), including William Haber.[37] Woodworth saw caseworkers as too interfering and noted "that unless we watch, social service workers will supervise the lives of those people after they get their pensions."[38] He argued that people were more able and willing to fool caseworkers, because the caseworkers did not know the residents well. Instead, he maintained, the supervisors were the ones to do the job: "I am convinced that at least one third of the welfare recipients wouldn't have the nerve to tell him the 'cock and bull' story they would tell the Emergency Relief Administration."[39] Critics of social work believed that experienced local officials were better qualified than "immature and inexperienced students of sociology and psychology" and "'young folks fresh from school'

---

35. WRSC Minutes, Hearing held November 10, 1936, Lansing; Box 1, Folder 9.
36. WRSC Minutes, November 20, 1936, WRSC Records, Box 1, Folder 10.
37. Fine, *Frank Murphy: The New Deal Years*, 417.
38. WRSC Minutes, Box 1, Folder 6, September 18, 1936, 17. Woodworth referred to OAA recipients in this statement.
39. WRSC Minutes, Box 2, Folder 1, December 16, 1936, 47–48.

who lacked the experience and 'mental reserve' to resist the appeals of the undeserving poor."[40] Thomas commented in one meeting that he "would like to see the person educated at the University of Michigan who can take over the duties [of superintendents of the poor and supervisors] . . . You would only have an administration building filled with employees."[41] Thomas directed those comments at Haber and Dunham, both of whom were on the University of Michigan's faculty. He asserted that social work would only create a large, expensive system to administer relief, a system that would be rooted in academics at the expense of local officials. Another supervisor agreed, arguing that the demands for professional social workers were intended "to keep the parasitical social workers in jobs and build up a huge bureaucracy."[42]

The preference for business expertise, rather than professional social work, highlights the contrasting views of what training and background were needed for relief administration. Home rule advocates largely rejected social work in public relief. Social workers, many critics claimed, were too "soft" in their administration of relief, and were unable to spot people seeking help when none was needed. Business expertise was key, local officials reasoned, because welfare administration was a business. A social worker's role was not in the administration of relief, according to Milton Van Geison, president of the State Association of Superintendents of the Poor.[43] Van Geison believed social work should be confined to the "problem families in the localities . . . to work amongst those problem families and try to build their morale, rehabilitate them, and do whatever work becomes necessary in the social line." Welfare administration, then, should be along business standards, and Van Geison "firmly believe[d] in [his] opinion that the social worker should not be given one dime of money in the administration of that department."[44]

Anti-Semitism also appeared in the larger debates, when one supervisor commented that "a bunch of kike social workers . . . will be coming up her[e] . . . and telling us how to run our own affairs."[45] Anti-intellectual, antiuniversity, and anti-Semitic views also were voiced by legislators who criticized Haber in particular, and social workers in general, during the debates over the WRSC bills in 1937. Sidney Fine argues that such views also appeared in

---

40. Quoted in Fine, *Frank Murphy: The New Deal Years,* 416.
41. WRSC Minutes, August 21, 1936, WRSC Records, Box 1, Folder 5, 48, 54.
42. Quoted in Fine, *Frank Murphy: The New Deal Years,* 417.
43. Milton Van Geison worked as a city poor commissioner in Flint in 1932, was secretary of the poor commission in 1935, and was secretary of the poor commission in 1938 and 1939. He would be named to the new County Social Welfare Board by 1941. See *Polk's Flint City Directory* (Detroit: Polk & Company, 1932), 668; *1935,* 770; *1938,* 24; *1941,* 22.
44. WRSC Minutes, Box 1, Folder 8, October 22, 1936, 24.
45. Quoted in Fine, *Frank Murphy: The New Deal Years,* 417.

earlier debates about civil service reform and unemployment insurance, and were directed at the most feared Jewish social worker, William Haber, who was a key player in those issues as well. (Ironically, Haber was not a social work professional, but a professor of economics.)[46] This hostility toward Haber and educated social workers is hard to overstate.

Officials expressed similar criticisms in their interviews with WRSC staff for the local report. Overall cost and duplication of services were the key problems for one Saginaw Township supervisor, who was one of several Saginaw County officials interviewed by WRSC staff. He also echoed the views of Woodworth and Thomas when he said that social workers were overgenerous, and "took in everyone." As representatives of the poor department, he said, "We have to be harsh with some." The latter sentiment was shared by a farmer who had led the Kochville Township board for thirteen years. His first words to the investigator were that "he wished welfare was out of existence." He also believed the WRC took on cases for which he would not have elected to provide relief.[47]

Many critics of the centralization of relief and the New Deal programs lamented the effects of emergency-relief programs on the American values of self-support and independence. Integral to concerns about a growing preference for relief over work was the fear of a contagion of dependence. Both direct and work relief came under attack by critics of the emergency-relief programs. According to the critics, emergency-relief programs fostered dependency among Michigan residents, with too little emphasis on helping the unemployed become self-sufficient.[48] Opponents tended to favor more-traditional relief practices—often more-punitive methods—to ensure that "the dole" did not become a habit. Woodworth argued that people lost the ability to support themselves through the Works Progress Administration, and now needed to be retrained to work: "We cannot give them jobs where they stand and lean on their shovels."[49] Woodworth further likened the WPA and other federal relief programs to a narcotic or an addiction, insisting, "We had better put in a little cure."[50] Relief prompted people to say "'give, give, give,' and [relief] is spoiling the morale of a great many of the people, knocking the self-reliance

46. Quoted in Fine, *Frank Murphy: The New Deal Years,* 417.

47. WRSC Records, Sampling Survey of Local Relief Agencies, 1936, Box 7, Folder 7, Saginaw County.

48. Fine, *Frank Murphy: The New Deal Years,* 416–17; Fraser and Gordon, "A Genealogy of Dependency," 320–21.

49. WRSC Minutes, Box 1, Folder 6, September 18, 1936, 11.

50. WRSC Minutes, Box 1, Folder 6, September 18, 1936, p. 11. Woodworth's comments foreshadowed later emphasis on welfare dependency as an addiction, or "habit," that needed treatment. See Fraser and Gordon, "A Genealogy of Dependence," 325.

completely out from under them," according to a Midland County supervisor.[51] A Calhoun County supervisor lamented the demise of charitable donations and a willingness to contribute to private welfare programs and to help others; instead, former contributors told people to go to the state. The spirit of taking care of the community, he feared, was disappearing.[52] Local officials were also there, the supervisor contended, to "grab all [they] could."[53]

Gender continues to operate as a subtext in these hearings and the debates over who could best administer welfare. Social work symbolized the federal and state interference in local relief, and to many, that social worker was a female, or espoused decidedly female professional values, as described in chapter 5. The divide between two visions of precisely what professional values were needed for relief work again emerged in the reorganization debates. Conflicts over gendered professional values were evident. Social work's emphasis on service, compassion, and cooperation—largely female professional traits connected to feminized professions—ran counter to the male professional values articulated by many who opposed employing professional social work in the administration of relief. Social workers coddled relief recipients—in the male professional view—while local officials would not. Instead, in their narrative of relief, the male values of efficiency, individualism, and self-help were more appropriate for welfare administration.[54] For local officials in the 1930s, excluding women was not the goal, but the gendered values remained embodied, at least in the minds of proponents of home rule, in the ideals and practices of professional social work. They fought everyone—men and women—who practiced and advocated those values.[55]

Home rule advocates sought a wholesale return of relief administration to local governments, with all social work excluded. A Van Buren County superintendent of the poor, who testified at the October 23, 1936, WRSC hearing, claimed to speak for the county officials, saying "that they are standing

51. WRSC Minutes, Box 1, Folder 6, October 23, 1936, 106–7.

52. WRSC Minutes, Box 1, Folder 9, November 10, 1936, 27–28.

53. WRSC Minutes, Box 1, Folder 8, October 22, 1936, 113.

54. Muncy, *Creating a Female Dominion in American Reform, 1890–1935,* xiii–xiv, 8–10, 68–70; Brumberg and Tomes, "Women in the Professions," 283–84; and Fine, *Frank Murphy: The New Deal Years,* 416–17. Fine documents the negative views held by local officials of social workers, but he does not argue that a gender dimension existed in the arguments about economy and efficiency.

55. Gender signifies beliefs, practices, or values based on ideas about women and men that are often embedded in policy or institutions, beyond the interpersonal relationships between individuals. Socially constructed, such gendered meanings change over time and are powerful signifiers of power, according to Joan Scott, who has articulated the need for gender analysis at all levels of society including politics. See Joan Scott, "Gender: A Useful Category of Analysis," in *Gender and the Politics of History* (New York: Columbia University Press, 1988), 28–50.

pat, that the administration of relief shall be returned to local authorities."[56] He disputed earlier remarks by the county's WRC chair that the county put no money into relief. Not only had the county contributed some to the ERA, he said, but it had also funded hospitalization, medical care, and the county poor farm and infirmary. He stated simply, "We are taking care of Van Buren County."[57] A Saginaw superintendent of the poor echoed statements that the emergency was over and that "all relief should be turned back to the supervisors."[58] He shared Thomas's negative view of the commission's purpose and practices: "We are keeping up with this study of yours . . . we know all about what you are after and what will be recommended."[59]

Some local officials favored a limited role for county supervisors. Van Buren County's WRC chairperson opposed the supervisors taking complete control of relief. Although he was careful in his criticism, he clearly did not think the supervisors capable of administering relief effectively.[60] He saw the WRC as "a non-political organization which is trying to do a tough job in the most efficient possible manner." Consolidation of all relief into a single county unit, he felt, would solve the key remaining problem of duplication.[61] A Saginaw County supervisor argued that supervisors already had power, and were "the king bee, I would call them, of the township. In other words, they write the orders, so there isn't anyone that gets aid from 27 townships unless the supervisors write the order." He didn't see how they could wield any more power.[62] He asserted that supervisors should continue to be involved in the administration of relief, largely through representation on the county welfare board.

Some supervisors no longer wanted full responsibility for welfare administration. Berrien County (southeast of Van Buren County) supervisors submitted a resolution making a case for just what the WRSC eventually recommended: county departments run by civil service staff under a state department of welfare.[63] A member of the Livingston County WRC believed that the key to better administration was the caseworker: "The case worker . . . is the very genius of this new set-up, and ought to be continued at all possible extent." It was time

56. WRSC Minutes, October 22, 1936 hearing, 124. The hearing transcript erroneously lists Scamehorn as Scamehauser.

57. WRSC Minutes, October 22, 1936 hearing, 124.

58. "Sampling Survey of Local Relief Agencies," Box 6, Folder 7, Arthur Hauffe interview.

59. "Sampling Survey of Local Relief Agencies," Box 6, Folder 7, Arthur Hauffe interview.

60. WRSC Minutes, October 22, 1936 hearing, 117–18.

61. WRSC Minutes, October 22, 1936 hearing, 119.

62. WRSC Minutes, Box 1, Folder 9, November 10, 1936, 43. This supervisor also served on the county WRC, appointed the previous summer after the changes instituted by SERA.

63. WRSC Minutes, Box 1, Folder 8, October 22, 1936, 141–43.

to end the superintendents-of-the-poor era, he argued, and to use the better investigation methods of the caseworker. A rural Wayne County supervisor and another from Saginaw County shared this viewpoint. The latter maintained that the new agency saved him a lot of work and time, and he voiced no complaints about its operation.[64] These ideas were not widespread, but the hearing transcripts and WRSC interviews yield views different from those described by Thomas and Woodworth. County officials vehemently opposed to SERA and social work were vocal and visible, but were not the majority.[65]

Thomas and Woodworth led the opposition to the WRSC's final report, and Thomas announced his intention to author a minority report even before the commission had finalized the majority report, released in December 1936.[66] State funds appropriated for relief should be allocated to the counties to be "administered by responsible elective State and County officials," according to Thomas's minority viewpoint, and those funds would "be adequate when relieved of the burden of maintaining the tremendous and wasteful organization now maintained by Emergency Relief." Signatories of the minority report believed that local administration, without state supervision, would be far more economical.[67] The minority report also advocated that the county welfare commission, appointed by the county board of supervisors, would oversee all aspects of relief, including the federal categorical aids, but that only those federal programs should be subject to state supervision. County officials would select and hire all staff, without a civil service merit system, and also fix their salaries.[68]

The minority report was adopted by the State Association of Supervisors on January 27, 1937, at the organization's annual meeting in Lansing, with only 2 of the 402 delegates dissenting. The resolution called for local control of relief and minimum state interference, and soundly rejected the philosophy and specifics of the WRSC report.[69] The ideology of home rule was evident. Centralized relief administration, the resolution counseled, was too far removed from elected officials, thus subverting the democratic process. The

64. WRSC Minutes, Box 1, Folder 8, October 22, 1936, 140; "Recommendations of Various Local Officials," 3 Box 7, Folder 6; Sampling Survey of Local Relief Agencies, 1936, WRSC Records, Box 7, Folder 6.

65. This trend also is evident in the sampling surveys conducted in the case study counties by the WRSC staff.

66. WRSC Minutes, Box 1, Folder 12, December 3, 1936, 103; *Report of the Welfare and Relief Study Commission.*

67. "Minority Report," *Journal of the House,* January 28, 1937, 136, in WRSC Records, Box 13, Folder 7.

68. "Minority Report," 137.

69. "Supervisors Ask Tax Sale," *Lansing State Journal,* January 29, 1937, 12.

two reports set the stage for the passage of the 1937 welfare-reform legislation package, and the reaction against it.

Just four of the eighteen commission members refused to sign the final report. Two of the four opponents were local officials: Thomas and county supervisor Oliver Gibbs. Fred Woodworth also signed the minority report. Dr. Stanley Insley, of Detroit, did not sign the majority report but also did not endorse the minority report. While he criticized the administrative structure, he was not as focused on full home rule. His disapproval centered more on medical relief.[70] Two other key prominent local officials, Marquette Mayor Arthur Jacques and Kent County Probate Judge Clark Higbee, fully supported the final report. Jacques said, "It is certainly a wonderful step forward in the matter of handling welfare relief and humanitarian problems in this state."[71] He firmly believed that state supervision was acceptable if state funds were involved, and neither he nor Higbee shared the extreme home rule views of Thomas and Woodworth.[72] Both would play an active role in defending the welfare reorganization in the 1938 referendum.

The WRSC report resulted in a new legislative package to reorganize Michigan's welfare system. Both the incoming and the outgoing governor (Frank Murphy was elected governor in November 1936, defeating incumbent Frank Fitzgerald) indirectly endorsed the majority report in his respective speech at the inauguration.[73] Legislation was jointly introduced by a Democratic and Republican senator, and eventually passed both the senate and the house, being signed by Governor Murphy in late July.[74] Public Act 257 covered the state administrative structure, while Act 258 detailed the county organization and the ADC provisions. Act 257 created a single state Department of Public Assistance, governed by a five-member commission and headed by a director and deputy director. Supervisory powers over county administration were limited to only those programs that received federal funds (ADC, OAA, and AB), a provision required to comply with the Social Security Act and thereby make the state eligible for federal grants.[75] Act 258 called for a single county Department of Public Welfare governed by a board of three: one appointed by the state department and the other two by the board of

70. See Letter to Harold Smith from Stanley Insley, December 22, 1936, and February 13, 1937, WRSC Records, Box 9, Folder 11.

71. WRSC Records, Box 9, Folder 12, Letter from Jacques to Harold Smith, WRSC chairperson, July 7, 1937.

72. WRSC Minutes, August 21, 1936, Box 1, Folder 5, 45–47.

73. Dunham, "Public Welfare and Referendum in Michigan," 429.

74. Ibid., 429–31.

75. *Public and Local Acts of the Legislature of the State of Michigan, 1937* (Lansing: Franklin DeKleine Company, 1937), 442–43, 445.

supervisors. The county welfare board oversaw all aspects of welfare, from operating the county infirmary to administering the categorical aids.[76] The act abolished most existing relief positions, including superintendents of the poor.

Key differences between the WRSC's recommendations and the 1937 law included the removal of the civil service provisions for staff of both the county and state departments (although state employees would be covered under the recently passed civil service law) and a reduction in state supervision, except in those programs under federal guidelines. The director of the county department also had to be a three-year resident of the county.[77] Another important change was the participation of supervisors. Boards of supervisors were prohibited, under the law, from appointing fellow supervisors to the county social welfare board, a provision *not* recommended by the WRSC report. As with the early days of SERA, supervisors were cut out of the relief commission.[78] The exclusion of supervisors from social welfare boards, despite the elimination of civil service requirements for local relief staff, only magnified local opposition to the bills.

THE REFERENDUM

The two major organizations representing local officials, the State Association of Supervisors and the State Association of the Superintendents of the Poor, mobilized quickly and spearheaded a petition drive for a referendum vote.[79] The referendum focused on Act 257, which outlined the structure of the State Department of Public Assistance and its supervisory powers, which had been limited to the federally funded programs. The major opposition to the legislative package actually centered on Act 258, which specified the local administration of relief, including the exclusion of supervisors from welfare boards. That act, however, included appropriations for relief and, under Michigan law, could therefore not be placed on a referendum. Since Act 258's implementation was dependent on Act 257, opponents opted to place that act on the ballot instead. In this manner, if they managed to defeat that law, then they defeated

76. Fine, *Frank Murphy: The New Deal Years,* 418, 421; *Public Acts, 1937,* 450–52.

77. Dunham, "Public Welfare and Referendum in Michigan," 432–33; Fine, *Frank Murphy: The New Deal Years,* 418–19.

78. *Report of the Welfare and Relief Study Commission,* 26.

79. "County Poor Assail Welfare Law," *Manistee News Advocate,* August 19, 1937, 1, 5; "Convention of County Poor Chiefs Ended," *Manistee News Advocate,* August 20, 1937, 1, 4; and Letter from Milton Van Geison, President, Association of Superintendents of the Poor, to all superintendents of the poor, July 30, 1937, WRSC Records, Box 2, Folder 7.

all of them. By October enough signatures had been gathered, and the issue was placed on the November 1938 ballot.[80]

The next eleven months found both sides focusing on the referendum. Proponents organized a welfare-education committee, comprised of members of both political parties, in December 1937. They prohibited employees of relief agencies from actively participating in the campaign, which might be construed as self-interest on their part, a charge they made frequently against the superintendents of the poor. Their plans included promoting the law by distributing information through numerous organizations, including the Federation of Women's Clubs, the Parent-Teacher Association, and fraternal, religious, and service groups.[81] The committee published a pamphlet, *The Truth about Michigan's Welfare Referendum,* seeking to counter what it saw as misinformation circulated by the welfare-reform opponents.[82] Members of the group included state and local officials and representatives of organizations such as the American Association of University Women and the State Federation of Women's Clubs. Arthur Jacques, Marquette mayor and WRSC member, was on the state committee, along with Probate Judge Clark Higbee of Kent County, also a WRSC member.[83]

Cities and municipalities—represented through the Michigan Municipal League, which endorsed the law—tended to support the legislation, as it removed relief responsibility from their shoulders and made it a county concern. Counties also could not charge relief costs back to the local units—cities and townships—as they had in the past.[84] The city of Saginaw had already relinquished relief administration to the county in September 1936. The council believed that its relief work duplicated that of the county and that overhead could be reduced through a single county agency. The city continued to contribute relief funds, but no longer administered relief.[85] The city council unanimously adopted a resolution six months later seeking a consolidated welfare

80. Dunham, "Public Welfare and Referendum in Michigan," 434; Public Act 257 and Public Act 258, *Public and Local Acts of the Legislature of Michigan* (Lansing: Franklin DeKleine Company, 1937), 442–63; and Fine, *Frank Murphy: The New Deal Years,* 418–20.

81. Memo regarding committee formation dated July 21, 1938, WRSC Records, Box 2, Folder 7.

82. "The Truth about Michigan's Welfare Referendum," September 1938, WRSC Records, Box 2, Folder 8.

83. Welfare Education Committee letterhead, dated December 14, 1938, WRSC Records, Box 2, Folder 8; Ernest B. Harper and Duane L. Gibson, *Reorganization of Public Welfare in Michigan: A Study of Transformation of a Social Institution* (East Lansing: Michigan State College, 1942): 48.

84. Other groups who endorsed the laws were the Michigan League of Women Voters, the Michigan Federation of Labor, social workers, and several Detroit-based organizations. Fine, *Frank Murphy: The New Deal Years,* 421–22.

85. *Proceedings of the Council and Boards of the City of Saginaw,* September 8, 1936, 150.

system under state authority, funded by the state sales tax. Relief had drained the city's coffers for five years, and the city saw the state as the key means to secure financial help.[86]

Counties were less unified in their position on the referendum. Marquette County's board of supervisors took no formal stand on the referendum, and filed or tabled most communications from other counties seeking support for or against local control of relief.[87] The board was not actively working against the new legislation, although as a body it did not support the legislation either. Wayne County supervisors voted ninety-seven to eighteen in support of the Welfare Reorganization Act less than a month before the election.[88] Not surprisingly, Van Buren County's board of supervisors went on record endorsing the minority report early in 1937, although they took no formal action on the referendum.[89] Saginaw County's supervisors unanimously supported the home rule advocates.[90] Overall, eleven counties statewide endorsed welfare consolidation, including seven in the Upper Peninsula and four urban counties in lower Michigan (Muskegon, Kent, Oakland, and Wayne).[91]

The opposition's rhetoric depicted the referendum as a war defending democracy against centralized government. While the new law only partially curtailed powers of the local supervisors, they argued, more restraints would likely follow. The organizations representing the supervisors and the superintendents of the poor met in Sault Ste. Marie in July of 1938 to mobilize the final stretch before the November election, and in a letter to all supervisors and superintendents of the poor, Van Geison encouraged them to send delegates to the convention:

> This battle is in defense of local government . . . It will only be a short time until they will attempt to eliminate the Supervisors entirely, the same as they have the Superintendents of the Poor . . . Unless we take a definite stand and so decisively whip this attempt of encroachment upon local government, we will soon find all branches of local government under control of some State department. Therefore, it is your duty as public officials to protect the people at large who elect you to office.[92]

86. Ibid., March 22, 1937, 51.

87. "Board of Supervisors, Marquette County," July 20, 1938, 13.

88. *Official Proceedings of the Board of Supervisors, Wayne County, 1938*, October 18, 1938, 904. Those voting against the resolution represented both township and city officials. Six of those voting against the act represented Detroit.

89. Board of Supervisors, "Proceedings, Van Buren County," March 23, 1937.

90. *Proceedings of the Boards of Supervisors, Saginaw County,* June 29, 1938, 3.

91. Harper and Gibson, *Reorganization of Public Welfare in Michigan,* 49–50, footnote 3.

92. Letter from Milton Van Geison, president of the State Association of the Superintendents of the Poor and chair of the State Referendum Committee of Flint, dated June 23, 1938,

The extreme rhetoric of war and defense, furthering the argument that the state was seeking to usurp local government and the democratic process, continued at the convention held in late July. Several speakers, including Van Geison and William Thomas, assailed the new laws and the WRSC.[93] They also spoke to local service clubs, demanding home rule for counties.[94] Although officially a nonpartisan group, the associations' members were largely Republican, and the meeting was a pro-Republican, anti-Murphy event. Fitzgerald, who later gained the nomination for governor and won the November election, was a featured speaker at the convention, decisively condemning the legislation.[95]

Opponents of the welfare laws ultimately prevailed when Michigan voters defeated the welfare legislation by a vote of 572,756 to 497,569—a margin of about 75,000 votes—in what the *Detroit News* called "the most hotly-contested" proposal on the ballot.[96] The election attracted the largest number of Michigan voters in a nonpresidential election; about 53 percent of Michigan voters cast ballots in 1938, as compared to 33 percent in 1930.[97] The 1938 election was hailed by many political experts as a test of the New Deal; if so, a majority of Michigan voters rejected it. They reelected Republican Frank Fitzgerald, governor from 1934 to 1936, ousting Democrat Frank Murphy, the former Detroit mayor who had defeated Fitzgerald two years earlier. Republicans not only won the governorship, but also gained control of both the state senate and the house of representatives.[98]

Just eleven of Michigan's eighty-three counties approved the welfare laws. Seven of the eleven counties were in the Upper Peninsula and the other four were all urban counties (see table 7.1 and map 7.1). Marquette, Saginaw, and Van Buren all defeated the welfare legislation in their county votes, and only Marquette County's vote favored Democratic governor Murphy. Local offices

Proceedings of the Board of Supervisors, Saginaw County, June 27, 1938, 3.

93. "Superintendents of Poor Declare War on Social Service Bill," *Evening News,* July 27, 1938, 5.

94. "Would Scuttle Welfare Law of Michigan," *Evening News,* July 27, 1938, 2.

95. Fine, *Frank Murphy: The New Deal Years,* 420–21, 484–85; "Fitzgerald Lashes at Centralization," *Lansing State Journal,* July 29, 1938, 14; and "Fitzgerald Heads the Speakers Scoring Present Laws," *Evening News,* July 29, 1938, 1, 10.

96. "Referendum on Act 257, P.A. 1937," WRSC Records, Box 2, Folder 8; "Welfare Act Appears Lost," *Detroit News,* November 9, 1938, 1.

97. "Fitzgerald Lead Increasing with Third of Precincts In," *Detroit Free Press,* November 9, 1938, 1; Pollock and Eldersveld, *Michigan Politics in Transition,* 23. Michigan voter participation; in 1932 it was 63.7 percent; in 1936 it was 67.4 percent; and in 1940 it was 73 percent. No statistics for 1934 are included.

98. McSeveney, "The Michigan Gubernatorial Campaign of 1938," 97–99; Pollock and Eldersveld, *Michigan Politics in Transition,* 4–8.

TABLE 7.1
REFERENDUM RESULTS

County	Yes	No
Kent	23,816	22,843
Marquette	4,275	5,655
Saginaw	9,737	13,643
Van Buren	2,706	5,371
Wayne	234,208	172,643
State Total	497,569	572,756

Source: "Referendum on Act 257, P.A. 1937."

also followed the state trends as well; all three counties elected Republicans to county offices and the state legislature.[99]

Why the referendum failed is difficult to explain fully, although the fact that just 64 percent of voters casting ballots in the election opted to vote on it suggests that the issue was not all that important to many Michigan residents. Normally referendums attracted about three-quarters of voters who went to the polls, so the welfare count was lower than average.[100] Sidney Fine argues that referendums, although intended to bring a greater voice to citizens on specific issues, often served special interest groups, "and [have] required voters to decide issues they only dimly comprehend, if they comprehend them at all."[101] Some believed the issue was too complicated for the average voter to understand, or care about, and felt that many voters probably cast uninformed ballots. Two Michigan State College professors argued that part of the problem was the information provided by the proponents of the law, the welfare-education committee. The case the committee made was "too difficult for the average reader to comprehend, particularly in rural areas, but also and more important because it was not directed at underlying emotional beliefs, group

99. "Straight Vote Elects Van Buren Republicans," *Hartford Day Spring*, November 9, 1938, 1; "County Back in Republican Fold," *Saginaw Daily News*, 1.

100. Letter from WEC Executive Secretary John MacLellan to Harold Smith, December 14, 1938, WRSC Records, Box 2, Folder 8; and Harper and Gibson, *Reorganization of Public Welfare in Michigan*, 49.

101. Fine, *Frank Murphy: The New Deal Years*, 423–24. A 1940 study of the initiative and referendum in Michigan concluded that ballot issues had increased voter education in government. If such education was not adequate, report author James Pollock concludes, it "is not the fault of the initiative and referendum. It is largely the fault of public authorities for not having paid more attention to the problem of public education." James K. Pollock, *Direct Government in Michigan: The Initiative and Referendum* (Bureau of Government: University of Michigan, 1940). 18.

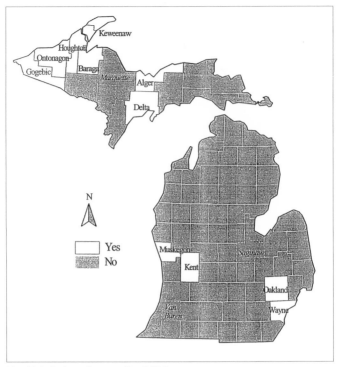

Map 7.1 Referendum results, 1938.

ideas, and accepted values of the rural population."[102] The professors' study of four counties during the referendum fight revealed that residents did not understand the emergency-relief programs even before the referendum, and thus supporters of the reorganization act faced an uphill battle to educate the public.[103]

Home rule advocates used rhetoric and ideas familiar to many voters, particularly those in more-rural areas. While proponents of the welfare law did not speak to the beliefs and values of the Michigan residents, especially those in rural areas, their opponents did. The extreme rhetoric of opponents certainly did not match the facts in the issue, and actually distorted what would happen if the legislation were to stand.[104] But in those distortions was a "message of real meaning."[105] The extreme hostility evident in WRSC minutes and hearings, the legislative debates, and the subsequent 1938 referendum points

102. Harper and Gibson, *Reorganization of Public Welfare in Michigan*, 48–49.
103. Ibid., 47–49.
104. Fine, *Frank Murphy: The New Deal Years*, 420.
105. Brinkley, *Voices of Protest*, 143.

to the entrenched belief in local government and the need to protect it. Fears about the centralization of the government were a critical part of the opposition's views, as well as a belief in the sanctity of local power and the importance of the community. The faith in local relief administration—the responsibility to care for the needy as communities deemed appropriate—was a long-held principle of American society, and retaining that responsibility, and power, was to many local officials an "affirmation of the ideal of community."[106]

Some proponents of home rule viewed the Social Security Act, even with the large amounts of money it would bring to the state and the burden it would lift from local communities for categorical relief, as further encroachment on local autonomy by the federal government, because of the strings attached to those funds, namely state supervision. In fact, both Thomas and Woodworth, the key proponents of home rule in the Welfare and Relief Study Commission, saw the act as unconstitutional, a violation of states' rights in the regulations that accompanied the money. "I think the grant-in-aid principle is all right but a grant that produces the dictation to the state when you say you have got to do so and so, you are taking certain liberties that are reserved to the state by the constitution," said Woodworth at one meeting.[107] In his mind, Michigan's compliance with the act's regulations, even on a temporary basis—in order to receive ADC and OAA funds—was a betrayal to the constitutional rights of state and local governments: "We just recently adopted a policy of purchasing submission to the Federal regulations."[108] The expanded power of the federal government came at the expense of the state government, and proponents of home rule argued that it was only the first step in the continued demise of local control.

But the claim that the election was a rejection of the New Deal masks the complexities at work. Many states saw election shifts in 1938, but for a variety of reasons. Although the Roosevelt administration and the Democratic Party suffered defeats throughout the country in the 1938 election, not all are explained by New Deal opposition. Jack Hayes maintains that voters in South Carolina did not reject the New Deal, which they generally supported, but did oppose issues that furthered black equality, including antilynching efforts and increasing blacks' access to relief programs. Race was a central issue, but many South Carolina residents supported numerous New Deal programs.[109] Several issues came into play in the defeat of both Governor Murphy and the welfare-reform law. Issues of home rule and fiscal localism were chief; rather

106. Brock, *Welfare, Democracy, and the New Deal,* 44–45; Brinkley, *Voices of Protest,* 144.
107. WRSC Minutes, September 18, 1936, WRSC Records, Box 2, Folder 6, 6.
108. WRSC Minutes, August 21, 1936, WRSC Records, Box 2, Folder 5, 50.
109. Hayes, *South Carolina and the New Deal,* 156–57.

than being altogether anti–New Deal, voters were rejecting the centralization of welfare, increased bureaucracy, and a loss of local autonomy. Taxpayers also continued to fight increased taxes and increased expenditures for relief. The emphasis on home rule and fiscal localism is particularly clear in the rural votes, which soundly denied the welfare law. Statewide, 52.5 percent of voters supported the law, but could not overcome the limited support (just 35.4 percent) among rural voters.[110] Throughout the state, support for Murphy, and for the welfare law, in urban areas could not overcome rural opposition.

Governor Murphy's role in the 1937 General Motors sit-down strike, and the rash of strikes that followed, played a role in his defeat. He was criticized for his failure to enforce the law and blamed for the labor unrest that followed the strike, an issue that also played in elections in other states, including South Carolina.[111] The strike was connected to the issue of relief. Strikers were eligible for relief, and thus the state's relief dollars supported the strike, much to the dismay of those opposed to both. Relief for striking workers was a contested issue throughout the decade, and never more so than in the General Motors strike. Murphy had long advocated providing aid to workers based on need, and not whether they were on strike. He had supported relief for strikers in Detroit as mayor, and also made his stance clear in his 1936 campaign. William Haber, administrator of SERA, shared that view, although county relief-commission officials likely would have denied strikers relief grants.[112] Home rule and local control again appear in this issue. State support of relief for strikers provided a clear link between the increased centralization of welfare and the strikes. Exacerbating this link were allegations of Communism in the strikes and labor organizations, both of which were intertwined with the issue of relief. Murphy's support of the Workers' Alliance—which sought to organize WPA workers and was alleged to have ties to the Communist Party, which was open in its backing of Murphy's reelection[113]—and his advocacy for the expansion of the WPA hurt his cause.

The WPA and politics, as well as accusations of using public programs for political patronage, were election issues in many states. Kentucky was among the most heated and visible. In that state, the New Deal was on trial, as investigations of using political favors in the funding and staffing of WPA projects became national news in the state's primary election. Investigation found that

110. McSeveney, "The Michigan Gubernatorial Campaign of 1938," 104–7. McSeveney argues that rural opposition to Murphy was linked to dislike of New Deal agricultural programs.

111. McSeveney, "The Michigan Gubernatorial Campaign of 1938," 108–11; Sidney Fine, *Sit-Down: The General Motors Strike of 1936–1937* (Ann Arbor: University of Michigan Press, 1969), 336–37; and Hayes, *South Carolina and the New Deal,* 150.

112. Fine, *Sit-Down,* 153–54, 202–4.

113. Lorence, *Organizing the Unemployed,* 220–22; Fine, *Sit-Down,* 337–38.

many local officials had used the WPA to secure votes.[114] Patronage was particularly rampant not only in Kentucky but also in West Virginia, Pennsylvania, Missouri, Tennessee, Mississippi, and Illinois.[115] It emerged as an issue as well in the 1938 election in Michigan, although to a much lesser degree. Accusations of politics in relief appeared in an Upper Peninsula congressional election, where Republican challenger John Bennett accused Democrat incumbent Frank Hook of using relief and the WPA to gain votes. The charges were significant, as the WPA and relief were critical in repairing the Upper Peninsula's dismal economy.[116] Bennett lost the election, though, and patronage remained a backseat issue behind concerns about home rule and fiscal localism.

IMPLEMENTATION OF THE 1939 LAW

The defeat of Act 257, and thus the entire welfare-reorganization package of 1937, opened the door for home rule advocates to shape successive legislation. At the 1939 meeting of the State Association of Supervisors in January, newly elected governor Frank Fitzgerald promised an end to expensive social work theories, "which are impractical and are paid for at a high cost to the taxpayers."[117] He did not entirely discount social workers, but maintained that "in the administration of welfare relief, more common sense and less socially minded ideas are needed."[118] Five months later the legislature approved Act 280 of 1939, a compromise bill, which took effect in 1940.[119]

The new commission was evidence of the partial shift in administration. Fitzgerald appointed key home rule advocates to the State Emergency Welfare Relief Commission, including Oliver Gibbs of the WRSC. The commission considered appointing Milton Van Geison, who had led the referendum fight, as SERA administrator, but instead retained George Granger as acting administrator.[120] Haber had served as the state's relief agency head until mid-1937, when he resigned to return to teaching at the University of Michigan. The

114. Blakey, *Hard Times in Kentucky*, 184–88; Jason Scott Smith, *Building New Deal Liberalism: The Political Economy of Public Works, 1933–1956* (New York: Cambridge University Press, 2006), 161–75.

115. Thomas, *An Appalachian New Deal*, 137–41.

116. Lorence, *Organizing the Unemployed*, 221–22.

117. "Governor Pledges Localized Relief," *Lansing State Journal*, January 25, 1939, 1.

118. Address by Frank Fitzgerald, *Proceedings of the Michigan State Association of Supervisors, Annual Meeting*, January 25, 1939, 34.

119. *Proceedings, Supervisors Annual Meeting*, January 26, 1939, 49–50. SEWC Minutes, January 27, 1939, 1, Box 2, Folder 7.

120. Harper and Gibson, *Reorganization of Public Welfare in Michigan*, 51–52.

New York Times article announcing his resignation said he refused to "play ball" with local politicians, and had implemented a civil service merit system—which the article equated with administrative efficiency—before the law required it.[121] His successor, George F. Granger, was a member of the American Association of Social Workers—another administrator with strong social work ties.[122] Like the welfare legislation passed in 1939, the state administration was a mix of ideologies.

The new law offered counties administrative options regarding welfare administration, including full-time working social welfare boards or part-time boards with a full-time director. All counties were to have a county social welfare board, with two members appointed by the board of supervisors, and the third member by the state social welfare commission.[123] Unlike the 1937 law, the 1939 law allowed supervisors to serve on the social welfare board. The vital decision facing counties was whether to adopt the dual system or the unified system. The dual system allowed counties to create a two-part welfare administration: one executive or board would administer direct relief, funded by state and local funds, with only minimal state supervision, and another executive would head the Bureau of Social Aid, which administered the categorical-aid programs under the Social Security Act. The latter, on the other hand, was directly supervised by the state, and workers were state employees. While the dual system was largely controlled by local officials, who were not bound by civil service rules and were relatively free of state supervision, under the unified system, counties had an integrated department of welfare, which administered all relief—both direct and categorical aids. The department was to be headed by a director and staffed by people selected under the civil service merit system; state supervision extended to all forms of relief.[124] The unified system followed the tenets of the 1937 law and the major recommendations of the WRSC, whereas the dual system exemplified the concept of home rule.

The law also allowed relief to be administered on a township basis, a practice one critic argued was a "relic of the poor laws and of horse and buggy days."[125] The State Association of Supervisors' President Oliver Gibbs told members the welfare law was not perfect, but was better than the one they

121. "Spoilsmen Foiled by Relief Head," *New York Times,* August 15, 1937, 38.

122. Membership listing, Michigan, 1936, American Association of Social Workers Records, Box 6, Folder 56.

123. *Public Acts of Michigan, 1939,* Act 280, Section 46, 527.

124. "Supervisors to Name New Welfare Board," *Hartford Day Spring,* October 11, 1939, 1, 4; Gene Alleman, "Supervisors Wrestle with Relief Problem," *Hartford Day Spring,* October 11, 1939, 8; Dunham, *The Michigan Welfare Reorganization Act of 1939,* 26–33; and Fine, *Frank Murphy: The New Deal Years,* 520.

125. Dunham, *The Michigan Welfare Reorganization Act,* 40.

helped to defeat, "because it places the administration of welfare in the hands of local officials who are in daily contact with the people and who know their needs better than any other group."[126] Michigan legislators created a dual system of administration, and although the New Deal's Social Security Act was a federal program—and many recipients saw a new ally in the federal government—local officials retained a significant role in their administration, and mediated all aid distributed through those programs.[127]

Most counties embraced the dual system, opting for a division between those services under direct state supervision and those with only minimal state involvement, which centered largely on direct relief. By February 1940, just fourteen of Michigan's eighty-three counties had implemented even a partially integrated system.[128] Most rejected state supervision coupled with civil service hiring systems and the use of trained, professional social workers. The minimum requirements for the social work administrator position under federal guidelines included at least four years of experience in social welfare, with at least one year in an administrative position. Administrators also had to have at least two years of college education, a portion of which was mandated to contain courses in social sciences. One report noted, "It is said on good authority in Lansing that not one county supervisor in Michigan could possibly qualify for the job of relief administrator." The same report reasons that the selection of the dual system by a majority of counties was "inevitable" for that reason.[129]

Michigan was not alone in its debate about the centralization of welfare, and was behind many states in its passage and implementation of welfare law to comply with the Social Security Act, in part because of the referendum debates. By January 1, 1939, a WPA study found that state supervision had expanded to include at least three types of relief in forty-five states, and about half of those states supervised five kinds of relief through a single agency. The increased state involvement in welfare was in part due to requirements under the Social Security Act, but two-thirds of the states played some supervisory role in general relief, the third track of welfare, and also provided funds for general relief, a significant change from pre-Depression years. But in at least ten states, general relief, although supervised by the states, remained under

---

126. "Welfare Law 'Not Perfect,'" *Lansing State Journal*, January 23, 1940.

127. Gordon, *Pitied But Not Entitled*, 294–99; Argersinger, *Toward a New Deal in Baltimore*, 208; Badger, *North Carolina and the New Deal*, 40, 47–48; Hayes, *South Carolina and the New Deal*, 45–48; Heinemann, *Depression and New Deal in Virginia*, 75–77; Lowitt, *The New Deal and the West*, 22–23; and Katznelson, *When Affirmative Action Was White*, 37–38.

128. Harper and Gibson, *Reorganization of Public Welfare in Michigan*, 55.

129. Alleman, "Supervisors Wrestle with Relief Problem," 8.

local control and included a return to poor law practices.[130] West Virginia's 1936 law was among the first enacted after the Social Security Act, and integrated all welfare functions into one state department, putting both the categorical-aid programs and general relief under the state's umbrella.[131] Illinois and Ohio both resisted the centralization of relief, and in the former state, local officials' organizations played a key role in the opposition.[132] Minnesota, like Michigan, separated general relief from the categorical aids, and it remained a local concern with minimal funding and no professional social workers as staff.[133] Some states, such as Virginia, achieved change simply by creating a local network of agencies under FERA, and retaining those for the categorical-aid programs of the New Deal. Virginia's 1938 Public Assistance Act included all programs under the Social Security Act. Although funding was limited and grants were below the maximum allowed, the new system represented an important change from before 1933.[134] Historians Thomas Coode and John Bauman make a case that the changes in Pennsylvania, particularly for rural counties, were profound despite their continued mix of state and local involvement. A state department ran all welfare programs, including the categorical aids, but institutional care remained a local concern. Local boards continued to play a role in all welfare. Coode and Bauman contend that local values, including the emphasis on independence and work, continued in the administration of relief: "It was perhaps ironic that the modernization of the relief and welfare systems in Snyder County, rather than undermining local beliefs ultimately harnessed them to a more efficient and able system."[135]

In Michigan, the counties of Manistee, Marquette, Saginaw, and Wayne all decided on a dual system, while Van Buren County supervisors surprisingly voted for an integrated department, despite their opposition to state supervision. Van Buren's decision came on a close thirteen to eight vote and was accompanied by a heated debate; one supervisor pointed out that the decision went directly against the home rule position the supervisors had defended for

130. Robert C. Lowe, *State Public Welfare Legislation,* Research Monograph XX (Washington, D.C.: U.S. Government Printing Office, 1939), 19–20, 29, 34. The limit of this study is that some states, including Michigan, had not yet instituted permanent change in their welfare laws.

131. Thomas, *An Appalachian New Deal,* 156–57.

132. Maurer, "Public Relief Programs in Ohio," 138–49; Cole, "The Relief Crisis in Illinois," 460.

133. Koch, "The Development of Public Relief Programs," 441–42.

134. Heinemann, *Depression and New Deal in Virginia,* 155–56, 161–63; Bucki, *Bridgeport's Socialist New Deal,* 172; Ferguson, *Black Politics in New Deal Atlanta,* 74; Argersinger, *Toward a New Deal in Baltimore,* 30–32; Badger, *North Carolina and the New Deal,* 49; and Smith, *The New Deal in the Urban South,* 62–64.

135. Thomas H. Coode and John F. Bauman, *People, Poverty, and Politics: Pennsylvanians during the Great Depression* (Lewisburg: Bucknell University Press, 1981), 82–86; quotation from 85.

so long.[136] Neither the newspaper accounts nor the minutes record why several supervisors reverted from their hard-line home rule stance. It is possible these supervisors feared that the dual system involved too much duplication of costs, and believed that the board's role in administering relief would be strong enough to retain a local voice. Conflicts among supervisors, evidenced in the early emergency-relief years, diminished and thus opened the way for more acceptance of change.[137] Marquette County's welfare committee recommended the dual system to supervisors because they believed the county's size warranted two executives, between whom they would divide the tasks. The board of supervisors agreed unanimously.[138]

Saginaw County—led by the vocal Charles Bois, an ardent opponent of the 1937 law and a vocal supporter of home rule—opted for the dual system, but, in contrast to Van Buren and Marquette, voted to have a full-time working board, rather than a separate administrator.[139] Saginaw County also appointed Bois, chairperson of the board of supervisors, as the member of the social welfare board to be endorsed by the state welfare commission.[140] Wayne County also selected the dual system of administration. The law permitted larger cities to administer their own direct relief, separate from the county, and Detroit chose that system, while the county operated through the Wayne County Department of Social Welfare and the Wayne County Bureau of Social Aid. All categorical-aid recipients went through the latter agency.[141] Wayne County's social welfare commission was a policy-making board, with a full-time director.[142]

Business expertise, or pre–New Deal relief experience, again was the preferred background for relief administrators. Many counties, including

---

136. "County Welfare Plan Is Approved," *Hartford Day Spring*, October 18, 1939, 4; "Proceedings, Van Buren County," October 12, 1939, 41.

137. Harper and Gibson, *Reorganization of Public Welfare in Michigan*, 55.

138. "Proceedings, Board of Supervisors, Marquette County," Vol. 8, September 20, 1939, 89–90.

139. *Proceedings, Board of Supervisors, Saginaw County,* October 9, 1939, 49–50.

140. Ibid., October 16, 1939, 110; October 25, 1939, 139; "Welfare Post Given to Bois," *Saginaw Daily News*, October 27, 1939. Forty-one other counties selected the dual organization system in the next year. Just five opted for a full-time working board. Arthur Dunham, Spender R. Gordon, Albert R. Renwick, Margaret F. Gordon, and Edward Dalton, *Public Relief in Three Michigan Counties: The Report of a Study of Public Relief in Houghton, Antrim, and Hillsdale Counties, Michigan* (Unpublished study, Washington, D.C.: Brookings Institution, 1940), 48.

141. *Journal of the Common Council, City of Detroit, 1939,* August 1, 1939, 1725; *Proceedings, Board of Supervisors, Wayne County, 1939,* July 27, 1939, 316–18; October 20, 1939, 87; *The Department of Public Welfare, 1930–1940* (Detroit: Department of Public Welfare 1940), 3, 22–23; Sullivan, "'On the Dole,'" 222–23; and Dunham, *The Michigan Welfare Reorganization Act of 1939,* 33.

142. *Proceedings, Board of Supervisors, Wayne County, 1939,* November 28, 1939, 992.

Marquette, Saginaw, and Van Buren, voted to hire nonprofessional social workers to head their county departments of public welfare. Marquette County hired a former poor-commission investigator as director of the County Department of Social Welfare in 1939. Marquette County did retain its WRC administrator on the DSW staff, in contrast to Saginaw County, but he had a business, and not a social work, background.[143] In addition to Bois, Saginaw County's board of supervisors appointed a former poor commissioner to the county social welfare board, instead of former WRC administrator Lucius Howlett.[144] Van Buren County also did not appoint former members of the WRC to its new commission, nor did it hire former poor commissioners.[145] Van Buren's social welfare board did retain its county administrator under the new system.[146] Detroit's Department of Public Welfare hired within its ranks, retaining Director G. R. Harris.[147]

Kent County is the most telling example of the retreat from professional social work. Kent County's WRC was once considered one of the most professional public agencies in the state, but looked to poor-relief officials to head its program in 1940. Supervisors appointed Ira Dean, a twenty-five-year superintendent of the poor, to the county social welfare board, and he also served as director of the social welfare department. Other board members included WRSC member and Superintendent of the Poor William Thomas, the most vocal of home rule advocates on the WRSC, and Probate Judge Clark Higbee, a WRSC member who supported the proposed changes. The commission had no interest in Family Welfare Association membership or in professional social work, developed during the early WRC years, and informed the FWA,

143. *Polk's Marquette-Ishpeming-Negaunee City Directory* (Detroit: R. L. Polk & Company, 1941), 333; "Proceedings of the Board of Supervisors, Marquette County," September 20, 1939, 89–90; October 9, 1939, 124.

144. *Official Proceedings of the Board of Supervisors of Saginaw County, Michigan,* October 16, 1939, 108–10; "School Annex Relief's Home," *Saginaw Daily News,* November 9, 1939.

145. "Proceedings, Van Buren County," October 12, 1939, 41; October 13, 1939, 44; "County Welfare Plan Is Approved," *Hartford Day Spring,* October 18, 1939, 1, 4.

146. Wilkinson replaced Harold Humphrey in August 1938 when Humphrey accepted a position in Lansing after earning the highest rating possible on the state's civil service examination. A former teacher, she had five years' experience as a caseworker. Because the county opted for an integrated system, they had to select someone (like Wilkinson) qualified under state and federal guidelines. "Voted $500.00 for County Relief in August," *Courier-Northerner,* August 12, 1938; "Supervisors Met Tuesday; Vote January Relief," *Courier-Northerner,* December 15, 1939.

147. *The Department of Public Welfare, 1930–1940,* 4; *Polk's Detroit (Wayne County) City Directory* (Detroit: Polk Publishing, 1936); *Polk's Detroit (Wayne County) City Directory* (Detroit: Polk Publishing, 1939); *Polk's Detroit (Wayne County) City Directory* (Detroit: Polk Publishing, 1940); and *Polk's Detroit (Wayne County) City Directory* (Detroit: Polk Publishing, 1941).

in late 1940, that it did not plan to pay dues or remain in the organization.[148] The FWA terminated Kent County's membership, ending the public agency's brief foray into professional social work.

A study of three Michigan counties in 1940 underscored the limited changes in relief administration that resulted from the New Deal programs. Only one county had trained social workers in its county social welfare department; the other two followed personnel guidelines only where they had to—in the categorical-aid programs of the Social Security Act, which had civil service requirements and state and federal supervision.[149] The study's authors argued that in two of the counties general relief in the post-Depression era was "scarcely distinguishable from the traditional archaic and discredited poor relief system."[150] The study's chief author was Arthur Dunham, a major framer of the WRSC report and the 1937 legislation; his criticisms of Michigan's relief programs continued in this study, and he found the 1939 law to be the foremost problem.[151]

Home rule advocates achieved their goal in fighting the referendum, thereby reshaping public welfare in their image. In rejecting professional social workers in welfare reorganization, county officials had rejected their methods and philosophy. Experiments in professionalizing public agencies, such as Kent County, did not last under the pressure of local officials. Fiscal localism also appears; supervisors wanted to be able to institute regulations to control costs so that relief did not become an out-of-control part of their budgets. Opposition to increased taxes, as well as the tax limitation of fifteen mills, was also a factor. Economy and efficiency, and not professional social work methods, were to define relief administration, and some counties, including Van Buren and Manistee, believed that relief needed to be stigmatized and punitive to discourage people from seeking it. Investigations were necessary for relief work, they acknowledged, but social workers did not need to be the people to do them. They also largely rejected women. Kent County was among the few that appointed a woman to its commission; most hired men, often with business experience, to lead their county social welfare departments. Women in public welfare tended to work in the Social Service Bureau, the county division that administered the categorical-aid programs of the Social Security Act.

148. Letter from Ira Dean to Margaret Wead, FWA, December 9, 1940, FSA Correspondence, FSA Records, Grand Rapids Folder.

149. Dunham et al., *Public Relief,* 92, 104, 274–75, 378–80, 400–409, 412–13.

150. Ibid., 104. Dunham's study is extremely critical of the new law and blames many of the relief-administration flaws on the law, and not the counties that administer it.

151. Ibid., 103–4. Raymond Koch states that such limited change also is evident in Minnesota's revised welfare program. Koch, "The Development of Public Relief Programs," 441–42.

Figure 7.1 Manistee County relief administrator Louise Armstrong with children of relief clients in Wellston. Photo from Louise Armstrong collection, courtesy Bentley Historical Library, University of Michigan.

Manistee County was a case in point. Manistee, like many counties, did not hire professional social workers to staff their agency. County relief administrator Louise Armstrong resigned in 1936, declaring that she could not work with supervisors under the new guidelines. She was harshly critical of the supervisors and the new appointees in her memoir.[152] By 1940 the county social welfare board was comprised of a former poor commissioner, a local barber and former county clerk, and WRC administrator Ole Hanson, a local businessman. Manistee's supervisors wanted control over relief; they wanted to be able to institute regulations—such as no aid for one who had a car—to control costs so that relief did not become an unmanageable portion of their budget. Manistee County officials rejected social workers, like Louise Armstrong, and the values they associated with both females and social work. Armstrong represented much of what supervisors loathed about emergency relief: trained,

---

152. Armstrong, *We Too Are the People,* 466–67; Fine, *Frank Murphy: The New Deal Years,* 407–8. Fine presents Armstrong's viewpoint uncritically in his analysis.

college-educated, "professional" outsiders representing the state government and telling local officials how to administer relief to their residents (see figure 7.1). The *Manistee Examiner* described Armstrong's legacy in this way, representing the mixed feelings that local residents felt about this strong woman who would not back down, and also the views that many home rule advocates exhibited toward social work and the social worker:

> We doubt if any other woman in Manistee county history ever held so important a trust, ever was the subject of so great political outcry, or ever stuck to her tasks so quietly yet determinedly. We now see it wasn't Mrs. Armstrong folks were fighting, it was the new state and national policy she represented. Going back to the simile of an invasion, we now realize she was an excellent soldier, winning her battle and consolidating her gains. Whether we admired the cause she was fighting for or whether we abhorred it, we must agree she filled her post well.[153]

The profession of social work enjoyed a brief and controversial career in public relief in Michigan, but did not remain in force after 1939. The actions of Michigan's county supervisors—including those in Manistee County—suggest that, in their eyes, the female social worker was the personification of FERA and SERA, a symbol of the government "invasion" that they so feared—and that they worked so hard to stop.

153. "Listening In," *Manistee Examiner,* June 10, 1938, in Armstrong Papers, Bentley Historical Library, Box 1, Clippings folder.

CONCLUSION

THE 1939 WELFARE Reorganization Act and the federal Social Security Act of 1935 shifted the organization and funding of relief, but brought limited actual change to Michigan's welfare system. The law resulted in a dual system of administration in most counties, with separate departments for the categorical-aid programs, governed by federal guidelines, and the general-relief programs. Categorical-aid programs, funded in part with federal matching grants, were implemented slowly, and few grants provided adequate support for recipients. In addition, families on WPA, and those who received ADC, OAA, or AB, often could not receive any supplemental aid in some counties, despite the low grants under those programs. Categorical-aid recipients continued to be subject to means testing and financial investigation. ADC, OAA, and AB were on the assistance track of welfare, and were not administered as entitlement programs. But while immediate change was limited, and continuities persisted, the events of the 1930s began a process of centralization at the state level that would continue for the next three decades.

The 1939 reorganization law was a compromise between old and new practices, and the lack of a consensus rendered the law unsatisfactory to people on both sides of the relief issue. Debates over welfare administration continued. Many counties continued to struggle with the financial burden of relief despite federal and state funds. Local officials did not have full control over all aspects of relief, including the categorical-aid programs. The state, when computing matching formulas for categorical-aid grants, did not consider the expenses of the county infirmary or of soldiers' and sailors' relief or medical and hospitalization costs, all programs that continued to be the full responsibility of counties. Local officials also wanted the state to earmark at least one-third of revenues from the 1933 sales tax for local relief. Supervisors attending the state association meeting in January 1940, just weeks after the new law was implemented, strongly endorsed resolutions on all those issues.[1]

Many local officials and their organizations wanted to return home rule to all areas of relief. The new law, in creating the ADC program, which was subject to federal guidelines, effectively eliminated mothers' pensions, a locally funded and administered program.[2] Some officials resented this shift, despite the accompanying federal funds. Melville McPherson, chair of the state tax commission and a vocal home rule proponent, even advocated a return to locally administered mothers' pensions, rather than the ADC program with its federal matching funds. He argued at the 1940 supervisors' meeting that more-efficient local administration, in conjunction with a larger OAA federal grant, would offset the $3.5 million ADC grant the state would receive.[3] Saginaw County's Arthur Hauffe, a former superintendent of the poor and member of the county's social welfare board, advocated a wholesale return to the pre-Depression system. The reorganized relief administration resembled the WRC too much, he insisted.[4] Both the State Association of Supervisors and the State Association of County Social Welfare Boards (the successor to the Association of Superintendents of the Poor) sought changes in the Social Security Act to allow local officials control over the categorical-aid programs. At its 1942 meeting the Michigan State Association of Supervisors urged Michigan's federal representatives to seek amendments to the Social Security Act to permit state and local, rather than federal, control, and reiterated, the following year, the power of supervisors in welfare administration.[5]

Most local officials did not mourn the demise of the professional caseworker in general relief. Social workers, who played such a central role in

---

1. "Local Control on Dole Given Dickinson O.K.," *Lansing State Journal*, January 24, 1940; "Supervisors Ask One-Third of Sales Tax," *Lansing State Journal*, January 25, 1940; and *Proceedings of the Michigan State Association of Supervisors Annual Meeting*, January 25, 1940, 79, 83.

2. The 1939 law did not explicitly eliminate mothers' pensions, but the federal funds for ADC were the key reason for a switch to that program. Landers and Tharp, *Administration and Financing of Public Relief*, 19–20.

3. "Local Control," 4.

4. "System No Good, Hauffe Declares; Urges Old Plan," *Saginaw Daily News*, October 30, 1940.

5. The organization evolved into the Michigan County Social Services Association. *Proceedings of the Michigan State Association of Supervisors*, 1943, 26, 45.

the battle over the 1938 referendum, largely disappeared from general-relief administration thereafter. Ira Dean, Kent County's social welfare director and a longtime poor-relief commissioner and outspoken home rule advocate, proudly stated that he required only a high school education of his staff, which was comprised of "nine young fellows about twenty-eight years old." They did not need a college education, he said, and "I defy anyone to pick better trained social welfare workers." He rejected the help of "the Kent County Social Welfare group" in setting standards and selecting personnel, because "we feel we can pick our own personnel, and we have reduced our administrative costs thirty-one percent."[6] Many counties reduced their costs by relying on supervisors' recommendations on the eligibility of applicants, rather than having employees conduct extensive investigations. Kent County opted for the "professional" relief worker as defined by local officials. The absence of social workers was not one of the flaws of the 1939 law, according to Dean and other home rule advocates.

Not all counties were unhappy with the new system, although a majority sought a revision of the matching-grant formula to include all local welfare expenditures, as well as an increase in the state's relief contribution. Ironically, Van Buren County's supervisors, among the most critical of the WRC and SERA in the early years of the New Deal, expressed few problems with the new system. They were the only county among the four to select the integrated relief system, placing their entire relief administration under the state's supervision. Their director, Louise Wilkinson, a former WRC caseworker, had to meet civil service requirements to hold her post, but had the board's support from the time of her appointment as administrator in 1938.[7] The county, which had faced a seventy-five-thousand-dollar deficit just a few years before and had suspended all poor relief and mothers' pensions, had recovered financially in the meantime, and the county treasurer told the supervisors at the 1940 budget meeting that the county was in its best financial shape in years.[8] Marquette and Van Buren officials did not fundamentally change their relief systems, or their personnel, in the years immediately following the new law's passage.

Detroit continued to operate a welfare department separate from the county system after the 1939 law. But all categorical-aid programs transferred to the Wayne County Bureau of Social Aid. Probate Judge D. J. Healy resisted

---

6. *Proceedings, Supervisors Meeting,* January 24, 1940, 46.

7. Wilkinson remained head of the department until her retirement in 1966. See "Field Report, Nov. 1965–January 1966," Field Service Correspondence, Archives of Michigan, Box 8, Folder 2.

8. "Supervisors O.K. Finance Budget," *Courier-Northerner,* November 1, 1940, 1.

the transfer of mothers' pensions from the probate court, but those cases were nevertheless moved to the BSA beginning in January 1940.[9] The DPW continued to provide aid for those waiting to transfer to ADC, OAA, and AB.[10] The county chose a dual system, with the BSA separate from the DSW, and established a part-time, policy-making board with a full-time director.[11] Wayne County supervisors were committed to maintaining the standard of living in the shift from mothers' pension to the ADC program, and agreed to provide supplementation from county funds to make up for the minimal ADC grants, as did the Detroit DPW.[12]

Saginaw County faced a difficult year in welfare administration. Early budget projections called for an additional twenty-five thousand dollars to run the reorganized system.[13] Repeated requests from the county for added funds to cover deficits angered city officials, who came to believe that the reorganized system, under county administration, was still too expensive.[14] The savings promised through local administration by home rule advocates, including many Saginaw County officials, failed to materialize. Instead, the city had spent double the amount in 1939–40 than it had in previous years, and city officials questioned the county's ability to administer relief.[15] Rumblings of discontent spread to the finance committee, which was upset at reports that administrative costs for the social welfare board were 25 percent, three times the rate of the WRC in the 1930s. Committee members called the costs "disgraceful," arguing that "no business could carry an administrative burden of 25 percent."[16] An investigation and subsequent reorganization followed. Instead of a three-member full-time board, supervisors established a three-member commission, with only one member serving full-time—as a director. They appointed to the social welfare board two "dollar-a-year" commissioners, in addition to Grover Stine, a former county clerk, as full-time director.[17]

9. *Proceedings, Wayne County Board of Supervisors, 1937,* January 14, 1938, 867–69; January 21, 1938, 872–83; *Proceedings, Wayne County Board of Supervisors, 1938,* November 28, 1939, 982; and Susan Stein-Roggenbuck, "'Wholly within the Discretion of the Probate Court': Judicial Authority and Mothers' Pensions in Michigan, 1913–1940," *Social Service Review* 79.2 (June 2005): 308–9.

10. Sullivan, "'On the Dole,'" 223–24.

11. *Proceedings, Wayne County Board of Supervisors, 1939,* November 28, 1939, 992.

12. Ibid., October 18, 1939, 651; *Proceedings, Wayne County Board of Supervisors, 1940,* September 19, 1940, 530; "Minutes, Detroit Public Welfare Commission," December 24, 1939, 119; and Sullivan, "'On the Dole,'" 224.

13. "New Relief Setup Adds on $25,000," *Saginaw Daily News,* October 31, 1939.

14. *Proceedings of the Council and Boards of the City of Saginaw,* January 2, 1940, 1 and 8; January 22, 1940, 20; February 19, 1940, 47.

15. *Proceedings, City of Saginaw,* July 15, 1940, 213–14.

16. "Relief Budget Costs Scored," *Saginaw Daily News,* October 18, 1940, 1.

17. "County's Relief Chief Dismissed," *Saginaw Daily News,* November 8, 1940, 1; "Relief

Saginaw County's intense conflicts over its new relief system were unique among the counties studied, although it was likely not the only one to under-take changes in the first year of the new system. One criticism of the new law was that it allowed too many administrative choices, but personality conflicts exacerbated Saginaw's problems. Clashes over relief administration calmed after the 1940 reorganization.[18]

The 1939 law effectively segregated general relief (later to be General Assistance) from other federal programs. General relief included those in need who did not fit the categorical-aid programs, including those who were disabled or too ill to work, but too young to qualify for OAA.[19] Funded by local and state dollars, general relief became the "third track" of welfare, often administered entirely by local officials,[20] who established their own eligibility and administrative guidelines. State officials had only limited supervision over those programs, although the state provided at least 50 percent of the funding.[21] Recipients of general relief, for the most part, faced a return to the pre–New Deal practices of poor relief when they sought aid from their local county social welfare boards. Relief applicants continued to face a maze of agencies, both public and private, to secure the help they needed. They also did not have the same avenues of protest—state and federal officials—as cat-egorical-aid recipients. General relief was strictly a local concern, and recipi-ents could appeal only to their local agency and township or city supervisor. A single agency did not guarantee change. Even states that merged the programs

Shake-up Shifts System," *Saginaw Daily News,* November 13, 1940; "Supervisors Limit Officers' Fees," *Saginaw Daily News,* November 14, 1940; and *Proceedings, Saginaw County,* November 12, 1940, 154–56.

18. Public officials later joined private welfare agencies from the Saginaw Council of Social Agencies in establishing a central index of relief and welfare. The council paid half the cost, and the county the other half, implementing a mechanism to facilitate coordination between public and private welfare agencies. "Food Stamps Plan Opposed," *Saginaw Daily News,* January 10, 1941.

19. Single women suffered perhaps the worst, as they likely worked in programs not cover-ed by Old Age Insurance (the program now popularly known as Social Security). Thus their only avenue of support was OAA, or general relief if they were not yet eligible for an old-age grant. See Kessler-Harris, "Designing Women and Old Fools," 102, 104–5.

20. Minnesota followed a similar trend, and historian Raymond Koch argues that the decade saw little change in the general-relief practices. Raymond L. Koch, "The Development of Public Relief Programs in Minnesota, 1929–1941" (PhD dissertation, University of Minnesota, 1967), 442–43.

21. Landers and Tharp, *Administration and Financing of Public Relief,* 27. Allocation per-centages were set by the State Social Welfare Commission, and some counties received up to 95 percent of their relief funds from the state. The formula was based on the county's financial situation and its relief needs. In 1940, Marquette, Saginaw, Van Buren, and Wayne all received 50 percent funding from the state. "Minutes, State Social Welfare Commission," November 29, 1940, 96–98.

into one department, localization, accompanied by minimal state funding, limited the changes. Jerry Thomas argues that West Virginia, which did create a single Department of Public Assistance for all relief, also saw regression in its relief programs: "What happened in West Virginia when the state and counties resumed control of relief reflected a national pattern of harsher administrative practices, reduced relief grants, and lower personnel standards."[22] Michigan's funding was more generous than many states, but local officials sought to minimize general-relief costs as much as possible.

Fiscal localism emerges in the development of this third track of welfare. Many counties, including Saginaw, used their restored authority over general relief to institute punitive measures to discourage relief applicants, reinforcing distinctions between the federal programs and general relief. A key argument for home rule was that local officials could administer programs more efficiently and economically than professional social workers, and thus could more effectively contain the contagion of dependence. Restricting eligibility for relief was a strategic means to minimize local expenditures. Saginaw County's Charles Bois proudly told supervisors at the 1940 meeting that Saginaw's board sought "to perfect a system whereby we can catch up to chiselers. We have a Congress . . . and a Legislature in Michigan . . . to make laws and we have five million people to figure out how to break them."[23]

To limit potential chiselers, several counties placed restrictions on what services or goods rendered an applicant ineligible for relief. Both Saginaw and Manistee counties refused aid unless applicants turned over their automobile license plates; when their need for relief ended, the license plates were returned. No relief was granted to anyone who owned a telephone; exceptions were made if someone other than the applicant paid the bill or if the applicant was elderly or ill.[24] Faced with a deficit early in their fiscal year, Manistee County supervisors refused to grant aid to anyone frequenting places that served alcohol, a practice also implemented in Van Buren County.[25] When costs continued to climb, Manistee County supervisors further restricted eligibility in 1940. Recipients had to maintain gardens and supervisors prohibited newly married couples from receiving relief for a period of one year. The supervisors also denied any supplementation for WPA workers, regardless of their family size, as well as ADC and OAA grant recipients. In addition, the supervisors told the social welfare board not to exceed budgeted amounts;

22. See Thomas, *An Appalachian New Deal,* 156–57.

23. *Proceedings, Michigan State Association of Supervisors,* January 24, 1940, 43–44.

24. Ibid., 44–45; "Proceedings, Board of Supervisors, Manistee County," February 1, 1940, 401.

25. "Relief Clients Must Cease Spending for Beer," *Courier-Northerner,* October 14, 1938.

when the money ran out, relief would stop. They sought more careful investigation of cases before relief was granted, and by January of 1941 the supervisors also wanted to see regular lists of recipients.[26] The 1939 law forbade the publication of recipients' names, but some counties persisted in that practice anyway, prompting the Social Welfare Commission to remind counties of that prohibition, stating that "it does not approve of any action which will tend to stigmatize recipients of public relief."[27] Fiscal localism, particularly with respect to economy and efficiency, was the guiding principle of relief administration in many counties.

Several counties continued to rely heavily on township supervisors to screen applicants. A member of the Ottawa County social welfare board reported in 1942 that the staff was small "because we depend upon getting information direct from supervisors in the local units, who we feel know better the conditions of each of those applicants . . . We go by the recommendation of the supervisors."[28] A 1944 study of the role of the boards of supervisors in the administration of relief found that supervisors played a central part in eight counties. In some cases supervisors were simply consulted on applications, but in several counties supervisors were the investigating officials and determined the amount of relief granted. Such actions violated the 1939 law, but continued regardless.[29]

The responsibility of relatives to provide support for family members remained a feature of welfare in both the categorical aids and general relief for three decades. The administration of that policy, and the formulas used in computing the amount expected, changed, but the Social Welfare Commission stayed committed to the responsibility of families to contribute. Many of the changes sought to make it easier for caseworkers to determine the ability of relatives to help family members. The expectation of adult children living in the household shifted from the 60 percent rule to the setting of a "reasonable" room and board rate.[30] In the 1950s, the twenty-dollar-per-week limit on relatives' contributions was rescinded to reflect rising incomes and costs of

26. "Proceedings, Manistee County," vol. 14, April 11, 1940, 408–9; April 12, 1940, 411; January 16, 1941, 501.

27. Minutes of the Michigan Social Welfare Commission, November 28, 1940, 92; Box 1, Folder 1.

28. *Proceedings of the Michigan State Association of Supervisors*, 43rd Annual Meeting, January 27, 1942, 16–17.

29. The Michigan attorney general ruled two years earlier that the law did not grant supervisors the power to grant relief or make investigations. Minutes, Michigan Social Welfare Commission, Box 2, April 12, 1944, 163; May 19, 1944, 179–84.

30. Minutes, Michigan Social Welfare Commission, Box 2, Folder 2, August 28, 1945, 16–17.

living. The legislature also passed a judicial-review option whereby relatives could have the decision of the agency reviewed by the probate court; while the review took place, the contribution would not be budgeted into the recipient's grant. If the family did not request a review, the contribution was considered in the budget whether it was paid or not.[31] The commission sought to alleviate the burden on caseworkers in this area of administration by simplifying budgeting procedures and the required correspondence. The mandatory rechecking of relatives by caseworkers was also moved back to every two years instead of being annual.[32] By 1968 local officials requested the removal of the responsible-relative provisions from welfare law, because of the difficulty in administering them and the lack of uniformity.[33] The responsibility of relatives to support family members narrowed significantly in 1970, when state law required support only of spouses and parents.[34]

The status of welfare recipients did not change significantly, although the targets shifted in the coming decades. The ADC program came under increasing fire as caseloads escalated in the 1960s, and the recipients increasingly were nonwhite and unmarried. The demand for OAA diminished, and the program effectively disappeared in the 1970s. The single mother on ADC, therefore, became the picture of welfare, and increasing dissatisfaction with both ADC and welfare resulted in the state reforms of the early 1990s, and the 1996 welfare-reform law. While the responsibility of relatives to support family narrowed primarily to spouses and parents, with increasing attention to "deadbeat dads," the emphasis on individual behavior and work increased. As with the 1939 law, the most recent reforms, rather than creating an entirely new system, reshaped existing ones, producing even greater complexity for both caseworkers and recipients. The 1996 reforms added about one-third more rules, and many state manuals doubled in size.[35] Although the goal was to foster the movement of people from welfare to independence and work, the outcome has been mixed, according to Sharon Hays: "What we have achieved with the decline of the welfare rolls is, in fact, the *appearance* of independence."[36] The

31. *Eighth Biennial Report, Michigan Social Welfare Commission, July 1954–June 1956* (Lansing: December 1956), 14–15; Minutes, Michigan Social Welfare Commission, Box 3, Folder 4; May 24, 1954, 122–23.

32. *Tenth Biennial Report, Michigan Social Welfare Commission, July 1956–1958* (Lansing: December 1958), 15–16.

33. "Resolution, District X," dated March 11, 1968, approved at Michigan County Social Services Association meeting, 1968, I–2 and I–16; Michigan County Social Services Association Records (hereafter cited as MCSSA), Box 12, Folder 4, Archives of Michigan.

34. Public Act 88 of 1970, *Public and Local Acts of the Legislature of the State of Michigan* (Lansing: Speaker-Hines and Thomas, Inc, 1971), 263.

35. Hays, *Flat Broke with Children,* 47.

36. Ibid., 61.

larger discourse about welfare has again masked the complexities of a person's need for welfare, and equated the receipt of welfare with individual failing rather than larger structural issues or experiences, some beyond the control of the recipient.

The decades following the 1939 law saw an incremental increase in state control and shifts in the formula for funding direct relief. All counties struggled to finance their relief costs, and although the law called for a fifty-fifty match with the state, some counties secured much higher funding from the state. In mid-1940, seven counties paid just 10 percent of direct-relief costs and one paid just 5 percent. Just more than half of all counties paid 50 percent of their costs that year.[37] By 1956 the state paid more than 50 percent in just seven counties. The formula changed to require a minimum of 30 percent contribution by the state.[38] The state extended control over general assistance in 1967, when it enacted minimum standards for relief. The formula for funding shifted to 40 percent state and 60 percent local, but any county that expended the equivalent of a one-mill tax levy could secure state funding for any expenditures over that.[39] The centralization of general relief, sought in the debates of the 1930s, finally occurred in 1975, when the state assumed full administrative and fiscal responsibility for General Assistance.[40]

In the years following passage of the 1939 law, local officials and the organizations that represented them resisted further efforts to integrate Michigan's welfare system; instead, they fought to keep the dual-system option, and home rule, available to counties. A 1942 study of the state's welfare system, requested by Governor Murray Van Wagoner, identified duplication and the concomitant need to consolidate agencies as the key issue. The report recommended integration of both the State Department of Public Welfare and county agencies. The state commission included that recommendation in its 1942 report, and also encouraged that the county be the unit for relief administration.[41] Efforts

37. Minutes of the Michigan Social Welfare Commission, June 28, 1940, 291; November 29, 1940, 96–98.

38. Minutes, November 20, 1957, 3–4; *Ninth Biennial Report, Michigan Social Welfare Commission* (Lansing: December 1956), 65; Public Act 286 of 1957, *Public and Local Acts of the Legislature of the State of Michigan,* 396.

39. *Fifteenth Biennial Report, State Department of Social Services, July 1966–June 1968* (Lansing: December 1968), 47; *Annual Report, Michigan Department of Social Services, Fiscal 1969* (Lansing: December, 1969), 51. Five counties secured additional funding under the one-mill limit; that number increased to nine the following year.

40. *Report of the Michigan Department of Social Services for 1976,* 12; Public Act 237 of 1975, *Public and Local Acts of the Legislature of the State of Michigan,* 607–11.

41. "The Organization and Functioning of the System of Public Welfare Services in Michigan," submitted October 6, 1942, 1, 18–20. Box 1, Folder 7; Department of Social Welfare Records, Archives of Michigan; "Minutes, State Social Welfare Commission," December 31,

to encourage integration, however, were met with disinterest on the part of many counties, and the Michigan State Association of Supervisors passed a resolution opposed "to any county integration of welfare administration" in 1943. They also endeavored to bring the categorical-aid programs in line "with the conception of local home rule and self-government."[42] Efforts to encourage consolidation of the "dual system" into an integrated department (such as Van Buren County's) began in earnest in 1945; one year later thirty-three counties had reverted to that system.[43] The State Department of Public Welfare, divided into two administrations in the 1939 law, as were most counties, merged, by 1944, into a single department administering all types of welfare.[44]

Efforts to integrate at the local level continued, and the opposition of local officials waned somewhat by the 1960s. Many counties chose to merge their departments by 1965; eight counties did so in 1964 alone. Reducing administrative duplication was a major reason. Often applicants applied for one program (perhaps general relief) but were eligible for a categorical aid. The referral process slowed the application by weeks or up to three months. If the departments merged, one application could cover all programs. Medical-assistance programs further complicated the situation, particularly for the elderly. A single local welfare board overseeing all programs, with the state as an oversight, offered local officials the opportunity to play a greater role in the administration of the categorical-aid programs; some locals officials argued that merging could provide more local authority rather than less.[45]

The consolidation of Michigan's welfare services at the local level coincided with the 1963 revision of the state constitution, a change that strengthened executive authority and streamlined state administration, which was a trend shared by other states in this period as well. The constitution required organizing state government around no more than twenty departments (down from the estimated 130 that had existed). It mandated four commissions

---

1942, Box 1, Folder 3; *Michigan Social Welfare Commission Second Report* (Lansing: Michigan Social Welfare Commission, 1942), 1.

42. *Proceedings of the Michigan State Association of Supervisors*, 44th Annual Meeting, January 26–28, 1943, 26, 45–46.

43. See address by Social Welfare Commission member Carlton H. Runciman, *Proceedings of the Annual Convention of the State Convention of County Social Welfare Boards and County Boards of Supervisors*, 1946, 30.

44. *Fourth Biennial Report, Michigan Social Welfare Commission, July 1944–1946* (Lansing: December 1946), 9. The Director of Social Welfare also served as acting director of the Bureau of Social Security two years earlier, a practice made permanent in Public Act 217 of 1945. See *Third Biennial Report, Michigan Social Welfare Commission*, July 1942–June 1944, 1; Public Act 218 of 1945, *Public and Local Acts of the Legislature of the State of Michigan*, 288–89.

45. Minutes, Welfare Advisory Committee, December 10, 1965, 1–3; Records Relating to Public Assistance, Box 2, Folder 3, Archives of Michigan.

(education, civil service, civil rights, and state highways).[46] Controversy occurred over how many departments would be headed by commissions, rather than a single department director. Governor George Romney—reminding legislators that if a bill reorganizing state government was not passed in the 1965 session, the power to reorganize would rest with him—gained passage of a bill that included seven commissions and nineteen departments. All other departments were headed by single executives under direct authority of the governor, who appointed them. The senate could disapprove any appointment, but if it took no action, the appointment stood.[47]

The reorganization affected both state and local welfare administration. Under the 1965 law, the Department of Social Services became one of the nineteen departments in the executive branch. The law also abolished the Michigan Social Welfare Commission, placing all authority in the director of DSS.[48] The merging of county departments into a single agency administering both the categorical aids and direct relief became mandatory in 1965. In addition to creating a single county agency for all welfare programs, the law established a ten-member advisory committee comprised of representatives of the districts of the Michigan County Social Services Association.[49] The county association thus had control over who served on the committee. Its standing, however, was advisory only; it had no administrative or policy authority. Members of the county organization sought the reinstatement of the Social Welfare Commission, arguing that they had lost an important voice and resource in the development and administration of welfare, but to no avail.[50] Centralization of welfare services and state supervision was achieved, although local administration continued for all programs.

Michigan's experiences during the New Deal years reveal the limited, but also important, changes of those years. The New Deal federalized parts of the welfare system, although some services provided through the Social Security

46. Albert L. Sturm and Margaret Whitaker, *Implementing a New Constitution: The Michigan Experience* (Ann Arbor: Institute of Public Administration, 1968), 104, 109.

47. Sturm and Whitaker, *Implementing a New Constitution,* 105, 114–16; D. Duane Angel, *Romney: A Political Biography* (New York: Exposition Express, 1967), 123–24; and Robert W. Carr, *Government of Michigan under the 1964 Constitution* (Ann Arbor: University of Michigan Press 1967), 39–41.

48. Public Act 380 of 1965, *Public and Local Acts of the Legislature of the State of Michigan* (Lansing: Speaker-Hines and Thomas, Inc. 1965), 768–69; Sturm and Whitaker, *Implementing a New Constitution,* 115–17.

49. Resolution passed at the 1965 meeting of the MCSSA, Box 1, Folder 6, MCSSA Records; Public Act 401 of 1965, *Public and Local Acts of the Legislature of the State of Michigan* (Lansing: Speaker-Hines and Thomas, Inc. 1965), 803–19.

50. Report of the Partnership Committee, "Minutes of Michigan County Social Services Association, August 27–29, 1968, I–20; MCSSA Records, Box 12, Folder 4.

Act did exist in different forms before 1935. It injected needed federal funds into relief, and revealed the entrenched hardships of the ill, disabled, elderly, and single parents. Michigan created a third track of welfare, separating those who received general relief from those eligible for categorical aid. The New Deal also illustrates the importance of home rule ideologies, and the defense of local government, which both played out in very clear ways in the welfare-reorganization debates. Competing visions of what professional skills were necessary for relief administration were central to those debates, and for the short-term, professional social workers were excluded. Reorganization debates would continue, but the New Deal years began the process of centralization.

BIBLIOGRAPHY

PRIMARY SOURCES

Archival Materials

Archives of Labor and Urban Affairs, Wayne State University
    Michigan AFL-CIO Collection
    Wayne County AFL-CIO Collection
Archives of Michigan, Lansing, MI
    Case Records of Aid to Dependent Children, Marquette, Saginaw, and Wayne counties
    Case Records of Old Age Assistance, Marquette, Saginaw, and Wayne counties
    Case Records of Van Buren County Emergency Relief Administration
    Civilian Conservation Corps Records
    Field Service Correspondence
    Michigan County Social Services Association, 1946–76
    Minutes of State Emergency Welfare Relief Commission, 1933–39
    Minutes of the State Social Welfare Commission, 1939–64
    Narrative Field Reports, Public Assistance, 1937–49
    Records of the Welfare and Relief Study Commission
    Records of Isabella County Emergency Welfare Relief Commission, 1935–36
    Records of the St. Clair County Superintendents of the Poor
    Works Progress Administration Records
Bentley Historical Library—University of Michigan
    Children's Fund of Michigan—State Emergency Relief Administration
    Louise Armstrong Papers
    Michigan State Emergency Welfare Relief Commission Papers

William Haber Papers
William Haber Oral Biography Project: Edited Transcripts
Burton Historical Collections, Detroit Public Library
    City of Detroit Common Council Minutes, 1931–49
    Detroit Public Welfare Commission Minutes, 1927–49
    Mayor's Papers, Detroit, 1933–41
Franklin Delano Roosevelt Library, Hyde Park, NY
    Harry Hopkins Papers, field reports, Michigan
    Lorena Hickok, field reports, Michigan
Marquette County Historical Society
    Records of the Board of the Superintendents of the Poor, Marquette County
National Archives, Washington, D.C.
    Federal Emergency Relief Administration, 1933–36, Record Group 69 (State Series
    and New General Subject Series)
Social Welfare History Archives, University of Minnesota
    Family Service Association of America
    National Association of Social Workers, 1917–63
    National Social Work Assembly, 1911–56
Western Michigan University Archives, Kalamazoo, MI
    Administrative Records of the Van Buren County Emergency Relief Administra-
    tion, 1930–43
    Minutes of the Superintendent of the Poor and Poor Commission, Van Buren
    County, 1912–39

Public Documents and Records

Manistee County
    Minutes of the Board of Supervisors, Manistee County, 1929–45
Marquette County
    Minutes of the Board of Supervisors, Marquette County, 1929–45
Saginaw County
    Minutes of the Board of Supervisors, Saginaw County, 1933–45
    Minutes of the City Council of Saginaw, 1930–45
Van Buren County
    Minutes of the Board of Supervisors, Van Buren County, 1930–45
Wayne County
    Minutes of the Board of Supervisors, Wayne County, 1930–50

Periodicals

The Courier-Northerner
Daily Mining Journal
Hartford Day Spring

Manistee News-Advocate
Manistee Examiner
Saginaw Daily News
Social Work Today

Published Primary Sources

Abbott, Edith. *Public Assistance: American Principles and Politics, Vols. I and II.* New York: Russell & Russell, 1940.

Annual Abstracts of the Reports of the Superintendents of the Poor in the State of Michigan, 1891–1938. Lansing, MI.

Annual Reports of the Secretary of the Board of Agriculture, 1935–1955 (Lansing).

Annual Reports of the Superintendents of the Poor for the County of Wayne, 1895–1923.

Armstrong, Louise. *We Too Are the People.* Boston: Little, Brown and Company, 1938.

Baird, Enid. *Average General Relief Benefits, 1933–1938.* Washington, D.C.: U.S. Government Printing Office, 1940.

———. *Public and Private Aid in 116 Urban Areas 1929–38.* Public Assistance Report No. 3. Washington, D.C.: Social Security Board, 1942.

Biennial Reports of the Michigan Department of Social Services, 1965–1991.

Biennial Reports of the Michigan State Attorney General of the State of Michigan, 1914–1940.

Biennial Reports of the Michigan State Board of Corrections and Charities, 1913–1928.

Biennial Reports of the Michigan Social Welfare Commission, 1939–1964.

Board of County Auditors, Wayne County, *The Cost of County Government: An Analysis of the Wayne County Budget, 1925–1929.* Detroit: Board of County Auditors, 1929.

Bogue, Mary F. *Administration of Mothers' Aid in Ten Localities.* U.S. Children's Bureau Publication No. 184. Washington, D.C.: U.S. Government Printing Office, 1928.

Bromage Arthur W. and Thomas H. Reed, *Organization and Cost of County and Township Government.* Detroit: Detroit Bureau of Governmental Research, 1933.

Brown, Josephine Chapin. *Public Relief, 1929–1939.* New York: Henry Holt, 1940.

Bruce, Isabel Campbell and Edith Eickhoff. *The Michigan Poor Law: Its Development and Administration.* Chicago: University of Chicago Press, 1936.

Carothers, Doris. *Chronology of the Federal Emergency Relief Administration, May 12, 1933 to December 31, 1935.* Washington, D.C.: U.S. Government Printing Office, 1937.

Case, Herbert S., ed. *Who's Who in Michigan.* Munising: 1936.

Colcord, Joanna C. *Cash Relief.* New York: Russell Sage Foundation, 1936.

———. *Emergency Work Relief.* New York: Russell Sage Foundation, 1932.

Dunham, Arthur. *The Michigan Welfare Reorganization Act of 1939: An Analysis.* Lansing: Michigan Conference of Social Work, 1939.

———. *Public Relief in Three Michigan Counties.* Detroit: 1940.

———. "Public Welfare and the Referendum in Michigan." *Social Service Review* 12 (September 1938): 417–39.

Elderton, Marion, ed. *Case Studies in Unemployment.* Philadelphia: University of Pennsylvania Press, 1931.

Ellis, Mabel Brown. "Juvenile Courts and Mothers' Pensions in Michigan." Unpublished manuscript, 1917.

Employment on Projects in March 1936, WPA Including NYA. Works Progress Administration, 1936.

Fifteenth Census of the United States, 1930. Washington, D.C.: U.S. Government Printing Office, 1931.

50,000 Men: Report of the Work Division of the Michigan Emergency Welfare Relief Commission. Lansing: Michigan Emergency Welfare Relief Commission, 1935.

Final Report on the WPA Program. Washington, D.C.: U.S. Government Printing Office, 1948.

Findlay, A. C. "The Development of Community Resources in Flint, Michigan, During Depression Years." Flint Institute of Research and Planning, October 1938.

Fourteenth Census of the United States, 1920. Washington, D.C.: U.S. Government Printing Office, 1921.

Geddes, Anne E. *Trends in Relief Expenditures, 1910–1935.* WPA Research Monograph X. Washington, D.C.: U.S. Government Printing Office, 1937.

Granger, George F. and Lawrence R. Klein. *Emergency Relief in Michigan, 1933–1939.* Lansing: State of Michigan, 1939.

Haber, William and Paul L. Stanchfield. *Unemployment and Relief in Michigan.* Lansing: Franklin DeKleine Company, 1935.

———. *Unemployment, Relief and Economic Security: A Survey of Michigan's Relief and Unemployment Problem.* Lansing: 1936.

Harper, Ernest B. and Duane L. Gibson. *Reorganization of Public Welfare in Michigan: A Study of Transformation of a Social Institution.* East Lansing: Michigan State College, 1942.

Harris, Reba. *Mothers' Pensions in Michigan: Report of a Study Made by the State Welfare Department.* Lansing: State Welfare Department, 1934.

Healy, D. J. "Prevention of Juvenile Delinquency." *Probation in Theory and Practice, Michigan Probation Association 1937 Yearbook.* 37–40.

Hiller, Francis. "The Juvenile Court as a Case-Working Agency." *The Courts and the Prevention of Juvenile Delinquency: Annual Reports and Proceedings of the Twentieth Annual Conference of the National Probation Association.* Albany, NY: National Probation Association, 1926.

Hopkins, Harry L. *Spending to Save: The Complete Story of Relief.* New York: W. W. Norton, 1936.

Kirby, John B., ed. *The New Deal and Black America.* Frederick, MD: University Publications of America, 1984.

Landers, Frank M. and Claude R. Tharp. *Administration and Financing of Public Relief,* Michigan Pamphlets No. 17. Bureau of Government: University of Michigan, 1942.

Lowe, Robert C. *State Public Welfare Legislation,* Research Monograph XX. Washington, D.C.: U.S. Government Printing Office, 1939.

Lundberg, Emma O. *Public Aid to Mothers With Dependent Children.* U.S. Children's Bureau Publication No. 162. Washington, D.C.: U.S. Government Printing Office, 1926.

———. *State Commissions for the Study and Revision of Child-Welfare Laws.* U.S. Children's Bureau Publication No. 131. Washington, D.C.: U.S. Government Printing Office, 1924.

Matson, Opal VaLeta. *Local Relief to Dependents.* Detroit: Detroit Bureau of Governmental Research, 1933.

Michigan: A Guide to the Wolverine State. New York: Oxford University Press, 1941.

Michigan State Emergency Welfare Relief Commission. *Cost of Administration in the Emergency Relief Program.* Lansing: 1935.

———. *A Manual for Aid to Dependent Children.* Lansing: Michigan State Emergency Welfare Relief Commission, 1938.

———. *A Manual for Suggested Policies and Procedures for Use by County Relief Administrators.* Lansing: Michigan Welfare Emergency Relief Commission, 1938.

———. *Michigan Emergency Relief Administration Budget Manual.* Lansing: 1937.

———. *Unemployable Persons on the Emergency Relief Rolls in Michigan.* Lansing: 1935.

Michigan State Welfare Commission. *Reports of the Michigan State Welfare Commission 1921–28.*

Old Age Assistance in Michigan, 1933–1937. Lansing: 1938.

Mothers' Aid, 1931. U.S. Children's Bureau Publication No. 220. Washington, D.C.: U.S. Government Printing Office, 1933.

National Probation Association. *Report of a Study of Juvenile Courts and Adult Probation in Certain Counties of Michigan.* National Probation Association and Michigan State Conference of Social Work, 1926.

Pollock, James K. and Samuel J. Eldersveld. *Michigan Politics in Transition: An Areal Study of Voting Trends in the Last Decade.* University of Michigan Governmental Studies No. 10. Ann Arbor: University of Michigan Press, 1942.

Pollock, James K. *Direct Government in Michigan: The Initiative and Referendum.* Bureau of Government: University of Michigan, 1940.

Proceedings of the Annual Convention of the State Association of County Welfare Boards and State Association of Boards of Supervisors. Lansing, MI, 1946–55.

Proceedings of the Annual Convention of State Superintendents of the Poor and Keepers of Infirmaries, 1880–1930.

Proceedings of the Michigan State Association of Supervisors Annual Meeting, 1939–1968. Lansing, MI.

Public and Local Acts of the Legislature of the State of Michigan, 1906–1975. Lansing: Franklin DeKleine Company.

Relief Expenditures by Governmental and Private Organizations, 1929 and 1931. Washington, D.C.: U.S. Government Printing Office, 1932.

Report of the Welfare and Relief Study Commission. Lansing: December 1936.

Ricks, James Hoge. "The Place of the Juvenile Court in the Care of Dependent Children." *Social Service and the Courts, the Annual Report and Proceedings of the Fourteenth Annual Conference of the National Probation Association.* Albany, NY: National Probation Association, 1920. 124–29.

Schouten, John H. "Relief Expenditures in Michigan Cities during 1931 and 1932." Michigan Council for Governmental Expenditures. *Material for Independent Study and Application, Submitted to 40 Federated State & Local Organizations.* 1933.

Sinai, Nathan, Marguerite F. Hallo, V. M. Hogue, and Miriam Steep. *Medical Relief in Michigan: A Study of the Experience in Ten Counties.* Ann Arbor: Edward Brothers, Inc., 1938.

Thirteenth Census of the United States Taken in the Year 1910. Washington, D.C.: U.S. Government Printing Office, 1911.

Unemployable Persons on the Emergency Relief Rolls in Michigan. Lansing: Michigan Emergency Welfare Relief Commission, 1935.

Walker, Sydnor H. "Privately Supported Social Work." *Recent Social Trends in the United States: Report of the President's Research Committee on Social Trends.* Vol. II. New York: McGraw-Hill Book Company, 1933. 1168–223.

Whalen, Cecile M. *Tenure, Training and Compensation of Detroit Social Workers.* Detroit Bureau of Governmental Research Report No. 10. Detroit: 1938.

Williams, Edward Ainsworth. *Federal Aid for Relief.* New York: Columbia University Press, 1939.

Winslow, Emma A. *Trends in Different Types of Public and Private Relief in Urban Areas, 1929–1935.* U.S. Children's Bureau Publication No. 237. Washington, D.C.: U.S. Government Printing Office, 1937.

Woodworth, Leo Day. *Expenditures for Mothers' Pensions, 1931.* Michigan Council on Governmental Expenditures, 1933.

WPA Projects. Works Progress Administration, 1937.

SECONDARY SOURCES

Abramovitz, Mimi. *Regulating the Lives of Women: Social Welfare Policy from Colonial Times to the Present.* Boston: South End Press, 1992.

Alexander, Leslie. "Organizing the Professional Social Worker: Union Development in Voluntary Social Work, 1930–1950." PhD Dissertation. Bryn Mawr, PA: Bryn Mawr College, Graduate School of Social Work, 1976.

Alexander, Ruth M. *The "Girl" Problem: Female Sexual Delinquency in New York, 1900–1930.* Ithaca: Cornell University Press, 1995.

Amenta, Edwin. *Bold Relief: Institutional Politics and the Origins of Modern American Social Policy.* Princeton: Princeton University Press, 1998.

Angel, D. Duane. *Romney: A Political Biography.* New York: Exposition Press, 1967.

Argersinger, Jo Ann E. *Toward a New Deal in Baltimore: People and Government in the Great Depression.* Chapel Hill: University of North Carolina Press, 1988.

Barrett, James and David Roediger, "Inbetween Peoples: Race, Nationality, and the 'New Immigrant' Working Class." *Journal of American Ethnic History* 16.3 (1997): 3–44.

Bates, Barbara. *Bargaining for Life: A Social History of Tuberculosis, 1876–1938.* Philadelphia: University of Pennsylvania Press, 1992.

Begala, John A. and Carol Bethel, "A Transformation within the Welfare State." *The Council of State Governments* 65.1 (1992): 25–30.

Beito, David T. *Taxpayers in Revolt: Tax Resistance during the Great Depression.* Chapel Hill: University of North Carolina Press, 1989.

Bell, Winifred. *Aid to Dependent Children.* New York: Columbia University Press, 1965.

Berkowitz, Edward D. *America's Welfare State: From Roosevelt to Reagan.* Baltimore: Johns Hopkins University Press, 1991.

Bernstein, Irving. *The Lean Years: A History of the American Worker, 1920–1933.* New York: Da Capo Press, 1960.

Berry, Dean L. *The Powers of Local Government in Michigan.* Ann Arbor: University of Michigan Press, 1961.

Blackwelder, Julia Kirk. *Women of the Depression: Caste and Culture in San Antonio, 1929–1939.* College Station: Texas A&M University Press, 1984.

Blakey, George T. *Hard Times and New Deal in Kentucky, 1929–1939.* Lexington: University of Kentucky, 1986.

Bledstein, Burton J. *The Culture of Professionalism: The Middle Class and the Development of Higher Education in America.* New York: W. W. Norton, 1976.

Blee, Kathleen Marie. "The Impact of Family Settlement Patterns on the Politics of Lake Superior Communities." PhD Dissertation. Madison: University of Wisconsin, 1982.

Boyle, Kevin. *Arc of Justice: A Saga of Race, Civil Rights, and Murder in the Jazz Age.* New York: Henry Holt, 2004.

Brinkley, Alan. *Voices of Protest: Huey Long, Father Coughlin and The Great Depression.* New York: Vintage Books, 1983.

Brock, William R. *Welfare, Democracy, and the New Deal.* Cambridge and New York: Cambridge University Press, 1988.

Brown, JoAnne. "Professional Language: Words That Succeed." *Radical History Review* 34 (1986): 33–51.

Brown, Michael C. *Race, Money, and the American Welfare State.* Ithaca and London: Cornell University Press, 1999.

Brumberg, Joan Jacobs and Nancy Tomes. "Women in the Professions: A Research Agenda for American Historians." *Reviews in American History* 10 (June 1982): 275–96.

Bucki, Cecilia. *Bridgeport's Socialist New Deal, 1915–1936.* Urbana and Chicago: University of Illinois Press, 2001.

Burt, John S. "'Boys, look around and see what you can find.'" *Michigan History* 78.6 (November/December 1994): 10–15.

Canning, Kathleen. "Feminist History after the Linguistic Turn: Historicizing Discourse and Experience." *Signs* 19.2 (Winter 1994): 368–404.

Carr, Robert W. *Government of Michigan under the 1964 Constitution.* Ann Arbor: University of Michigan Press, 1967.

Case, Herbert S., ed. *Who's Who in Michigan.* Munising: 1936.

Chafe, William H. "Flint and the Great Depression." *Michigan History* 53 (Fall 1969): 225–39.

Chambers, Clarke A. *Paul U. Kellogg and the Survey: Voices for Social Welfare Thought and Social Justice.* Minneapolis: University of Minnesota Press, 1971.

———. "Women in the Creation of the Profession of Social Work." *Social Service Review* 60 (March 1986): 1–33.

Ciani, Kyle Emily. "Choosing to Care: Meeting Children's Needs in Detroit and San Diego, 1880–1945." PhD Dissertation. East Lansing: Michigan State University, 1998.

———. "Hidden Laborers: Female Day Workers in Detroit, 1870–1920." *Journal of the Gilded Age and Progressive Era* 4.1 (January 2005): 23–51.

Clinansmith, Michael S. "The Black Legion: Hooded Americanism in Michigan." *Michigan History* 55 (Fall 1971): 243–62.

Clive, Alan. *State of War: Michigan in World War II.* Ann Arbor: University of Michigan Press, 1979.

Cobble, Dorothy Sue. "Rethinking Troubled Relations between Women and Unions." In *U.S. Women in Struggle: A Feminist Studies Anthology*, ed. Claire Goldberg Moses and Heidi Hartman. Chicago: University of Chicago Press, 1995. 166–88.

Cohen, Lizabeth. *Making a New Deal: Industrial Workers in Chicago, 1919–1939.* Cambridge: Cambridge University Press, 1990.

Cole, Dwayne Charles. "The Relief Crisis in Illinois during the Depression, 1930–1940." PhD Dissertation. St. Louis University, 1973.

Coll, Blanche D. *Safety Net: Welfare and Social Security 1929–1979.* New Brunswick, NJ: Rutgers University Press, 1995.

Coode, Thomas H. and John F. Bauman. *People, Poverty, and Politics: Pennsylvanians during the Great Depression.* Lewisburg, PA: Bucknell University Press, 1981.

Connif, Ruth. "Welfare, Ground Zero: Michigan Tries to End It All." *The Nation,* May 27, 1996.

Cook, Blanche Wiesen. *Eleanor Roosevelt: Volume Two, 1933–1938.* New York: Viking Penguin, 1999.

Daniels, Roger. *Coming to America: A History of Immigration and Ethnicity in American Life.* New York: HarperCollins, 2002.

Davies, Margery W. *Woman's Place Is at the Typewriter.* Philadelphia: Temple University Press, 1982.

Dunbar, Willis F. and George S. May. *Michigan: A History of the Wolverine State.* 3rd rev. ed. Grand Rapids: William B. Eerdmans Publishing Company, 1995.

Edin, Kathryn and Laura Lein. *Making Ends Meet: How Single Mothers Survive Welfare and Low-Wage Work.* New York: Russell Sage Foundation, 1997.

Edsforth, Ronald. *Class Conflict and Cultural Consensus: The Making of a Mass Consumer Society in Flint, Michigan.* New Brunswick, NJ: Rutgers University Press, 1987.

Ehrenreich, John H. *The Altruistic Imagination: A History of Social Work and Social Policy in the United States.* Ithaca: Cornell University Press, 1985.

Feldberg, Georgina D. *Disease and Class: Tuberculosis and the Shaping of Modern North American Society.* New Brunswick, NJ: Rutgers University Press, 1995.

Ferguson, Karen. *Black Politics in New Deal Atlanta.* Chapel Hill: University of North Carolina Press, 2002.

Fields, Harold. "Where Shall the Alien Work?" *Social Forces* 12 (December 1933): 213–21.

Fine, Lisa M. *The Souls of the Skyscrapers: Female Clerical Workers in Chicago, 1870–1930.* Philadelphia: Temple University Press, 1990.

Fine, Sidney. *Frank Murphy: The Detroit Years*. Ann Arbor: University of Michigan Press, 1975.

———. *Frank Murphy: The New Deal Years*. Chicago: University of Chicago Press, 1979.

———. *Sit-Down: The General Motors Strike of 1936–1937*. Ann Arbor: University of Michigan Press, 1969.

Fraser, Nancy and Linda Gordon. "A Genealogy of Dependency: Tracing a Keyword of the U.S. Welfare State." *Signs* 19 (Winter 1994): 309–36.

Garcia, Juan. *Mexicans in the Midwest, 1900–1932*. Tucson: University of Arizona Press, 1996.

Gary, Robenia Baker and Lawrence E. Gary. "The History of Social Work Education for Black People 1900–1930." *Journal of Sociology and Social Welfare* 24, no. 1 (March 1994): 67–81.

Goodwin, Joanne. "'Employable Mothers' and 'Suitable' Work: Our Evaluation of Welfare and Wage-Earning for Women in the Twentieth-Century United States." *Journal of Social History* 29, no. 2 (Winter 1995): 253–74.

———. *Gender and the Politics of Welfare Reform: Mothers' Pensions in Chicago, 1911–1929*. Chicago: University of Chicago Press, 1997.

Gordon, Linda. *Heroes of Their Own Lives: The Politics and History of Family Violence*. London: Virago Press, 1988.

———. "The New Feminist Scholarship on the Welfare State." In *Women, the State, and Welfare*, ed. Linda Gordon. Madison: University of Wisconsin Press, 1990. 9–35.

———. *Pitied But Not Entitled: Single Mothers and the History of Welfare*. New York: The Free Press, 1994.

———. "Putting Children First: Women, Maternalism, and Welfare in the Early Twentieth Century." In *U.S. History as Women's History: New Feminist Essays*, ed. Linda K. Kerber, Alice Kessler-Harris, and Kathryn Kish-Sklar. Chapel Hill: University of North Carolina Press, 1995. 63–86.

Gray, Susan E. *The Yankee West: Community Life on the Michigan Frontier*. Chapel Hill: University of North Carolina Press, 1996.

Grossberg, Michael. *Governing the Hearth: Law and the Family in Nineteenth-Century America*. Chapel Hill and London: University of North Carolina Press, 1985.

Guest, Avery M. "The Old-New Distinction and Naturalization: 1900." *International Migration Review* 14.4 (1980): 492–510.

Hanawalt, Leslie L. *A Place of Light: The History of Wayne State University*. Detroit: Wayne State University Press, 1968.

Harms, Richard H. "Paid in Scrip." *Michigan History* 75 (January/February 1991): 37–43.

Hayes, Jack Irby, Jr. *South Carolina and the New Deal*. Columbia: University of South Carolina Press, 2001.

Hays, Sharon. *Flat Broke with Children: Women in the Age of Welfare Reform*. New York: Oxford University Press, 2003.

Heinemann, Ronald L. *Depression and New Deal in Virginia: The Enduring Dominion*. Charlottesville: University Press of Virginia, 1983.

Hodges, Jeffrey Alan. "Euthenics, Eugenics and Compulsory Sterilization in Michigan: 1897–1960." Master's Thesis. East Lansing: Michigan State University, 1995.

Hoffman, Abraham. *Unwanted Mexican Americans in the Great Depression: Repatriation Pressures, 1929–1939.* Tucson: University of Arizona Press, 1974.

Howard, Christopher. "Sowing the Seeds of 'Welfare': The Transformation of Mothers' Pensions, 1900–1940." *Journal of Policy History* 4, no. 2 (1992): 188–227.

Humphrey, Norman D. "The Detroit Mexican Immigrant and Naturalization." *Social Forces* 22 (March 1944): 332–35.

———. "Mexican Repatriation from Michigan: Public Assistance in Historical Perspective." *Social Service Review* 15 (September 1941): 497–513.

———. "The Migration and Settlement of Detroit Mexicans." *Economic Geography* 19 (October 1943): 358–61.

Hurl, Lorna F. "Gender and Auspice in the Development of Social Welfare in Michigan, 1869–1900." *Social Service Review* 70.4 (December 1996): 573–612.

Hurl, Lorna F. and David J. Tucker. "The Michigan County Agents and the Development of Juvenile Probation." *Journal of Social History* 30.4 (Summer 1997): 905–35.

Iacovetta, Franca. "Gossip, Contest and Power in the Making of Suburban Bad Girls, Toronto, 1945–1960." *Canadian Historical Review* 80.4 (December 1999): 585–623.

Iacovetta, Franca and Wendy Mitchinson. "Introduction: Social History and Case Files Research." In *On the Case: Explorations in Case History,* ed. Franca Iacovetta and Wendy Mitchinson. Toronto: University of Toronto Press, 1998. 3–21.

Igra, Anna R. *Wives without Husbands: Marriage, Desertion, and Welfare in New York, 1900–1935.* Chapel Hill: University of North Carolina Press, 2007.

Jones, Jacqueline. *Labor of Love, Labor of Sorrow: Black Women, Work and the Family, From Slavery to the Present.* New York: Vintage Books, 1985.

Josephson, Jyl J. "Gender and Social Policy." In *Gender and American Politics: Women, Men, and the Political Process,* ed. Sue Tolleson-Rinehart and Jyl J. Josephson. Armonk, NY: M. E. Sharpe, 2000. 133–59.

Katz, Michael. *In the Shadow of the Poorhouse: A Social History of Welfare in America.* New York: Basic Books, 1986.

———. *Poverty and Policy in American History.* New York: Academic Press, 1983.

———. *The Price of Citizenship: Redefining the American Welfare State.* New York: Henry Holt, 2001.

Katzman, David. "Ann Arbor: Depression City." *Michigan History* 50 (December 1966): 306–17.

Katznelson, Ira. *When Affirmative Action Was White: An Untold History of Racial Inequality in Twentieth-Century America.* New York: Norton, 2005.

Kessler-Harris, Alice. "Designing Women and Old Fools: The Construction of the Social Security Amendments of 1939." In *U.S. History as Women's History: New Feminist Essays,* ed. Linda K. Kerber, Alice Kessler-Harris, and Kathryn Kish Sklar. Chapel Hill: University of North Carolina Press, 1995. 87–106.

———. *In Pursuit of Equity: Women, Men, and the Quest for Economic Citizenship in 20th Century America.* New York and Oxford: Oxford University Press, 2001.

———. "Where Are the Organized Women Workers?" In *U.S. Women in Struggle: A Feminist Studies Anthology,* ed. Claire Goldberg Moses and Heidi Hartman. Chicago: University of Chicago Press, 1995. 110–33.

Kilar, Jeremy W. *Michigan's Lumbertowns: Lumbermen and Laborers in Saginaw, Bay City and Muskegon, 1870–1905.* Detroit: Wayne State University Press, 1990.

Kilar, Jeremy W. with Sandy L. Schwan. *Saginaw's Changeable Past: An Illustrated History.* St. Louis: G. Bradley Publishing, Inc., 1994.

King, Desmond. *Making Americans: Immigration, Race, and the Origins of the Diverse Democracy.* Cambridge, MA: Harvard University Press, 2000.

Klug, Thomas A. "Labor Market Politics in Detroit: The Curious Case of the 'Spolansky Act' of 1931." *Michigan Historical Review* 14 (Spring 1988): 1–32.

Koch, Raymond L. "The Development of Public Relief Programs in Minnesota, 1929–1941." PhD Dissertation. Minneapolis: University of Minnesota, 1967.

Kunzel, Regina. *Fallen Women, Problem Girls: Unmarried Mothers and Professionalization of Social Work.* New Haven: Yale University Press, 1993.

Ladd-Taylor, Molly. *Mother-Work: Women, Child Welfare, and the State, 1890–1935.* Urbana: University of Illinois Press, 1994.

Lankton, Larry. *Cradle to Grave: Life, Work, and Death at the Lake Superior Copper Mines.* New York: Oxford University Press, 1991.

Larson, Magali Sarfatti. *The Rise of Professionalism: A Sociological Analysis.* Berkeley: University of California Press, 1977.

Lee, Sharon M. "Racial Classifications in the US Census: 1890–1990." *Ethnic and Racial Studies* 16.1 (January 1993): 74–94.

Leighninger, Leslie. *Social Work: Search for Identity.* New York: Greenwood Press, 1987.

Lieberman, Robert C. *Shifting the Color Line: Race and the American Welfare State.* Cambridge, MA: Harvard University Press, 1998.

Leiby, James. *A History of Social Welfare and Social Work in the United States.* New York: Columbia University Press, 1978.

Leuchtenberurg, William E. *Franklin Delano Roosevelt and the New Deal.* New York: Harper & Row, 1963.

———. *The Perils of Prosperity, 1914–1932.* Chicago: University of Chicago Press, 1958.

Lindenmeyer, Kriste. *"A Right to Childhood": The U.S. Children's Bureau and Child Welfare, 1912–1946.* Urbana and Chicago: University of Illinois Press, 1997.

Little, Margaret Hillyard. "'He Said, She Said': The Role of Gossip in Determining Single Mothers' Eligibility for Welfare." *Journal of Policy History* 11.4 (1999): 433–54.

Lorence, James. *Organizing the Unemployed: Community and Union Activists in the Industrial Heartland.* Albany: State University of New York Press, 1996.

Lowitt, Richard. *The New Deal and the West.* Bloomington: Indiana University Press, 1984.

Lubove, Roy. *The Professional Altruist: The Emergence of Social Work as a Career, 1880–1930.* New York: Antheneum, 1983.

Lunbeck, Elizabeth. *The Psychiatric Persuasion: Knowledge, Gender and Power in Modern America.* Princeton: Princeton University Press, 1994.

Maurer, David Joseph. "Public Relief Programs in Ohio, 1929–1939." PhD Dissertation. University of Minnesota, 1962.

May, Martha. "The Historical Problem of the Family Wage: The Ford Motor Company and the Five Dollar Day." *Feminist Studies* 8 (Summer 1982): 399–424.

McColloch, Mark. *White Collar Workers in Transition: The Boom Years, 1940–1970.* Westport, CT: Greenwood Press, 1983.

McElvaine, Robert S. *The Great Depression: America, 1929–1941.* Rev. Ed. New York: Random House, 1993.

McLean, Robert N. "A Dike against Mexicans." *The New Republic* 49 (August 14, 1929): 334–37.

McSeveney, Samuel T. "The Michigan Gubernational Campaign of 1938." *Michigan History* 45 (June 1961): 97–127.

Melosh, Barbara. *The Physician's Hand: Work, Culture and Conflict in American Nursing.* Philadelphia: Temple University Press, 1982.

Mettler, Suzanne. *Dividing Citizens: Gender and Federalism in New Deal Public Policy.* Ithaca: Cornell University Press, 1998.

Meyer, Stephen III. *The Five Dollar Day: Labor Management and Social Control in the Ford Motor Company, 1908–1921.* Albany: State University of New York, 1981.

Miller, Karen R. "The Color of Citizenship: Race and Politics in Detroit, 1916–1940." PhD Dissertation. Ann Arbor: University of Michigan, 2003.

Mink, Gwendolyn. "The Lady and the Tramp: Gender, Race, and the Origins of the American Welfare State." In *Women, the State, and Welfare,* ed. Linda Gordon. Madison: University of Wisconsin Press, 1990. 92–122.

———. "The Lady and the Tramp (II): Feminist Welfare Politics, Poor Single Mothers, and the Challenge of Welfare Justice." *Feminist Studies* 24 (Spring 1998): 55–64.

———. *The Wages of Motherhood: Inequality in the Welfare State, 1917–1942.* Ithaca: Cornell University Press, 1995.

———. *Welfare's End.* Ithaca: Cornell University Press, 1998.

Mittelstadt, Jennifer. *From Welfare to Workfare: The Unintended Consequences of Liberal Reform, 1945–1965.* Chapel Hill: University of North Carolina Press, 2005.

Muncy, Robyn. *Creating a Female Dominion in American Reform, 1890–1935.* New York: Oxford University Press, 1991.

Nelson, Barbara J. "The Gender, Race, and Class Origins of Early Welfare Policy and the Welfare State: A Comparison of Workmen's Compensation and Mothers' Aid." In *Women, Politics, and Change,* ed. Louise A. Tilly and Patricia Gurin. New York: Russell Sage Foundation, 1990.

———. "The Origins of the Two-Channel Welfare State: Workmen's Compensation and Mothers' Aid." In *Women, the State, and Welfare,* ed. Linda Gordon. Madison: University of Wisconsin Press, 1990. 123–51, 413–35.

Nelson, Daniel. *Farm and Factory: Workers in the Midwest, 1880–1990.* Bloomington: Indiana University Press, 1995.

Odem, Mary E. *Delinquent Daughters: Protecting and Policing Adolescent Female Sexuality in the United States, 1885–1920.* Chapel Hill: University of North Carolina Press, 1995.

Ofman, Kay Walters. "A Rural View of Mothers' Pensions: The Allegan County, Michigan, Mothers' Pension Program, 1913–1928." *Social Service Review* 70.1 (March 1996): 98–119.

Ortquist, Richard T. *Depression Politics in Michigan, 1929–1933.* New York: Garland Publishing, 1982.

Patterson, James T. *The New Deal and the States: Federalism in Transition.* Princeton: Princeton University Press, 1969.

Piven, Frances Fox and Richard A. Cloward. *Regulating the Poor: The Functions of Public Welfare.* Rev. ed. New York: Vintage Books, 1993.

Pyle, Susan Newhof, ed. *A Most Superior Land: Life in the Upper Peninsula.* Lansing: TwoPeninsula Press, 1983.

Quadiagno, Jill. *The Transformation of Old Age Security: Class and Politics in the American Welfare State.* Chicago: University of Chicago Press, 1988.

Reisler, Mark. *By the Sweat of Their Brow: Mexican Immigrant Labor in the United States, 1900–1940.* Westport, CT: Greenwood Press, 1976.

Reynolds, Terry S. "We Were Satisfied with It." *Michigan History* 78.6 (November/December 1994): 24–32.

Rich, Adrena Miller. "Case Work in the Repatriation of Immigrants." *Social Service Review* 10 (December 1936): 569–605.

Roediger, David R. *Working toward Whiteness: How America's Immigrants Became White.* New York: Basic Books, 2005.

Romanofsky, Peter and Clarke Chambers. *Social Service Organizations.* Vol. I. Westport, CT: Greenwood Press, 1978.

Rose, Nancy E. *Put to Work: Relief Programs of the Great Depression.* New York: Monthly Review Press, 1994.

———. *Workfare or Fair Work: Women, Welfare, and Government Work Programs.* New Brunswick, NJ: Rutgers University Press, 1998.

Rosentreter, Roger. "Roosevelt's Tree Army: Michigan's Civilian Conservation Corps." *Michigan History* 70.3 (May/June 1986): 14–23.

Rossiter, Margaret W. *Women Scientists in America: Struggles and Strategies to 1940.* Baltimore: Johns Hopkins University Press, 1982.

Rothman, David J. *Conscience and Convenience: The Asylum and Its Alternatives in Progressive America.* Boston: Little, Brown and Company, 1980.

———. *The Discovery of the Asylum: Social Order and Disorder in the New Republic.* Boston: Little, Brown and Company, 1971.

Rubin, Lawrence A. *Bridging the Straits: The Story of Mighty Mac.* Detroit: Wayne State University Press, 1985.

Salmond, John A. *The Civilian Conservation Corps, 1933–1942.* Durham, NC: Duke University Press, 1967.

Sapiro, Virginia. "The Gender Basis of American Social Policy." In *Women, the State and Welfare,* ed. Linda Gordon. Madison: University of Wisconsin Press, 1990. 36–54.

Schackel, Sandra. *Social Housekeepers: Women Shaping Public Policy in New Mexico, 1920–1940.* Albuquerque: University of New Mexico Press, 1992.

Schoen, Johanna. *Choice and Coercion: Birth Control, Sterilization, and Abortion in Public Health and Welfare.* Chapel Hill: University of North Carolina Press, 2005.

Schwartz, Bonnie Fox. *The Civil Works Administration, 1933–1934: The Business of Emergency Employment in the New Deal.* Princeton, NJ: Princeton University Press, 1984.

Scott, Joan. "Gender: A Useful Category of Analysis." In *Gender and the Politics of History.* New York: Columbia University Press, 1988. 28–50.

Semark, Douglas L. *A History of Van Buren County, Michigan, 1982.* Hartford, MI: Van Buren County Historical Society, 1983.

Shapiro, Ann-Louise. *Breaking the Codes: Female Criminality in* Fin-de-Siècle *Paris.* Stanford: Stanford University Press, 1996.

Shaw, Stephanie J. *What a Woman Ought To Be and To Do: Black Professional Women Workers during the Jim Crow Era.* Chicago: University of Chicago Press, 1996.

Shaw, Wilfred B., ed. *The University of Michigan: An Encyclopedic Survey.* Ann Arbor: University of Michigan Press, 1941–. http://www.hti.umich.edu/u/umsurvey/ (accessed July 13, 2006).

Sheridan, Clare. "Contested Citizenship: National Identity and the Mexican Immigration Debates of the 1920s." *Journal of American Ethnic History* 21 (Spring 2002): 3–35.

Simons, Marian Gertrude. "Public Welfare Administration in Michigan." Master's thesis. University of Chicago School of Social Administration, 1931.

Singleton, Jeffrey. *The American Dole: Unemployment Relief and the Welfare State in the Great Depression.* Westport, CT: Greenwood Press, 2000.

Sitkoff, Harvard. *A New Deal for Blacks: The Emergence of Civil Rights as a National Issue.* New York: Oxford University Press, 1978.

Skocpol, Theda. *Protecting Soldiers and Mothers: The Political Origins of Social Policy in the United States.* Cambridge: Harvard University Press, 1992.

Smith, Douglas L. *The New Deal in the Urban South.* Baton Rouge: Louisiana State University Press, 1988.

Smith, Jason Scott. *Building New Deal Liberalism: The Political Economy of Public Works, 1933–1956.* New York: Cambridge University Press, 2006.

Social Security in America. Washington, D.C.: U.S. Government Printing Office, 1937.

Spano, Rick. *The Rank and File Movement.* Washington, D.C.: University Press of America, 1982.

Stadum, Beverly. *Poor Women and Their Families: Hard Working Charity Cases, 1900–1930.* Albany: State University of New York Press, 1992.

Stein-Roggenbuck, Susan. "'Wholly within the Discretion of the Probate Court': Judicial Authority and Mothers' Pensions in Michigan, 1913–1940." *Social Service Review* 79.2 (June 2005): 294–321.

Strom, Sharon Hartman. "Challenging 'Woman's Place': Feminism, the Left, and Industrial Unionism in the 1930s." *Feminist Studies* 9 (Summer 1983): 359–86.

———. "'We're No Kitty Foyles': Organizing Office Workers for the Congress of Industrial Organizations, 1937–1950." In *Women, Work and Protest: A Century of US Women's Labor History,* ed. Ruth Milkman. Boston: Routledge & Kegan Paul, 1985. 206–234.

Sturm, Albert L. and Margaret Whitaker. *Implementing a New Constitution: The Michigan Experience.* Ann Arbor: University of Michigan Press, 1968.

Sturtevant, Deborah. "A Poor Farm Withstands the Test of Time." *Michigan History* 76, no. 5 (September/October 1992): 13–17.

Sugrue, Thomas. *The Origins of the Urban Crisis.* Princeton, NJ: Princeton University Press, 1996.

Sullivan, Martin Edward. "'On the Dole': The Relief Issue in Detroit, 1929–1939." PhD Dissertation. University of Notre Dame, 1974.

Swain, Martha H. *Ellen S. Woodward: New Deal Advocate for Women.* Jackson: University Press of Mississippi, 1995.

Tanenhaus, David S. *Juvenile Justice in the Making.* New York and Oxford: Oxford University Press, 2004.

Tebbutt, Melanie. *Women's Talk? A Social History of "Gossip" in Working-Class Neighborhoods, 1880–1960.* Brookfield, VT: Ashgate Publishing Company, 1995.

Tentler, Leslie Woodcock. *Seasons of Grace: A History of the Archdiocese of Detroit.* Detroit: Wayne State University Press, 1990.

Tharp, Claude R. *A Manual of City Government in Michigan.* Ann Arbor: University of Michigan Press, 1951.

———. *Social Security and Related Services in Michigan, Their Administration and Financing.* Ann Arbor: University of Michigan Press, 1946.

Thomas, Jerry Bruce. *An Appalachian New Deal: West Virginia in the Great Depression.* Lexington: University Press of Kentucky, 1998.

Thomas, Richard W. *Life for Us Is What We Make of It: Building Black Community in Detroit, 1915–1945.* Bloomington: Indiana University Press, 1992.

Thompson, Lyke. "The Death of General Assistance in Michigan," In *The Politics of Welfare Reform,* ed. Donald F. Norris and Lyke Thompson. Thousand Oaks, CA: Sage Publications, 1995. 79–108.

Thurner, Arthur W. *Strangers and Sojourners: A History of Michigan's Keweenaw Peninsula.* Detroit: Wayne State University Press, 1994.

Trattner, Walter I. *From Poor Law to Welfare State: A History of Social Welfare in America.* New York: Free Press, 1989.

Traverso, Susan. *Welfare Politics in Boston, 1910–1940.* Amherst and Boston: University of Massachusetts Press, 2003.

Trelaor, Wilbert H. "A Bond of Interest." *Harlow's Wooden Man: Quarterly Journal of the Marquette County Historical Society* XIII, no. 5 (Fall 1978): 1–30.

Trolander, Judith Ann. *Settlement Houses and the Great Depression.* Detroit: Wayne State University Press, 1975.

Trout, Charles H. *Boston, the Great Depression, and the New Deal.* New York: Oxford University Press, 1977.

Valdes, Dionicio Nodin. *Barrios Nortenos: St. Paul and Midwestern Mexican Communities in the Twentieth Century.* Austin: University of Texas Press, 2000.

Vander Hill, Warren. "So Many Different People." In *A Most Superior Land,* ed. Susan Newhof Pyle. Lansing: TwoPeninsula Press, 1983.

Vargas, Zaragosa. *Proletarians of the North: A History of Mexican Industrial Workers in Detroit and the Midwest, 1917–1933.* Berkeley: University of California Press, 1993.

Walkowitz, Daniel J. "The Making of a Feminine Professional Identity: Social Workers in the 1920s." *American Historical Review* 95 (October 1990): 1051–75.

———. *Working with Class: Social Workers and the Politics of Middle-Class Identity.* Chapel Hill: University of North Carolina Press, 1999.

Ware, Susan. *Beyond Suffrage: Women in the New Deal.* Cambridge: Harvard University Press, 1981.

———. *Holding Their Own: American Women in the 1930s.* Boston: Twayne Publishers, 1982.

Weber, Devra. *Dark Sweat, White Gold: California Farm Workers, Cotton, and the New Deal.* Berkeley: University of California Press, 1994.

Willrich, Michael. *City of Courts: Socializing Justice in Progressive Era Chicago.* New York and Cambridge: Cambridge University Press, 2003.

———. "Home Slackers: Men, the State, and Welfare in Modern America." *Journal of American History* 87, no. 2 (September 2000): 460–89.

Wolcott, Victoria W. *Remaking Respectability: African-American Women in Interwar Detroit.* Chapel Hill: University of North Carolina Press, 2001.

Zunz, Oliver. *The Changing Face of Inequality: Urbanization, Industrial Development, and Immigrants in Detroit, 1880–1920.* Chicago: University of Chicago Press, 1982.

INDEX